Colonel Richardson's Airedales

The Making of the British War Dog School 1900-1918

Bryan D. Cummins

Colonel Richardson's Airedales: The Making of the British War Dog School, 1900-1918
© 2003 Bryan D. Cummins

National Library of Canada Cataloguing in Publication Data
Cummins, Bryan David
Colonel Richardson's Airedales/Bryan D. Cummins

Includes bibliographical references and index.
ISBN 1-55059-248-3

1. Richardson, Edwin Hautenville, 1863-1948. 2. Dogs – Training. 3. Dogs – War use. 4. Dog trainers – Great Britain – Biography. I. Title.
SF422.82.R52C85   2003   636.7'0886   C2003-910490-7

Detselig Enterprises Ltd.
210-1220 Kensington Rd. N.W., Calgary, Alberta, T2N 3P5
Phone: (403) 283-0900/Fax: (403) 283-6947
E-mail: temeron@telusplanet.net
www.temerondetselig.com

All rights reserved. No part of this book may be reproduced in any form or by any means without permission in writing from the publisher.

We acknowledge the financial support of the Government of Canada through the Book Publishing Industry Development Program (BPIDP) for our publishing activities.

We also acknowledge the support of the Alberta Foundation for the Arts for our publishing program.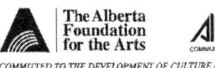

ISBN 1-55059-248-3
SAN 115-0324
Printed in Canada

Cry "Havoc," and let slip the dogs of war...
Shakespeare
Julius Caesar
Act III, Scene I

Dedication

Colonel Richardson's Airedales could only be dedicated to one person: the late Colonel Richardson. In addition to bringing into existence the British War Dog School, which ultimately saved thousands of Allied lives during World War I, he is recognized today as being the founder of the modern working dog movement in Britain. Without him, the use of police patrol dogs would have been long delayed, as would have the use of tracking Bloodhounds. Airedale fanciers around the world also owe him a huge debt for having established their breed as one of the finest police, military and all 'round service dogs in the world. Dogs of his breeding and training were to be found around the globe during the first part of the 20th century.

It took Colonel Richardson two decades for the government to acknowledge that what he was proposing for the British army was not only feasible, but also necessary. Largely ignored for much of his life, he has too often been neglected since his death. It is now more than half a century since he passed away, and it is time for this story to be told. I hope that he would have liked this tribute to his life's work.

TABLE OF CONTENTS

Acknowledgements 9
Preface 11

PART ONE: WAR DOGS THROUGH HISTORY
1) War Dogs of Old 15
2) The Modern War Dog Movement 1870-1914 33

PART TWO: COLONEL RICHARDSON'S AIREDALES
3) Colonel Edwin Hautenville Richardson: a brief biography 59
4) An Uphill Battle 73
5) The British War Dog School is Born 97
6) British War Dogs in France .105
7) The Dogs 125
8) The Training 137
9) The Heroes 147
10) Epilogue: World War II 155

Appendix A 171
Appendix B 183
Appendix C 195
Appendix D 197
Endnotes 199
References 203
Index 205

Acknowledgements

Colonel Richardson's Airedales could not have been written without the help of a number of people.

First off, I would like to thank Karen Clouston, who has done so much for the Airedale. She generously provided me with some early archival documentation for which I am most grateful. Her enthusiasm and support for this project is greatly appreciated.

Joanne Briggs, an anthropology student at Trent University and my research assistant, did an exceptional job in tracking down archival and other elusive material for me. She also created the wonderful art that graces the cover of *Colonel Richardson's Airedales*. I am most grateful for her untiring and diligent assistance.

I cannot thank my friend David Lafleche enough for the fine job he did in helping me acquire many of the illustrations for this book. He was always there, taking up the slack, when I was unable to do so myself. Thanks, Dave.

I would like to thank the staff at the Imperial War Museum (IWM), London, England. They were most professional and were of invaluable assistance. In particular, I would like to thank Emma Crocker, Tony Richards and Janice Mullins for their help, generosity and prompt replies to my queries. I would be remiss if I did not thank the gentleman in the Reading Room, whose name I never learned, who directed me to the other archival sources at the IWM. With his guidance I was able to locate, in the video archives, a remarkable 1918 film of Colonel Richardson's messenger dogs in training. It was an incredible find and I am most grateful for the time he spent with me and for his gentle persistence that I keep looking through these other sources.

Dominique Collon, at The British Museum, was most helpful. She gave me a tour of the Ancient Near East Galleries at the museum and provided me with her own insights on the possible use of ancient war dogs. I thank her for all help and knowledge.

Phyllis Wayne generously lent me one of her exceptionally scarce images of Colonel Richardson's war dogs so that I could include it in this book. I thank her for her generosity.

I would like to thank Mr. Monty Hunt, of Kent, England. Mr. Hunt was with the War Dog School during World War II. In recent years, he has donated to The Imperial War Museum, London, a number of volumes containing pictures and text relating to his years in the service. These are a virtual treasure trove for anybody interested in military history generally, and the use of service dogs specifically. Mr. Hunt generously shared with me much of his material, for which I am most grateful.

Partial funding for *Colonel Richardson's Airedales* was provided by The Canadian Union of Public Employees (3908) Professional Development Fund, Trent University. I am most grateful for their generous assistance.

A special thank you must go to Ted Giles, Linda Berry and the staff at Detselig Enterprises for their work in making the book a reality.

Finally, a very special thank you to Tricia, not only for her support, but for reminding me that I had promised myself, many years ago, that I would one day write *Colonel Richardson's Airedales*. With her encouragement and support, I kept that promise to myself.

Preface

Ernest Gray, in his *Dogs of War* (1989), writes the following in reference to the Royal Air Force Police Dog School and the Army Dog Training School.

Two famous English dog schools, whose dogs are in demand all over the world, are situated in the Midlands, not so far distant from each other as the crow flies. Each should have a portrait of Colonel Richardson in a conspicuous position, as the outstanding English pioneer in training dogs of war.

His suggestion is not unfounded, for without Richardson's commitment, determination and tenacity, Britain would probably still be without a military dog program. As it was, England entered the First World War as the only major European nation that did not have an active military dog program. The others – including Germany, France, Italy, Sweden, Belgium, Bulgaria, Russia and Holland – all had canine units functioning in various capacities. While this oversight might seem minor, the tremendous number of lives saved and the significant freeing of personnel for other military endeavors, eventually proved Richardson to be right: there was a need for highly trained dogs in the military. As it was, Britain finally developed a war dog school more than halfway through The Great War.

The fact that Britain did not have a war dog program is remarkable for a number of reasons. For one, the English had used canine allies as far back as the Roman era. Caesar remarked upon the huge Mastiffs that fought alongside their masters when he invaded the British Isles in 55 BC. Centuries later, Henry VIII sent hundreds of Mastiffs to help his allies in their battles. As well, given the military and imperial might of Britain over the centuries, it is curious that it did not capitalize upon the use of the dog during times of war. By way of contrast, Spain, with whom England competed for colonies, used them very successfully (if barbarically) in its conquest of the Americas. And, given the renowned (and somewhat clichéd and stereotypical) love of dogs by the British, it would seem that the development of a military dog program was logical. It would be tempting to suggest that it was this very love of the dog that precluded training and sending them into battle, but it must be remembered that the same people developed bear, bull and badger baiting – not to mention pit dog fighting – to its highest (or perhaps that should be lowest) levels of development. Whatever the reasons, and they are elusive, Britain entered World War I with no formal military dog program in place. It would only be after the dogs had proven themselves, in an unofficial capacity, that the authorities came around.

It was then-Major (later Colonel) Edwin Hautenville Richardson who single-handedly brought about the War Dog School. It would seem that there was almost an inevitability to it: he was a military officer, a dog fancier, trainer and breeder, and a staunch patriot of the old school. More than that, however, he was a man of vision and he was aware of social and political winds of change. With these qualities, and an unyielding belief that what he was striving for was correct, needed and ultimately for the good of all, he prevailed. This is the story of the battles he had to endure and the success that he finally attained.

PART ONE
War Dogs Through History

CHAPTER ONE
War Dogs of Old

Exactly when dogs began to accompany armies into battle is open to question. A number of writers have argued that dogs were an integral part of ancient warfare, the importance of military dogs in ancient times being that, without the advantages of gunpowder, the military dog was a most effective weapon, fighting side by side with his owner/handler. Others strongly disagree.

The first generally undisputed dates for the use of war dogs begin with the Romans. Prior to that period, the evidence is more flimsy and thus open to debate. Cynologists, those who study the dog and its history, tend to be more liberal in their interpretations of the available data. Archaeologists and historians tend to be more bound by the conventions of serious scholarship and are less quick to reach conclusions based upon scant evidence.

The Ancient World

Among most dog fanciers, the most oft-cited evidence for the early use of war dogs is alleged to come from the ancient Near East. Assyria was an ancient empire of western Asia, named for the original city-state of Ashur (or Assur), located on the upper Tigris River. In the early 2nd century BC, it began to expand northwards. Nineveh and Nimrud eventually became co-capitals of the empire. From this region, armies spread out as far as lower Mesopotamia and present day Syria, Iran, Turkey. There was constant enmity with Babylon, although there also appears to have been much cultural borrowing from it as well. The Assyrians were noted warriors, armed with iron weapons and – the cynologists maintain – also with fierce war dogs. Its period of greatness, from roughly 883 to 612 BC, was an era of constant militarism, resulting in an empire that at its peak stretched from the Nile to close to the Caspian Sea and from Cilicia to the Persian Gulf.

Cynologists argue that the Assyrians used war dogs in their numerous military campaigns. The evidence they present comes from one of the most renowned depictions of dogs from early times. It is from the North Palace of Ashurbanipal in Nineveh and dates to about 645 BC. Cynologists claim that it depicts soldiers and what can only be described as a Mastiff or Mastiff type dog. The soldiers are marching as if to battle, with the huge, powerful dogs straining on their leads, eager to engage the enemy. The detail of the mural is quite remarkable, the dogs' musculature, ribs and fine detail of their heads and muzzles quite explicit.

This understanding of this (and similar) material housed at The British Museum (and elsewhere) has been unquestioningly accepted by most cynologists. In other words, it is assumed that the dogs – which are, indeed, Mastiff like – were war dogs. Trew, in "With War Dogs Through The Ages" (1941), submits an illustration with a caption that states "In the British Museum there are bas-reliefs showing Babylonian war dogs, circa. 650 B.C. that are like Mastiffs." He is not alone. Lloyd, who wrote an important piece for Vesey-Fitzgerald's *The Book of the Dog* (1948), also uses these early images as evidence that Mastiffs were used as war dogs by these ancient civilizations. He writes that among the early references to dogs in combat are those recorded by Hammurabi, King of Babylonia, whom he describes as "a great and talented organizer of empire who employed dogs of war." His warriors, Lloyd contends, were accompanied into battle by huge "hounds." The evidence he presents are the bas-reliefs from ancient Babylon that depict "powerfully built animals somewhat similar to Mastiffs" that may be found at the British Museum.

Archaeologists and other scholars, including those at The British Museum, which houses the Nineveh pieces, disagree. They claim that the figures leading the dogs are hunt attendants. Dr. Dominique Collon, of the Department of the Ancient Near East, The British Museum, maintains that there are no pictorial or textual references to dogs used in war in Babylonia or Assyria. She suggests that the big Mastiffs depicted on the terra cotta plaques and on Assyrian reliefs could have been used for war, but are shown only in hunting scenes. Moreover, she suggests, they would not have been too effective in battle against bow and arrow. On the other hand, she acknowledges, they were used as guard dogs and models of them were buried in the doorways of Assyrian palaces (Collon, pers. comm., 2003).

The Celts

The Celts occupy a curious place in both the public and academic imagination. For the former, they are hazy and unknown, but omnipresent. For the latter, it seems to be a perpetual struggle to demystify and clarify the very important role that the Celts played in Western and world history. They were an ancient central and western European people who dominated much of that part of the world in the second half of the first millennium BC until their domination by the Romans in the first century BC.

It is likely that the Celts employed war dogs. Green, in *Animals in Celtic Life and Myth* (1992:66), states that a crucial role in Celtic warfare was played by animals, including dogs. While cavalry and chariot units employed horses and other equines – such as mules, donkeys and ponies – dogs were also put into battle. She states that horses and dogs fought together in the war between Ulster and Connacht. As well, there exists a wood block print of a Celtic warrior in Gaul, equipped with a spear, a shield and a "Mastiff" dog. What is interesting is that one could make the case that this warrior is accompanied by a Dogue de Bordeaux (or French Mastiff – see below) or its ancestor. In Ireland, it is alleged that the awesome Irish Wolfhound was used by Irish chieftains in their battles.

Roman War Dogs

It is not until the Roman Empire that we start to uncover more comprehensive records of the use of war dogs. The Romans apparently adopted the use of war dogs after having encountered them in their own wars of conquest. When the Roman consul, Marius, fought at the battle of Versella against the Teutons in 101 BC, he was met with a horde of war dogs. The Romans had already overcome the defending forces, but then had to deal with this new enemy. Remarkably, according to Richardson in *British War Dogs*, the dogs were organized and handled by the "blonde-haired women of Wagenburg," who apparently had no reservations against turning the ferocious animals against the Romans. These canine gladiators delayed his victory and almost cost him the battle. The Teutonic peoples apparently used dogs regularly in battle and large, powerful animals were highly prized. Sometimes, their war dogs were supplied with complete suits of armor, including body covering and headpieces.

Building on these experiences, the Romans introduced their own innovations to war dog technology. They outfitted them with spiked armor, or heavily padded their bodies and mounted firepots on their backs. The dogs would then be loosed under mounted soldiers, causing the horses to rear, throwing their riders. Once the men were on the ground, the dogs would set upon them, rendering them to pieces. It is the Romans who are generally credited with organizing the first systematic use of military dogs. In addition to the offensive use of animals, they would place cordons of sentry dogs around their defenses to warn of enemies. They also served as guards for their camps and for the ramparts of their towns.

The Romans would also initiate a form of attack training that was not all that different from what is conducted today. The idea was that the dogs would learn to attack men armed with swords. Dogs would be held while their owners would be engaged in mock combat. Soldiers, armed with swords, would pretend to attack the dog's owner. The dog would then be loosed to attack his owner's assailants. In this way, the dogs became not only brave, but also protective of their owners and most effective at meeting the most dangerous form of aggression, an armed man.

Spanish War Dogs in the New World

Undoubtedly, the most sadistic and successful use of war dogs was during the conquest of the New World by the Spanish. Varner and Varner have documented well that grisly history (1983). When Columbus set sail for the second time in September, 1493, he took with him 20 purebred Mastiffs and Greyhounds.[1] It had been suggested to him by the ship's surgeon that the dogs could be used as tasters, thereby preventing the men from consuming any poisonous food that they might encounter on their travels. It became apparent that the dogs had other uses, as well. Because the "licentious behaviour" of some of his men had evoked hostility among some of the natives, Columbus discovered that the large and imposing dogs might have some value other than tasting food.

The use of dogs as military weapons in the New World began on May 5, 1494, when Columbus set ashore in Jamaica for fresh water and wood. The natives appeared hostile to the Europeans, so three ships drew near to the shore and soldiers fired a volley from their crossbows. Following this initial display of arms, they went ashore, slashing many of the natives and continuing to fire. As they fled in terror, a dog was let loose. It mauled several people. Thurston, in *The Lost History of the Canine Race*, claims that the dog "fatally mauled a half dozen natives within a matter of minutes." Varner and Varner state that "one dog against the Indians was worth ten men." Whether or not this is true, the Spaniards quickly appreciated the value of dogs in the New World. More dogs were shipped to the colonies, ostensibly for protection of supplies and personnel. Ultimately, they were used for pursuing and killing natives, for both "sport" and out of perceived necessity.

The dogs incited fear in the hearts of the local people. They had never witnessed anything like these huge, ferocious animals that – from all accounts – were able to run down and kill people, even adult males, with ease. There was no end to the cruelty involved. Varner and Varner refer to a letter from 14 Dominican priests who describe how the Spanish used dogs in the most horrific fashion. They describe how "some Christians" came across a native woman with a nursing child in her arms. As their dog was hungry, they tossed the infant to the dog, who killed and devoured it in front of the mother. They also recounted how the natives were used as slave labor, forced to march "sixty or seventy leagues," carrying heavy loads, and without food. To make sure that they didn't escape, the Spanish would accompany them with Mastiffs. To make sure that the dogs wouldn't bruise their paws, they were carried on hammocks that were strung between the shoulders of natives. In other words, the dogs that were used to prevent natives from escaping were carried by those same natives. The dogs were prized and esteemed by the Spanish because "If an Indian fled, a dog would catch him and tear out his entrails before the Christians overtook him," according to Varner and Varner. In Cuba, chained convoys of local people were maintained, one being released whenever a dog or dogs needed to be fed. The idea was that the pursuit of a fleeing native would enhance and refine the dogs' killing instincts.

Throughout the Spanish colonies, the stories are similar in their barbarity and sheer wantonness. Out of this madness, there emerged legendary characters, notorious for their viciousness and cruelty. One of them is a dog, Becerrillo, or "Little Bull Calf." Recorded in history as a "Greyhound," there is little likelihood, based on his exploits, that he was. Thurston (1993) suggests (based on engravings of the dog) that he was a Mastiff/Greyhound cross.[2] Elsewhere in the same volume she posits that he was an Alaunt. The Alaunt, now extinct, is somewhat of an enigma. The Duke of York, writing in *The Master of the Game* (1406, cited in Fleig, 1996), described the dog as being similar to the Greyhound except that it had a very large and broad head with heavy flews and ears. Its primary purpose was bull baiting and hunting wild boar. Furthermore, he said, they were completely unpredictable and took offense at everything. Richardson, in *British War Dogs*, suggests that the Alaunt (or Allan or Allande) probably originated in southern Europe, the result of a cross between a Wolfhound and a Mastiff, as they had speed, strength and "a very determined disposition." Given their qualities, Richardson suggests that they were frequently employed as war dogs and were raised to be as fierce as possible and to protect their owners against all enemies. He cites Ulysses Aldrovandus, who described the Alaunt in 1607. They were

> *terrible and frightful to behold and more fierce and fell than any Arcadian curre...In build he resembles the hound. He ought to be gentle to his own household, savage to those outside it, and not to be taken in by caresses. He should be robust, with a muscular body, and noisy in his deep bark, so that, by his bold baying, he may threaten on all sides, and frighten away prowlers. He should have a fierce light in his eyes, portending the lightning attack on the rash enemy. He should be black in his coat, in order to appear more fearful to the thieves in the daylight, and being of the same shade as the night itself, to be able to make his way quite unseen by enemies and thieves.*

All in all, the Alaunt sounds like a most formidable and dangerous animal.

Just as we are uncertain of Becerrillo's lineage, we similarly are unaware of his place of birth. Thurston claims that he came from the kennels of Diego Columbus, Christopher's brother, but Varner and Varner claim that his origins are uncertain. Regardless, by 1511, when he appeared in Puerto Rico, he already had a reputation and the battle scars from arrows to corroborate it. His son, Leoncico (Little Lion) was equally well known and shared a similar notoriety for viciousness and violence.

Becerrillo has been attributed with almost human intelligence. It is said that he was able to distinguish among Carib, Arawak, "Christian" and good and evil. Should a man escape, Becerrillo was said to be able to track him into a crowd of 200 people, find the man and lead him out by the wrist if he complied. Should the escapee resist, Becerrillo would kill him instantly. Legend maintains that the natives were so fearful of this one dog that they would prefer to fight 100 soldiers without him than ten with him.

The story is told of how the soldiers were intending to have some sport at the expense of an elderly woman. She was given a note to take to the governor and, should she refuse to do so, she would be tossed to the dogs. She set out and after going a brief distance, Becerrillo was released with the command to "take her." The woman, seeing the beast approaching, fell to the ground and is said to have uttered "Oh, my Lord Dog. I am on my way to bear this message to the Christians. I beseech thee, my Lord Dog, do me no harm." Becerrillo, it is said, looked into her eyes, sniffed her and then urinated on her, allowing her to continue. When Juan Ponce de Leon heard of this incident, he commanded that the woman be allowed to return free to her people for, he maintained, the charity of a man must not be exceeded by that of a dog.

Becerrillo enjoyed privileges unknown to most men. Because the Spanish feared for his life, he was guarded by the soldiers. He wore a spiked collar (finely made) and when going into battle wore a protective coat, called an *escaupil*, similar to those of Celtic war dogs. He received a pay equivalent to one and a half that of a bowman, plus a share of spoils, including slaves, gold and food, all of which were entrusted to his handlers.

He met his end the way he lived his life – violently. When he and his handler were attacked, the dog followed the Caribs into the water where they had fled in terror. Becerrillo was out of his element (literally) and impeded by the water and rendered somewhat defenseless without his protective coat. Ripping and slashing, he was eventually stabbed with poisoned arrows, by one of the very men he had bitten. He killed his assailant and then swam to shore, seeking help. The soldiers were able to drain and cauterize his wounds, thereby preventing the madness that typically accompanied such injuries, but the dog died shortly thereafter. Becerrillo was buried in secrecy out of fear that the natives would learn of his demise. Becerrillo, they thought (or so the Spanish believed the natives thought), was invincible.

English War Dogs

Henry VIII is said to have provided war dogs for Charles V in the 16th century. These were 400 iron-collared dogs, said to have been Mastiffs. They were set upon the French dogs and proved superior, driving the French animals from the field in defeat. They were also apparently used as some embryonic form of scout dogs, accompanying the soldiers when they went on reconnaissance missions. The dog's fine sense of smell alerted the Spanish to potential ambushes before they could occur. So well did they perform that the dogs were held up as examples to the Spanish soldiers. Curiously, Jager, in *Scout, Red Cross and Army Dogs* (1910), described these English Mastiffs as "terriers" whereas the Elizabethan, Dr. Caius, described the animals as "vast, huge, ugly, and stubborn." Each animal had "a good yron coller after the fashion of that countrey."

English war dogs were not restricted to repelling Roman invaders and to battles on the Continent, however. They were also used in the British Isles. Legend has it that 50

1888 engraving depicting slavering Mastiff in spiked collar simply titled "War." Compare this dog with the photograph of the Mastiff on page 28. (author's collection)

Mastiffs were once used in the hunt for Robin Hood and his men. Given that Robin Hood himself is a legendary person, some believe to be a composite of a number of historical figures, this is somewhat debatable. Nonetheless, it is but one indication of a larger truth: dogs were used by the authorities in England against their own people. Mastiffs, for example, were employed during the Wars of the Roses. The English also turned them against the Irish and the Scots. During the reign of Elizabeth I, the Earl of Essex took with his army 800 dogs, supposedly Bloodhounds provided by Her Majesty, to help him in the suppression of the Irish rebellion.[3]

French War Dogs

Napoleon is another of those legendary commanders who used dogs (or is *claimed* to have used dogs) in battle even though he is alleged to have not particularly liked the species. He employed them in his Egyptian and Italian campaigns. During his Egyptian campaign, he capitalized on the pariah dogs that lingered around the camps, feeding on scraps and whatever else they could find. As they scavenged on the perimeters of the fortifications, they also were quick to sound the alarm at any strange movements. He began a more systematic use of dogs shortly thereafter. Just prior to the Battle of Aboukir, July 25, 1799, he ordered General Marmont to collect a large number of fighting dogs and arrange them in front of his fortifications.

At least two dogs appear in the history of Napoleon's wars. One, allegedly a Barbet,[4] might actually have brought a brief cessation to a battle. The scene was the Battle of Castiglione, which occurred in 1796. Richardson, in *British War Dogs*, quotes from Williams' *Sketches of the French Republic*:

> ...Buonaparte [sic] coming to the spot where the thickest of the combat had taken place, where the French and the Austrians lay strewn in horrible profusion, he perceived one living object amid those piles of corpses which was a little Barbet dog. The faithful creature stood with his forefeet fixed on the breast of an Austrian officer....his eyes...were riveted on those of his dead master. The tumult seemed neither to distract the attention nor change the attitude of the mourner, absorbed by the object to which he clung. Buonaparte, struck with the spectacle, stopped his horse, called his attendants around him, and pointed out the subject of his speculation.
>
> "The dog," said Buonaparte, "as if he had known my voice, removed his eyes from his master, and throwing them on me for a moment, resumed his former posture; but in that momentary look there was a mute eloquence beyond the power of language. It was a reproach, with all the poignancy of bitterness." Buonaparte felt the appeal;....[and] gave orders to stop the carnage immediately.

One might be forgiven for suggesting that this story, somewhat apocryphal in tone, sounds Disneyesque. Further casting doubt upon the veracity of the tale is that in his memoirs (cited in Gray, 1989), Napoleon relates a similar story purported to occur at The Battle of Marengo, which occurred in 1800.

The other dog, which was actually quite well known in an earlier era, was not nearly so anonymous. His name was Moustache and, again, there is disagreement about his breed. Some have called him (yet again) a Poodle, while others are less certain. Regardless, it appears that he was born in Calais in 1799 and was originally owned by a grocer. He ended up with some Grenadiers and was soon as much a part of the regiment as the soldiers. He forever ingratiated himself when he gave warning of the enemy. During the Italian campaign in 1800, a detachment of Austrians was intent on surprising the French in the Valley of Balbo. The weather was stormy, and the Austrians were advancing without any possible chance of being detected. Moustache, patrolling the French camp, detected their presence, presumably by their scent. He sounded the alarm and the Austrians retreated. The next morning, it was determined that Moustache, who had hitherto been living on scraps, should be given the rations of a grenadier. He was also given a proper grooming, a collar that bore the name of his regiment, and the barber was ordered to groom him properly once a week.

Moustache is renowned for two other notable accomplishments. He detected the presence of an Austrian spy who had somehow managed to infiltrate the French camp through donning a disguise. Later, he was engaged in a major battle, although having recently suffered a bayonet wound to the shoulder. As the flag bearer fell dead, surrounded by a half dozen of the enemy, Moustache ran to his aid and attempted to seize the ensign out of the hands of one of the enemy. He was again about to be bayoneted, this time fatally by a five or six Austrians, when his companions-in-arms intervened with a blast of grapeshot. With a burst of energy, he ripped the standard from the hands of the deceased foe and carried it back to his company. For this deed, he was decorated by Field Marshal Lannes.

The story is told that Moustache was mistakenly hit on the head by a chasseur, whereupon he deserted his regiment and attached himself to some dragoons. He went with them into Spain where, on March 11, 1811, he was killed by cannon fire at the storming of Badajoz. He was buried with full military honors, including his collar and medal. A plain stone, inscribed with *Ci Git le Brave Moustache*, was placed over his grave. Later, the Spanish broke the stone, removed the bones and had them burnt.

War Dogs on the American Frontier

Throughout the 18th century, there were several efforts made to employ dogs in battle on the American frontier. Benjamin Franklin was one of the earliest advocates, suggesting the use of dogs for detecting Natives who might otherwise be concealed in the bush. In a letter written in 1755, he explained how they might be used (cited in Downey's *Dogs for Defense*, 1955):

> *Dogs should be used against the Indians. They should be large, strong and fierce; and every dog led in a slip string, to prevent their tiring themselves by running out and in, and discovering the party by barking at squirrels, etc. Only when the party come near thick woods and suspicious places they should turn out a dog or two to search them. In case of meeting a party of the enemy, the dogs are all then to be turned loose and set on. They will be fresher and finer*

for having been previously confined and will confound the enemy a good deal and be very serviceable. This was the Spanish method of guarding their marches.

Franklin's suggestions here anticipate the use of scout dogs two centuries later. What is not stated, but is somewhat implied, is that the dogs were also expected to run down and maim, if not kill, the enemy. Small dogs can detect and alert their handlers to the presence of the enemy as well as large dogs. Franklin's explicit preference for "large, strong, and fierce" dogs suggests that their role was to be more than the detection and "confounding" of the enemy.

Nearly a decade later, John Penn, the Lieutenant-Governor of Pennsylvania from 1763 to 1771, again urged the use of dogs. On June 28, 1764, he wrote to James Young, pay master and Commissioner of Musters in Philadelphia (cited in Downey, 1955).

You will acquaint the Captains that every Soldier will be allowed three Shillings per month who brings with him a strong Dog that shall be judged proper to be employed in discovering and pursing the Savages. It is recommended to them to procure as many as they can, not exceeding ten per Company; Each Dog is to be kept tied and led by his owner.

A third attempt was made later that decade by William McClay, in a letter he sent to the State of Pennsylvania's Supreme Executive Council. It was sent on April 27, 1779 (Downey, 1955).

I have sustained some Ridicule for a Scheme which I have long recommended, Vis, that of hunting the Scalping Parties with Horsemen and Dogs. The imminent Services which Dogs have rendered to our people in some late instances, seems to open People's Eyes to a Method of this kind. We know that Dogs will follow them, that they will discover them and even seize them, when hunted on by their Masters.

History informs us That it was in this Manner That the Indians were extirpated out of whole Countrys in South America. It may be objected That we have not proper Dogs. It is true that every new thing must be learned; But we have, even now, Dogs that will follow them, and the arrantest [sic] Cur will both follow and fight in Company. I cannot help being of the opinion that a Single Troop of Light Horse, attended by Dogs (and who might occasionally carry a footman behind them, that the pursuit might not be interrupted by Morasses or Mountains), under honest and active officers, would destroy more Indians than five thousand Men stationed in forts along the Frontiers; I am not altogether singular in this opinion, could not such a Thing be tried?

The American colonists never used dogs in any systematic manner during the 18th century. And, more "Indians" would be "destroyed" by disease over the ensuing decades than any number of dogs could have accomplished.

Hamer, in *Dogs at War* (2001) states that the US Army, during the second Seminole War of 1835-1842, used Cuban Bloodhounds[5] to track natives in thick swamps of western Florida and Louisiana. The natives had the upper hand in this environment, where they had fled the soldiers who were trying to capture them. This, according to Hamer, was the first recorded use of dogs by the US army. Thirty-three Cuban Bloodhounds and five handlers were put to work tracking down the natives as the US sought to remove them from the land and relocate them to Oklahoma. The government did not have total support for their effort, however, nor for their use of the dogs. Quakers from New York, Pennsylvania and Louisiana petitioned the government by way of protest.

Historically, it has been suggested that during the American Civil War, few dogs were employed in any significant way. Those that were used were mainly pets or mascots, often dogs that were found as strays and then kept by the troops. At best, it has been stated that a few were used as messengers and both sides had camp dogs that served as sentries, although never in any official capacity.

However, this stance might actually minimize the importance of dogs during the War Between the States. Thurston, in *Lost History of the Canine Race*, notes that dogs that "were inclined toward viciousness found employment in the military as prison guards." She refers to 13 such dogs kept by Captain Henry Wirz at the Andersonville Prison in Georgia. The dogs were kept for the express purpose of recapturing Union soldiers who had escaped. Apparently, prisoners who attempted escape were frequently mutilated or killed by the dogs. The most notorious of the 13 dogs was Spot, an innocuously named Cuban Bloodhound who tipped the scales at 150 pounds. Numerous attempts were made on Spot's life, but he survived them all and lived out his life as a civilian with his captain.

Thurston's brief discussion of these Civil War dogs is especially interesting in light of a contemporaneous illustration. An engraving from *Harper's Weekly*, November 26, 1863, titled "The War in the Southwest – Guerillas Hunting Union Men With Blood-Hounds" (see illustration) suggests that perhaps more use was made of dogs than has been recorded by history. Given that hounds (or, more likely, hounds crossbred with other dogs) were used to track runaway slaves and escaped prisoners, it should come as no surprise that – perhaps – they were also employed during the Civil War. This is not to suggest that there was systematic use of dogs; rather, a more frequent, albeit casual use, likely occurred. Note in the engraving how the dogs were used not only for detecting Union soldiers, but are also attacking them.

One must issue a cautionary note, however. There is the distinct possibility that the illustration is propaganda, or even fantasy. If such incidents actually occurred, and if they were used as propaganda from a Confederate stance, it might have been used to rally the Southern side in their war against the north, showing a successful routing of the enemy. If from the Union side, it might have been used as a means of disparaging the Confederates, showing them in a negative light, turning vicious dogs on the northern troops. Yet again, there is the possibility that such events never did occur and the scene is simply the figment of somebody's imagination. Stranger things have happened in the history of military art.

It should also be noted that such actions are completely antithetical to the Bloodhound's character. The breed is renowned for its good nature (the name comes from being a "blooded" or purebred dog, not from any affiliation with blood letting). Despite the title, the dogs depict-

Illustration from <u>Harper's Weekly</u>, November 1, 1863.

ed in this engraving in all likelihood were crossbred hounds of some type. Possibly, they were Cuban Bloodhounds. Regardless of the breed, it depicts an interesting aspect of the Civil War.

Despite the successes of camp sentries, prison guard dogs and the possible occasional use of Bloodhounds by both sides, none of the dogs employed during the Civil War were formally trained. They were, for the most part, family pets that accompanied their owners into battle, or strays picked up en route.

Ancient War Dog Breeds

Military forces today typically employ a handful of breeds for work. These include the ubiquitous German Shepherd Dog, the Belgian Malinois (now rapidly overtaking the German Shepherd as the war and police dog of choice) and, on occasion, the Doberman Pinscher (the Marines "Devil Dog" in World War II), the Rottweiler and Labrador Retriever (used primarily for mine detection). Over the centuries, however, other breeds have been used, or have been claimed to have been used, as war dogs. For the most part their histories are murky.

The Molossus

From ancient Greece comes what many people believe to be the ancestor of all contemporary Mastiff type dogs, the Molossus.[6] The Molossis (spelled with an "i", not a "u") were a Greek people who had as the centre of their homeland ancient Epirus. Here developed a large, aggressive breed of dog that is now known as the Molossus. It is believed that pilgrims to the Holy Oak of Dodona (a shrine to Jupiter) took many of these dogs back with them to their homelands, where it contributed to the development of other breeds. The Molossus was used for guarding the herds and, possibly, for warfare. As such, it might have contributed to other war dogs in the region.

The essential question, however, is where and how the Molossus originated. Some believe that it is a descendant of Tibetan dogs that Alexander the Great brought back to Greece and which had subsequently found a home in Molossis. Others contend that the breed developed *in situ*, over time. Aristotle referred to the Molossus, noting that it was used to protect the herds and was distinguishable from all other dogs by virtue of its size and indomitable courage. This suggests that the Molossus was a distinct breed, or at least a distinct type, by the third century BC. However, there are conflicting view about exactly what the Molossus looked like.

Fleig, in his *Fighting Dog Breeds* (1996), does an admirable job of scouring the earliest literature about the breed. He quotes Marius Terentius Varro, who died in 27 BC. He described the Molossus the following way. "The lower jaw is undershot. From it grows two teeth, one on the left, the other on the right, which are only slightly exposed…These dogs have large heads and drooping ears, a strong nape and neck…The tail is thick, the bark sonorous, the jaws large; the color usually is white, so that it can be distinguished from predators at night." This a remarkable description because, with the exception of the undershot jaw and protruding teeth, it very much describes any member of what has been called "the great white family of guardians."[7] If this early description is true, the Molossus very well might be the ancestor of all or most of these breeds.

However, there is conflicting evidence, in both text and art, that suggest a different appearance of the Molossus. The evidence suggests that the Molossus was dark in color and that some had pendant, or drop, ears. Most large, muscular dogs have a drop or pendant ear, unless surgically altered. Witness, for example, the Mastiff, Neapolitan Mastiff and Dogue de Bordeaux. Those who see a prick ear (standing naturally erect without the benefit of cropping or other alteration) point to a figure of what is purportedly a Molossus that is housed at the Vatican. The statue, called the Nikias, depicts a dog with erect, or pricked, ears. Many historians and cynologists, however, perceive the ears as having been cropped, and not naturally pricked. Those who don't, see the statue as evidence of the Molossus developing independently in the region, with a possible breeding with the indigenous wolf of the region. Hence, their acceptance of the erect ear, inherited from their wild ancestor.

However, many scholars view the small terra-cotta dog, found in the palace of King Assurbanipal (668- 636 BC) at Nineveh, as representative of the typical Molossus. Clearly a

Mastiff type, the dog is a large-framed, muscular, massive-skulled, broad-muzzled animal, with pendant ears.

How might we explain this discrepancy? Some people have suggested that the Molossus was, in fact, a Mastiff type and that because of its ferocity and courage was bred with shepherds' dogs to increase their abilities as flock guardians. So, in essence, the dog's genes were passed on and, to some extent, the confusion over the name. As well, scholars have noted there might very well have been two types of Molossus, each corresponding to the descriptions that we have today. One – the large, white dog – was the flock guardian. The other, large, dark animal was the guardian of the home and, when needed, the war dog.

How might we account for the different color and ears? Some people have suggested that they represent crossbreeding, i.e., either black or white is indicative of breeding with other breeds. For example, those who suggest that the Molossus was the descendant of the Tibetan Dog, i.e., the Tibetan Mastiff, suggest that the white dogs were clearly the product of crossbreeding. Others suggest the opposite, that the black dogs are clearly impure.

It is possible that neither is true. For centuries, shepherds in Europe and Asia have cropped their dog's ears as a means of protecting them from wear and tear in battles with wolves and other predators. Even today, one comes across pictures of Akbashes and Kangals (a Turkish livestock guardian) with cropped ears. On the other hand, as Fleig notes, the dogs that were used to guard human settlements were usually dark in color. With no threat from predators, other than thieves and trespassers, there was no need to crop the ears of these dogs. So, the flock guardians, with their occasionally cropped ears, were generally white so that the shepherd could easily distinguish his dog from a wolf at a distance, while the guardian of the house and courtyard, with their pendant ears, were dark in color so that they were hard for thieves to discern in the darkness. It is possible that these were simply the same breed (or type) in different guises to meet different purposes.

In all likelihood, not only the Molossus name, but also the breed itself spread across Europe and much of Asia. The Molossus, or its descendants, found its way to other parts of Greece, Italy and elsewhere. It is conceivable that all of the aforementioned livestock breeds are descendants of the Molossus, as are the Neapolitan Mastiff and Dogue de Bordeaux.

The Mastiff

There are few extant breeds that can legitimately claim to be linear descendants of the war dogs of old. Two that can are the Mastiff (sometimes called the English Mastiff) and the Neapolitan Mastiff. Both breeds are assumed by most cynological scholars to be directly related, if not identical, to war dogs of centuries ago.

The Mastiff lays claim to being Britain's most ancient breed. Some scholars believe that the breed is indigenous to the British Isles while others argue that the breed is related to a Mastiff type used by the Assyrians for the hunting of lions and other formidable game, as well as for military purposes. Yet others have noticed the similarity between the British breed and the massive Molossus of the Greeks. For those who subscribe that the Mastiff has its roots elsewhere, the

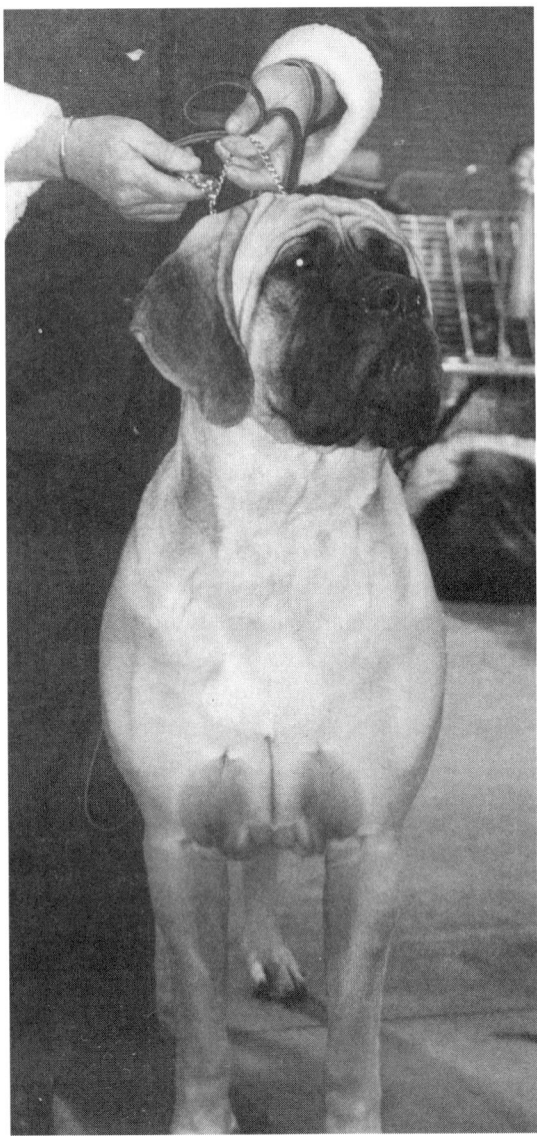

A handsome adult Mastiff bitch. (Photo courtesy of Tricia Lore)

belief is that the dog was introduced to Britain by the Phoenicians in the 6th century BC, via the Scilly Islands and Cornwall. Still others combine these two stances, suggesting that there existed an indigenous Mastiff type whose size and power was enhanced by crossbreeding with the "Asiatic Mastiff" introduced by the Phoenicians. Regardless, there is little doubt that the Mastiff is an ancient breed, dating back at least two thousand years and possibly even longer, and that it functioned as an adjunct to ancient armies. When Julius Caesar invaded what is now Britain in 55 BC, he encountered Mastiffs that had been turned against his army, armed with spikes and wreaking havoc among the Roman horses. Caesar would eventually take some of the British dogs back to Rome with him, where they would entertain Romans in the arenas with their combat against other animals.

Many dog fanciers today lament that the Mastiff is not the dog that it once was and that it has become a lethargic, phlegmatic caricature of what was once a noble and magnificent animal. If such is the case (and such wistful yearnings for days long gone are always suspect), it is probably because today's Mastiff is a much larger animal than it used to be and also because today's fanciers breed for the show ring and the home, not for estate guardians and war dogs. The result is that male Mastiffs today typically weigh in excess of 82 kilograms (180 pounds), and often well over 90 kilograms (200 pounds). Bitches typically weigh 68 (150 pounds) or more. Minimum height for a male, according to the breed standard, is 30" (76.2 cm) at the shoulder for males, 27.5" (69.85 cm) for females. The Mastiff Club of America states a general range of 160-230 pounds for males and 120-170 pounds for females. By comparison, a century ago, a good-sized male Mastiff would be the size of today's average bitch. For example, Dalziel, in his *British Dogs* (1889), cites measurements for typical show dogs of the era. Beaufort, a male, weighed 165 pounds and stood 29.5" at the shoulder, while Jack Thyr stood 28.5" and weighed 156 pounds. Wodan, a noted dog of the period, weighed 160 pounds and stood 30" at the shoulder. The largest male noted by Dalziel was His Lordship, who stood 33" and weighed 180 pounds. Weights and heights for bitches were 136 pounds (29.5" at the shoulder), 120 pounds (29"), 128 pounds (26") and 135 pounds (27").

Although somewhat smaller in size in centuries past, Mastiffs are prominent all through British history. They had a fearsome reputation as guardians, hunters, fighters and warriors. They guarded cattle against predators and thieves as well as being all-round watchdogs on estates of the wealthy, the powerful and the nobility. As hunters, they were used on the largest of British big game, hunting wolves and bears, before both were hunted to extinction.

Mastiffs were used in the cruelest of blood sports, including bear, bull and lion baiting. Bear baiting has been documented as far back as 1050, and possibly occurred even earlier, although it was particularly popular from the time of Edward I to Henry VII. During the 16th century, it became something akin to a national pastime. Bulls were also baited, and although this particular "sport" was less popular than bear-baiting, it persisted longer, undoubtedly because bulls were easier to come by than bears which, after being rendered extinct in the British Isles, had to come from the Continent. Hutchinson in his massive (three volumes and 1998 pages) and masterful *Dog Encyclopaedia* (1934/35), informs us that Paris Garden, near London's Blackfriar's Bridge, had at its height a stable of 20 bears and 70 Mastiffs but only three bulls. Boars, and even horses and donkeys, were baited by Mastiffs.

The scale of these bloody endeavors was truly impressive, if only because it is hard to conceive of such barbarity occurring with such widespread acceptance. Huge numbers of bears and Mastiffs were kept throughout various parts of Britain, solely for the amusement they provided. Royal performances were held in a number of localities, including Greenwich and Kenilworth. It had the royal endorsement, for during Henry VIII's reign, a special office was created: Master of the Royal Game of Bears and Mastiff Dogs. It was maintained until 1642 when it was abolished by order. The last master of note was Edward Alleyn, the well-known actor and founder of Dulwich College. During his tenure there was a master and two keepers of the Royal Game of Bears and Mastiffs.

Bear-baiting probably reached its peak of popularity during the reign of Elizabeth I, when bears and dogs were taken to Whitehall, and continued through the reigns of James I and Charles I, until temporarily abolished.

The "sport" was such that the bear was often outmatched. The spectacle unfolded with a bear held in place by a collar to which was attached a chain which, in turn, was attached to a stake in the middle of the ring. Four Mastiffs were then unleashed at the unfortunate bruin. Being Mastiffs, they would rush the bear, which frequently was able to kill or disable one or two of the dogs in their initial onslaught. Oftentimes, the remaining Mastiffs would retreat momentarily out of harm's way. The bear's defeat was almost – but not always – a foregone conclusion, however, for every time a dog was rendered *hors de combat*, another was released to replace it. The bloodletting continued until the bear was killed or disabled or — very infrequently — proved himself invincible. As many as 13 bears have been released in succession in one afternoon, suggesting that the toughest of staked bears was no match for an endless onslaught of large, fresh, powerful dogs. So popular was the activity that the successful bears, i.e., those that were able to survive a number of encounters, were well known by name. One, Sackerson, who was famous during the time of Elizabeth, was mentioned by Shakespeare in *The Merry Wives of Windsor*.

Lion baiting was less common, undoubtedly due to the difficulty of obtaining lions and replacing them after they had done their bit for human entertainment. The most oft-cited case took place during the reign of James I, when a lion dispatched two Mastiffs but was overcome by the third. The first dog had been seized by the cat and dragged around the cage. Much the same happened to the second. The third Mastiff was able to get hold of the lion's lower jaw and was able to maintain its grip for some time, until weakened by the cat's claws. The lion then leaped over the bodies of the first two dogs and retreated to his den, from where it refused to come out. The Mastiff so impressed the royalty that the King's son, Prince Henry, took him home and nursed him and, in a gesture to his noble battle, would not allow the dog to ever fight again. He spent the rest of his days as the pampered pet of the court.

Perhaps the most oft-cited account of the Mastiff war dog is that of Sir Peers Legh, Knight of Lyme Hall, near Stockport, Cheshire. He was at the Battle of Agincourt on October 25, 1415. He had taken into battle with him his favorite Mastiff, a bitch. When he fell during the conflict, the bitch stood over him, protecting him for many hours until he was picked up by his comrades and taken to Paris where he subsequently died of his wounds. The Mastiff was returned to Lyme Hall. Legend has it that her descendants have been perpetuated to this day, the Lyme Hall strain of Mastiffs having been bred true for nearly six centuries.[8] In the estate castle there hangs a stained glass window depicting Sir Peers and his devoted Mastiff.

The Neapolitan Mastiff

The Neapolitan Mastiff is one of the most formidable looking animals in the world today. Generally standing between 60 and 72 centimetres at the shoulder and weighing between 50 and 80 kilograms, it is a massive, low-slung brute, typically black or grey in color. But it is the massive head, with copious amounts of jowl, that contribute to the breed's truly intimidating appearance. If an even more awe-inspiring effect is needed, breeders usually crop the animal's ears close to dog's elephantine skull.

Cathy Flamholtz, in *A Celebration of Rare Breeds* (1986), discusses the military history of the Neapolitan Mastiff (simply called the "Neo" by his fanciers). She suggests that the breed is descended from the Tibetan Mastiff (virtually all Mastiff breeds are believed — rightly or wrongly — to have the Tibetan Mastiff as their ancestor) and probably made his appearance in what is now Italy in about 300 BC, accompanying Alexander the Great on his wars of conquest. She cites a passage from the second century AD that, with the exception of coat length, describes the Neo.

An adult Neapolitan Mastiff bitch. (Photo courtesy of Tricia Lore)

The guard dog of the house should be black (or dark) so that during the day a prowler can see him and be frightened by his appearance. When night falls, the dog, lost in the shadows, can attack without being seen. The head is so massive that it seems to be the most impressive part of the body. The ears fall toward the front, the brilliant and penetrating eyes are black or grey, the chest is deep and hairy, the hind legs are powerful, the front legs are covered with long thick hair and he is generally short-legged with strong toes and nails.

While we can never be certain, there is a strong possibility that the Neapolitan Mastiff, or its ancestor, was the Roman war dog. It is believed that over the centuries, the descendants of the ancient Roman war dog survived around Naples, eventually becoming today's Neo. Shortly after World War II, a handful of fanciers dedicated themselves to keeping the breed alive by building on the best examples of the breed that they could find. The result is today's Neapolitan Mastiff.

The Dogue de Bordeaux

We are less certain of the Dogue de Bordeaux's history, but it is likely that the breed also has a history as a war dog long ago. Carl Semencic, the author of *The World of Fighting Dogs* and *Pit Bulls and Other Tenacious Guard Dogs*, alludes to the possible close relationship between the Neo and the Dogue, and that therefore the latter was also used for combat. While he does not state whether that "combat" was with humans or other animals, he acknowledges that the Neo was used for both, suggesting that he recognizes the dual purpose of the Dogue, as well. Semencic supports the belief that the Dogue is an ancient breed, having existed in France (hence its other name, the French Mastiff) in its present state prior to the time of Christ. Somewhat similar to the Bullmastiff of England, the Dogue is a more formidable looking animal and is generally acknowledged as being more aggressive, a legacy of his fighting background. In centuries past, the breed was pitted against bears, bulls, wolves and anything else that offered a challenge. One Dogue is alleged to have killed a jaguar in a fight.

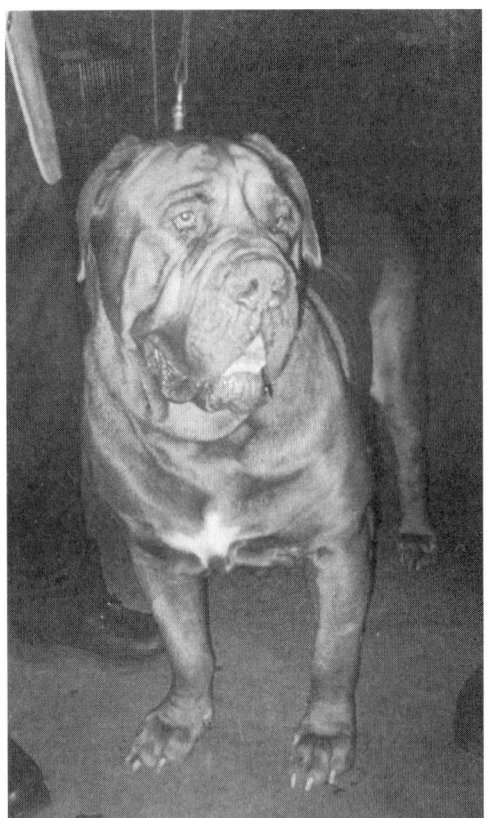

A massive 77 kilogram (170 pound) adult male Dogue de Bordeaux. (Photo courtesy of Tricia Lore)

In addition to being comparable in size (and possible blood relationship) to the Neapolitan Mastiff, the Dogue shares equal billing with that breed as the most fearsome appearing dog in the world. One study in the United States found that males in that country averaged 142 pounds, while bitches averaged 121.4 pounds. The Dogue has the largest head of any breed in the world. In one American study, the heads of adult males averaged 26" in circumference, while those of adult bitches averaged 24". Recognized colors of the Dogue are mahogany (red-brown), golden and fawn. A mask, preferably red, is preferred, although black masks are accepted. As is the case with the Neapolitan Mastiff, the Dogue is a formidable animal that is more than capable of dealing with the strongest of men in a confrontation. The breed became somewhat popular after the release of the movie *Turner and Hootch*. Hootch was a Dogue de Bordeaux.

CHAPTER TWO
The Modern War Dog Movement 1870-1914

The modern war dog movement may be said to have begun in 1870, when there was a concerted effort on the part of many European nations to fully implement a systematic, coherent and permanent war dog program. The result was that World War I saw the first large-scale use of the military dog. By comparison, everything that had occurred before was, to a large degree, haphazard, incidental and directionless. Those who had used the dog had, for the most part, relied on the animal's keen senses to detect the enemy or, once the enemy had been detected, relied on large, powerful, ferocious dogs to run down and kill him.

When The Great War erupted, there were those, particularly in England and the United States, who saw no place for canine soldiers. The nature and technology of warfare had changed and, in some eyes, the idea of military dogs was somehow anachronistic. Ironically, perhaps, more dogs than ever before were put into service between 1914 and 1918, with total estimates as high as 75 000 dogs seeing combat.[9] Their roles were greatly expanded over what had been before. Today, in the 21st century, although dogs may no longer be message carriers or ambulance dogs, they now serve in more capacities than could ever have been imagined at the turn of the last century. Sophisticated technology has not rendered the dog obsolete.

An interesting summation of the state of the use of military dogs at the end of the 19th century appeared in *Journal of the Military Service Institution* (U.S.), September, 1896. It is worth citing in full for the information it presents and for the American perspective on the use of war dogs.

> *Herr Karl von Donat must feel gratified to observe that the idea originated by him of using dogs in war has been successfully followed out. It is stated in the* Avenir Militaire *that there are great numbers of dogs under training for employment in the German autumn manoeuvres at a place near Cologne. These dogs are fitted with saddles, in which are carried* eau de vie *and the first necessaries for the wounded. They are taught to lower themselves beside men lying on the ground, so as to allow the contents of their saddles to be reached, and as they are trained to look for and find wounded men they will be messengers of mercy on the field of battle pending the arrival of medical aid. Scotch Collies are said to be the best dogs for the purpose; and so they may well be except for their uncontrollable propensity to give tongue. This has, according to reports, been overcome, and if so there will be a large and very useful field for the employment of dogs on outpost duty and in many other circumstances.*
>
> *Some years ago Lieutenant Jupin urged the use of war dogs on the attention of the French military authorities, but with very small success. This is deplored by the writer in the* Avenir Militaire, *who can see that every means should be resorted to with the view of keeping pace*

with the enterprising but careful military powers across the Rhine. That power experimented with war dogs in the autumn manoeuvres of 1895, and was sufficiently satisfied with the results obtained to continue and extend them in 1896. The consequence is that Germany will be the first in the field in respect to the knowledge and practice of this adjunct of warfare, and if any advantage is to be got out of it the plodding pains of Germany will get it. Where do we stand in this matter – we who have the best dogs, the greatest number of dog shows and dog enthusiasts, and who can train dogs to do anything and everything? Why, we stand nowhere. Our imitation of the German army is confined to matters which do not suit our national tastes, but when it comes to a branch of field service in which we are naturally fitted to be facile princeps *we do not get a chance to try.*

With over a century of hindsight, this is a most interesting article. For one, the United States, despite this early admonition to get on board with the Germans, did not organize a military dog program until halfway through World War II. As well, while Karl von Donat might have urged the use of dogs in combat, he certainly did not originate the idea, as discussed in the preceding chapter. Nonetheless, Germany is to be credited for giving rise to the *modern* use of war dogs.

Germany

Lloyd, in his useful "The Dog in War" (Vesey-Fitzgerald, 1948), states that Germany was far ahead of other nations in developing service dogs. He suggests, as well, that perhaps the Continental nations were ahead of Britain generally because they had long recognized the utility of the dog in such tasks as hauling milk-carts (Britain had laws forbidding the use of dogs as draught animals). This explanation is insufficient, however, for Britain had long used dogs as sheepherders, hunters and in other activities, including the barbaric blood sports. In the 19th century (and even into the 20th), clandestine dogfights continued. A more likely explanation is that in the late 19th century, the sun still failed to set on the British Empire and there was a smug sense of world domination that failed to recognize any need for military dogs.

Germany has long stood at the forefront of the service dog movement. One might speculate as to why this is so but Richardson, in *War, Police and Watch Dogs* (1910), offers us his view. He states that both sides in the American Civil War used dogs and it was from this that the Germans got the idea of incorporating them into their own military. Richardson was a keen student of military history, and especially of the history of the use of war dogs, but this assertion seems somewhat suspect. For one, military dogs were not used in any meaningful way during the Civil War. There was no institutionalization of service dogs and any use was incidental and haphazard. Their primary use, when it did occur, was in the form of camp dogs that acted as informal sentries. For Germany to take this casual use and to build upon it, when there were so many other, more meaningful uses demonstrated throughout history, is dubious. Furthermore, Vesey-Fitzgerald, in *The Domestic Dog* (1957:139), claims that Germany had opened its first war dog school in 1848.

Postcard of German officer and his Airedale. (Author's collection)

Regardless, in the late 1860s the German army began to seriously organize dogs for military purposes. By 1885, the first extensive experiments were well underway with the training of dogs for sentry purposes. When the century began to wane, a neat system was well developed around the concept of Village Clubs. These were organizations, subsidized by the government, that encouraged the breeding and training of suitable dogs for military work. In some instances, there were clubs that specialized in the breeding and training of specific breeds. To that end, competitions were arranged and inter-club matches held with a "grand championship" awarded. Top dogs were rewarded with reputations and large amounts paid for their progeny and in stud fees. Thus, there were major incentives for serious training, the focus of which was always for a serviceable dog suitable for military service. Today, the descendants of these clubs are the various Schutzhund clubs and other working dog organizations found in Germany and elsewhere.

Ignoring, if we may, Vesey-Fitgerald's undocumented claim that Germany's first military dog school opened in 1848, we may say with certainty that the legitimate first school opened nearly four decades later.[10] In 1884, the world's first military war dog school was established at Lechernich, near Berlin. Dogs were trained as sentries, scouts, ambulance dogs and messengers. The first training manual was published in 1885 (see discussion below). The dog units themselves were first mentioned officially in 1884 and then again in 1886. The head trainer of the school, Herr von Bungartz, would introduce the use of the Red Cross dog (also called mercy dogs, ambulance dogs or, in the case of Germany, "sanitary dogs" or Sanitatshunde) to search the field for wounded soldiers. Richardson, incidentally, owed a lot to Bungartz, for it was with one of the dogs trained by Bungartz, an animal named Sanita, that Richardson started his own kennel.

Sixty dogs had been sent from Germany to work with the troops during the Herrero campaign (1904-1907) in German West Africa. While there, numerous experiments were conducted in the field. After these dogs proved their worth time and time again by alerting their handlers to potential ambushes, dog training and breeding received an additional impetus under royal and official patronage. All the dog clubs were amalgamated under one large umbrella organization called Der Verein fur Deutsche Schaferhunde. The Crown Prince was president and military officers were placed in charge of the organization. Branches were established throughout Germany and Austria and trials were constantly held to demonstrate the breadth and extent of training methods and standards. The association maintained and updated annually a list of dogs under training. Each dog was duly noted with comments pertaining to its training, performance and titles won. The book was available to anybody who wanted to buy it. Richardson, in *British War Dogs*, maintains that the whole association was ultimately a "war organization" and

German soldiers and Airedale carrier dog with food. Note the dog's clamped tail. (Courtesy of the Imperial War Museum, London, Neg. #Q23700)

German messenger dogs with special carrier pigeon attachments. Western Front. (Courtesy of the Imperial War Museum, London, Neg. #Q48444)

that each branch was ordered to keep a secret register of all dogs considered especially suitable for military purposes.

The ultimate result of Germany's efforts was that, through rigorous training and constant experimentation with training methods and breeding, as well as with different breeds, the country had a jump on the rest of the world in terms of military and other service dogs when World War I broke out. Those dogs that were already in the army went directly to the front with their regiments. Owners whose dogs had been approved at trials and were listed in the associations' record books were ordered to mobilize at once. These represented the reserve army of dogs.

As the movement gained momentum and as war loomed on the horizon, dogs were recruited from all over Germany and Austria and sent to training establishments where they were rigorously trained by highly qualified specialists under the direction of expert military officers. When they were fully trained they were drafted to army kennels from where they were then selected and sent to the front lines as need demanded. With the first advance into France and Belgium, the German troops scooped up as many suitable dogs as they could and sent them to Germany for training. At the same time, they didn't neglect dogs in their own countries, offering to buy suitable animals from their owners at up to 50 marks per dog.

Man of the German medical corps with his dog, searching the battlefield at the Rotenturm Pass, Romania. (Courtesy of the Imperial War Museum, London, Neg. #Q55202)

As was the case in France, the German war dog effort was greatly aided by media attention. Through both written accounts of their heroics and illustrations of same, Germany's public was kept well aware of the accomplishments of its dogs on the battlefield and were encouraged to interest themselves in the matter. Richardson contends that this widespread use of the media made work easier for dogs, trainers and handlers "as the full object of their utilization would be understood by all ranks, and all would unite together to assist the good work."

With unprecedented thoroughness, Germany carefully laid out instructions for the breeding, rearing and training of war dogs. We are fortunate that copies of some of these manuals have survived. One, translated and published in the *United Service Journal* in 1904, clearly indicates that dogs had been fully integrated into the German military as a valuable auxiliary by that date, and provides us with insight into how they were trained and utilized. Airedales, because of their record as police dogs, were deemed the "most perfect" breed for military purposes.[11] Jaeger Battalions were assigned at least two dogs to a company, with a maximum of 12 to the battalion. Dogs were to be purebred and the greatest care was taken to prevent accidental breedings of different breeds.

Every aspect of the working dog's life was addressed in the manuals. Many of the guidelines contrast vividly with the standards adopted by today's breeders and trainers. Tails were to be docked within the first four weeks of the puppy's life (most breeders today do it between three and five days) under the supervision of the attending officer. Dogs, of course, were accustomed to gunfire. This was done by taking them to target ranges. On the other hand, dogs were severely discouraged from barking and no dog destined for service was allowed to chase wild animals. In a battlefield context, either habit could have very serious repercussions.

Training began in their seventh month with exercises on lead (among most trainers today, there is the belief that it is virtually impossible to start training too early, with many trainers offering "puppy kindergarten classes" for dogs under six months, and many people believe six to nine weeks is not too young to start training and routines). Only the trainers and their assistants were allowed to associate with the dogs. Punishment was discouraged, although it was emphasized that the trainer must never yield to the will of the dog. A pat and a "well done" were the rewards that the pupil received. It was believed (or at least stated in the manuals) that stubbornness was a rare trait in dogs and seldom, if ever, found in purebreds. Such a contention, of course, runs counter to much of today's wisdom. Trainers were inspired to bring out the best in their charges, with prizes being awarded to those whose dogs earned top grades.

Another training manual, found by youngsters playing in the abandoned farmhouse of a young French woman,[12] provides intriguing insights into the training techniques of the German army during World War I. The last owner of the manual had typed a translation as well as scribbling another translation in a notebook. The cover of manual itself was interesting:

> *Do Not Carry Into The Front Line Trenches*
> *For Army Use Only*
> *The Use of Courier Dogs With Appendix*
> *Instructions Adapted to Courier Dogs*

Issued with the approval of the Chief of Staff of Field Forces (I. C. #67613, op. of Oct. 19, 1917. From the Chief of Signal Corps, Nov. 1917.

While the translation of the article is rough (as will momentarily be shown), it does provide interesting insights. According to the manual, the purpose of the "courier dogs" was "the saving of human energy and lives through the employment of dogs by means of quick conveyance of written messages." They were considered "an organic part" of the Troop-Signal-Division of the infantry with up to 12 dogs assigned to an infantry regiment and up to six to an independent battalion. On the Eastern Front, each separate army chief-of-staff had at his disposal one courier dog kennels [sic] that consisted of one officer, "attendants" and dogs. On the Eastern and Southern Fronts, only the General Army Staff was supplied with a courier dog kennels [sic].

Training time was expected to be from three to five weeks, and only men who were willing and who were genuinely fond of dogs were to be requisitioned for the positions of trainer. Outside officers and men were strictly forbidden to interfere with the dogs in any way or to occupy themselves in any manner with their training. Any violations of these rules were to be strictly punished. As far as possible, the changing of training personnel was to be avoided. It was believed that the dog performs trustworthily only with fully experienced trainers and assistants and people known to him. In cases of emergency, the fully experienced substitute assistant was to fill the breech. It was recognized that the successful training and employment of the dogs rested upon these requirements.

Strict guidelines for the care and feeding of the dogs were laid out in the manual. Dogs that failed to perform, bitches in heat, and sick or wounded animals were to be returned to their respective headquarters for other dogs. They were to be provided with regular veterinary inspections to ward off contagious diseases. Ideally, these inspections were to follow the regular horse inspections. At the main kennels, there were separate rooms for sick animals and a "roomy, segregated kennel for contagious diseases."

Regular baths were to be provided, with follow-up drying with towel and with a thorough brushing. Baths were permitted in winter only if there was a warm room available for the dogs to rest in following the bath. All dogs were to be provided with shelter, specifically a dry, draft-free, bullet-proof "couch" [presumably this is an error in translation and probably meant "kennel"]. When in dugouts [presumably it is meant "trenches"] they were to be provided with a small "excavation." They were also to be kept chained to avoid them becoming lost. Dogs were to be brushed and combed daily and fed only by their trainers. Very specific guidelines regarding the quality and quantity of food are laid out in the manual, right down to the last gram.

The manual identified German Shepherd Dogs, Scotch Terriers [sic] and Airedale Terriers as the primary breeds used as courier dogs.[13] Clearly, this is an error in translation and the "Terrier" should have been "Collie." Richardson, it will be recalled, was inspired to begin his own military dog training when he observed German agents buying Sheepdogs in Scotland and, during his tour of German training facilities prior to the war, he noted the large number of Collies and Airedales being used by Germany.

Courier dogs were to be used under certain conditions. These included in difficult ground such as swamp, mountains or snow; upon discovering detachments of the enemy, when the telephone could not be used because of the possibility of being overheard. In addition to their messenger duties, courier dogs could also be employed to lay down telephone wires, to forward carrier pigeons and to convey munitions and sustenance when technical signal methods failed.

The Germans were aware of the limitations of messenger dogs, suggesting that the distance the dogs be expected to run not exceed two kilometres. To ask more of them was unrealistic. Furthermore, the dogs did the work because running to and fro, as their training entailed, was more rewarding than being confined. Therefore, coercion could not be a training method, for

German veterinary service. Treatment of wounded messenger dogs at a dog hospital. (Courtesy of the Imperial War Museum, London, Neg. #Q55272)

the dogs would resent any such treatment. Two or three practice runs daily kept the dogs conditioned and in readiness for work.

The dogs would inevitably face a number of obstacles in the course of their work. To that end, it was expected that they would be trained in all kinds of topography and to face all kinds of gunfire. Certain distractions, however, could not possibly be foreseen. This would include such things as a bitch in heat (which few dogs could resist), a particularly painful wound, or "drum fire." Even under such distractions, some dogs proved their mettle and carried out their duties.

Veterinary surgeon E. E. Bennett, of the Army Veterinary Department, and Colonel Richardson both provide some interesting observations of the types of experiments and training being conducted by the Germans in the late 19th and early 20th centuries. Bennett referred to trials carried out by the Berlin Sporting Club some time in the 1880s to determine the relative speeds of dispatch carriers. Cyclists competed against dogs over a two kilometre distance on "an ordinary road." A Pointer registered the fastest speed, covering the distance in a most impressive two minutes, forty-five seconds, being followed closely by a succession of Setters and Mastiffs.[14]

The leading cyclist took four minutes, a few lengths ahead of a Poodle. Two tricyclists finished last, taking five and six minutes respectively to complete the distance. Earlier tests had concluded that dogs were second only to pigeons in terms of the speed with which messages could be carried across country and they far outdistanced cavalry in the rapidity with which they covered the ground.

Richardson's observations of the German dogs prior to World War I are equally revealing of the type of experimentation and testing that were being conducted. He witnessed trials of the 15th German Army Corps. Messenger dogs were sent day and night from outposts to headquarters at distances from 1000 to 1200 "paces" and typically covered the distance in times of from two to three minutes. However, as he noted in his report of the trials, "the course the dogs took was over ground where it would have been impossible for the pedestrian to leave the footpath."

The German thoroughness in training and testing is apparent in some of the exercises that Richardson witnessed. To test sentry dogs, soldiers were sent out at night with the order to try and steal past the sentries. Despite extreme care taken by the "intruders," in no case did anybody ever succeed in passing a sentry with a dog. In every instance, the dogs gave warning as soon as the person approached within "150 to 200 paces" of the line of sentinels.

Patrol dogs were likewise tested. Incredibly, the dogs never gave notice if the animals knew the approaching patrol. However, if by any chance a stranger or strangers approached, the dogs alerted their handlers immediately. Likewise, in the testing for "ambuscades," it was noticed that the dogs (which would be what we now refer to as "scout dogs," leading the troops through unfamiliar territory) ignored the presence of soldiers of a troop known to them, passing them in an unconcerned manner, but immediately gave warning in the case of strangers.

Germany had introduced the concept of the ambulance dog in which the animal would carry a light harness that contained bandages, wound dressings and a mild stimulant (Richardson would later copy this idea in his own training). They recognized that during the heat of battle, wounded men often would crawl away to hidden places to avoid detection by the enemy, and by doing so were often overlooked by their own men who searched the battlefield afterwards. The ambulance dog would thus save many lives by being able to detect and hopefully save the wounded.

Lloyd notices an irony in these early dogs of the German service dog enterprise: most of the dogs in the German army were imports from England. The German Shepherd Dog, so beloved by the police and military for most of the 20th century, had not yet been developed to a fine state (the parent club for the breed in Germany wasn't founded until 1899) and so the Germans looked to Britain for sheep dogs of various kinds and the Airedale which, over the decades, always produced a higher percentage (if not total number) of working dogs than the German Shepherd.

When war broke out in 1914, Germany had at least 6000 dogs ready for immediate service, thanks to their Village Clubs. By one estimate, one branch of training alone – rescue dogs, i.e., ambulance or Red Cross dogs – saved at least 4000 wounded German soldiers during World War

I. In total, it is estimated that Germany put 30 000 dogs into combat during The Great War, primarily as messenger and ambulance dogs (U.S. Army Military History Institute Archive, ref # 4248).[15] Of these, it is estimated that 7000 died in the line of duty.

The Airedale arrived in Germany in 1893 (the same year that Germany initiated the idea of the ambulance dog) and was rapidly employed as a police and military dog. In 1900, the Germans used the breed in the Boxer Rebellion as messengers, munitions carriers, patrol dogs and as ambulance dogs, seeking wounded people. In 1914, after evaluating other potential breeds, the Airedale was the only breed designated "Kriegshund" or "war dog." Put another way, the English Airedale was considered the pre-eminent breed for military purposes. Military authorities turned to the Delegate Commission, the representative body for German breeders, for their opinion about what breed, or breeds, should be used in war time. They ignored the German Shepherd Dog. Max von Stephanitz, the founder of the German Shepherd Dog, wrote:

Thus it came about that – although shepherd dogs who had been tried out in one special regiment finished all their tests with full honours – English dogs were chosen as War dogs for German rifle battalions....English Airedale Terriers were enlisted side by side with Scotch collies. Therefore, when the newly founded SV (German Shepherd Dog Club) offered their breed, proved their existence and wanted to place dogs at the disposal of the authorities, all vacancies in Prussia were already filled. It was only in Bavaria that vacancies could be found for some dogs.

Thus, the English Airedale found itself at war against the nation that created it. The breed was assigned to the Jaeger battalions of both the German and Austrian military, where the dogs worked as sentry, ambulance and messenger dogs. At least two dogs were assigned to each company. In a prescient note, Richardson, in *War, Police and Army Dogs* (1910), includes a picture of Airedale sentries with a German rifle regiment. He captioned it with "English Dogs in the German Army. Airedale Terriers Used as Sentries With a German Rifle Regiment. *England, Take Note!*"

France

Downey, in *History of Dogs for Defense* (1955:9, 10), cites an interesting passage from Lieutenant Jupin of the French army who wrote *Les Chiens Militaire dans l'Armee Francaise*, published in Paris in 1887. It would seem that he might have been influenced by what was being conducted in Germany at the time, and his words seem somewhat urgent.

In order to assure the perfection of breeds destined for the Army, a military kennel, similar to that of the Acclimatization Gardens, and entrusted to special keepers, will be called upon in this case to play the same role as that of the military pigeon lofts and the stud farms which strive, each with some specific objective, to improve carrier pigeon strains and horse stock. Members of kennel clubs (societies of dog-lovers) will take charge of raising the puppies.

Postcard from 1914 showing "Ambulancier [Red Cross] dogs starting for the Front." (Author's collection)

At the time, he was the proverbial voice crying in the wilderness, and it would be 30 years before serious heed was paid to his suggestion. When the time did arrive, France followed much of his advice.

The French were probably second only to the Germans in terms of the number of dogs employed during World War I, with perhaps as many as 5000 seeing service. Prior to The Great War, efforts at mobilizing a war dog program were somewhat tentative and semi-official, limited to experiments with a small number of dogs over several years. However, dogs were usefully attached to the Chasseurs and Alpine regiments and were used with great success in Algeria, Madagascar, Dahomey and Tunisia as sentries and guards. The French government had established a training centre at Fontainebleau in 1910.

In 1914, one of the French dog clubs sent a number of dogs to the front, but the whole effort was lacking in management, organization and official sanction, so much so that it nearly completely crashed. Then, in December, 1914, the newspaper *Le Temps* drew attention to the fact that the Germans had a very large number of dogs employed with the military and asked the obvious question of why France could not do the same for their troops. The article drew a number of replies from French officers and men who took the same position, noting the many and useful ways in which dogs could be put to service and urgently requesting that trained animals be supplied to them. The hesitant, semi-official steps that had been taken by the French to this point were moved up a notch when General Catselnau accorded facilities for the employment of the dogs with the army. However, this new effort was also almost doomed to failure because of contrary and confusing direction and "difficulty of obtaining authority to demand suitable men as keepers for the dogs," according to Richardson in *British War Dogs*. The scheme was again, in Richardson's words, within "measurable distance of failure." But as Germany continued to exploit the military dog to the full, the French press again demanded why their country did not do the same.

This all changed in December of 1914 when a M. Megnin, a well known dog trainer, was granted permission by General de Maudhuy to establish a training kennel for the French army. Granted official support, four kennels and a large dog training facility were subsequently established at Satory. The commander was a Major Malric, who had a considerable interest in the use of war dogs and who, in fact, had tested the use of sentry dogs in Madagascar. Dogs were trained in three areas, as sentries, messengers and as pack dogs. This would later expand as the war progressed.

French dog clubs were asked to co-operate, which they did with remarkable zeal. Each took over a certain section of the country from which they sought the most suitable dogs and best breeds available for the war effort. Many were strays and gifts. The French did not discriminate on the basis of breed. Much as Richardson would later do, it was the dog, not the breed (or lack thereof) that was important. Among the purebreds, the Continental shepherd dogs (Beauceron, Briard, Belgian and German Shepherds) all proved their worth, with the Briard earning a leg-

French troops with war dogs on outpost duty on the Western Front, July, 1916. (Courtesy of the Imperial War Museum, London, Neg. #Q53878)

endary reputation as an ambulance dog. And the burly Great Pyrenees, another indigenous French breed, proved its worth as a draught worker. Some Collies and Airedales were also imported from England. Very few dogs were rejected, for with the array of tasks that were available to recruits, it was almost inevitable that a dog would find its niche. Those that were not alert enough for sentry work, aggressive enough for guard duty, or bright enough to become a messenger, could always be put into a harness for draught work.

The French were incredibly innovative in their use of dogs. Generally speaking, they were trained in five broad areas: as ambulance dogs to seek the wounded, as messengers (called "courier and dispatch"), as patrol dogs (often attached to an "outpost" where they were highly successful at detecting the approach of an enemy), as sentries and as draught animals.

Even within these roles, their work was highly original. The ambulance dogs (also called "sanitary dogs" or "Red Cross dogs") were used extensively by the French and gained considerable fame. They worked in conjunction with the French ambulance service, carrying first aid kits and leading stretcher bearers to wounded men. In this capacity, they performed a sort of battlefield triage for they are alleged to have had a talent for determining which men could still be helped and which were too far gone. However, the practice was discontinued. The dogs bore the international Red Cross insignia on their backs, but it was not respected and the dogs were often shot by the enemy, but not before more than 2000 French lives were saved by these remarkable animals.

Inspection of French Red Cross dogs before leaving for a forward area, Western Front, 1914. (Courtesy of the Imperial War Museum, London, Neg. #Q53509)

Carrier dog and his load of grenades. Military kennel at Camp de Satory, May, 1918. (Courtesy of the Imperial War Museum, London, Neg. #Q55074)

Draught dogs had a number of variations of the traditional hauling or packing. A pair of dogs could haul 200 kilos of supplies or munitions while a pack dog was expected to carry 12 to 15 kilos of gear. The Great Pyrenees (or Pyrenean Mountain Dog), another indigenous breed, was capable of carrying a load of 500 cartridges on its back in its capacity as ammunitions carrier. During the winter, draught dogs might be expected to haul sledges of supplies in snow covered areas, while in summer they might pull small carts on narrow gauge tracks. The Americans had no military dog program during World War I, but they filled a vital need when the French government put out an urgent request for sled dogs. Some 400 dogs were sent from Alaska to haul ammunition and supplies in snowy regions. So extensive was the French use of sled dogs that in 1918, there were more than 8000 sled dogs working for the army in the Vosges Mountains alone (Trew, 1941).

In addition to these tasks, the French put their dogs to work as guards in factories and other installations. And, in an often under-appreciated role, terriers were put to work in storehouses, cantonments and trenches, killing the rats that ate the food, carried disease and prevented sleep. Jager, in *Scout, Red Cross and Army Dogs*, states that by 1917, there were over 4000 French dogs serving on three German fronts and in occupied countries. These worked primarily as patrol, sentry, police, messenger and medical (or ambulance) dogs.

The effectiveness of the French war dogs is suggested by just a couple of examples. While many French ambulance dogs served wonderfully well, one in particular, Prusco, is renowned for having found more than 100 wounded soldiers after a single battle. According to a 1917 issue of *Red Cross Magazine*, he is reputed to have also dragged soldiers into craters or trenches to protect them. The value of the canine sentry dogs is best exemplified by two dogs that served with the Ninth Regiment of Cuirassiers. One night, they growled a warning a full 40 minutes before the garrison was aware of the approach of two strong enemy patrols that had intended a raid on their lines.

Despite the constructive and original uses to which French war dogs were put, they sometimes received criticism. Jager, in *Scout, Red Cross and Army Dogs* (1917), quotes an unnamed writer who called into question the wisdom of training ambulance and messenger dogs when greater emphasis should have been placed on sentry and patrol animals. Ambulance dogs, this critic suggested, demanded too much work and responsibility on the part of the handlers, while the messenger dog ran too great risk of literally running into the hands of the enemy. On the other hand, there was no limit to the value of the sentry and patrol dog, it was claimed. Time, of course, proved this Monday morning quarterback completely wrong, as both the messenger and ambulance dogs proved their worth and saved thousands of lives.

The media did their part in keeping military dogs in front of the public. Newspaper headlines, accompanied by illustrations, kept the public abreast of the important job the animals were performing. Eventually, from these humble beginnings, the role of canine soldier expanded to the point that by war's end, every French Army Corps had its completely organized, fully staffed and equipped camps of dogs, administered like every other recognized arm of the service.

Belgium

Belgium, like Germany, was a pioneer in the use of service dogs and, in fact, the city of Ghent is generally recognized as the birthplace of the modern police dog movement. Trainers today still speak of the "Ghent system" of police dog training. In 1899, the Ghent police force began supplying all their officers with dogs, an idea that caught on across the continent. With this background, it is not surprising that Belgium was also at the forefront of the military dog movement, as well. Prior to 1914, the Belgians, like the French and Germans, had army dog schools in place. Before war broke out, the Belgians had trained dogs being used as sentries with several regiments, including the carabineers. When World War I did break out, the Belgians also put patrol and messenger dogs into effective use.

Dogs were also used as munitions carriers, hauling machine guns, a task very much in keeping with the Belgian history of draught dogs for hauling milk carts and other conveyances. While other European nations had a centuries-old tradition of draught dogs, Belgium probably used them far more than any other country. Lest we think that this was somehow immeasurably cruel,

Belgian dog carts and guns leaving for the fighting line, 25th October, 1918. (Courtesy of the Imperial War Museum, London, Neg. #Q48445)

the use of the dogs was strictly controlled and monitored. The dogs were, generally speaking, well treated and respected. There were laws that governed their use and standards enacted for the type of cart, harness and dogs that were to be employed. In reality, the Belgian and other European dogs had an easier time of it than northern sled dogs. Loads rested on the axle of the cart, so that the load was resting on the wheels and not on the shoulders or backs of the dogs. There were specifications about the harness, which had to be broad and across the chest, where the dogs did their pulling. Failure to comply with any of the regulations pertaining to the carting dog could result in being stopped by the police.

With this history, it is not surprising that Belgium made ample use of their famed draught dogs when war erupted. Given the fact that dog transport was very common, training was not that extensive. The major hurdle was getting dogs used to the sounds of gunfire (large and small) at close range. That, and the frantic speed with which the dogs were pressed into action, presented the most difficult challenges.

This consideration for the dogs' well being continued – as much as possible under the conditions – throughout the war. Dogs were fed daily and were given water at least three times a day. Attention was paid to their grooming, with the dogs being brushed and combed every day if possible. Inevitably dogs were killed in action, and many more wounded. However, veterinary hospitals were established behind the lines to care for those that were sick or injured. And, in a grim reminder that casualties were unavoidable, there were stations where replacement dogs could be swiftly placed in harness to replace their dead or wounded comrades.

The Belgians put 12 companies of dog-drawn machine guns into use during the First World War. Five hundred big, brawny dogs were employed to haul the guns and ammunition wagons. After a while, it was found difficult to maintain this type of work, as the harnesses and carts were adapted to dogs of a particular size only and it was not an easy task to find dogs of proper stature and conformation. As well, because the dogs worked in pairs, it was necessary to find animals of near identical size.

It is hard to overestimate the contributions of these dogs to the war effort, for they were almost always at the front lines. They were at the battles of Liegeand, Namur, Antwerp and Louvain. Other nations were most impressed with the Belgian draught dogs that worked as teams during the war. At the siege of Liege, four gun teams were almost trapped by the Germans. But despite the loss of many of the gun crew, the surviving dogs were able to get back to the Belgian base with the guns.

Belgium was almost completely overrun during World War I and the recruiting of dogs of this specialty was nearly impossible, and so the requirements of the French army absorbed whatever dogs were available and suitable for draught purposes. However, a kennel was started in France and placed under the direction of an expert officer to cater to the need of the Belgian army. Richardson, in *British War Dogs*, observes that while sentry dogs and some messengers were trained at this facility, the majority of the animals were trained for draught work. Reflective, perhaps, of his English heritage and bias (Britain deeming it illegal to place a dog in harness), Richardson voiced the opinion that, while useful, draught dogs need roads to be most efficient, and that therefore on the battlefield, a pack dog makes more sense and is better suited.

Finally, Belgium, as did other nations, had trained "ambulance dogs," albeit in limited numbers, to seek out the wounded. These were of various breeds, including Dutch Shepherds and Airedales.

Russia

It is believed that the Russians used dogs as sentries during the Crimean War. However, they seriously began using military dogs in 1904, during the Russo-Japanese War. They got their start with the help of the British, in particular then-Major Richardson. They had learned of his work as a trainer of service dogs. The Russian Embassy in London made an official request for Richardson to supply a number of ambulance dogs to work with the Russian troops. They were quite pleased with their work.

Gray, in *Dogs of War*, cites an article from the Russian newspaper *Neva*:

Attached to the medical department of the Russian army on the Shao, are a number of dogs, which are of great help in the work of seeking out the wounded after the battle, especially on broken ground and at night-time. They are a kind of sheep-dog, bred by a certain major 'Ottonville' (Richardson) and have been trained to go about over the battlefield when the fight is over. They carry on their backs a small parcel, marked on the outside with a red cross and containing a length of bandage and small flasks of brandy and of water.... On finding a wounded man, the dog allows him, if he is able, to unfasten the packet and make use of the contents; if he can then manage to walk, the dog leads him to where the field hospital is at work, to give him proper medical dressing, if not, the dog trots off with his cap to fetch searchers whom it guides to the man it has found. The dogs are said to show great intelligence in their work, and may be compared to the famous dogs of St. Bernard.

The Russians employed dogs in a number of ways during the Russo-Japanese War, in addition to the ambulance dogs. Sections of the strategic Manchurian Railway were destroyed by bombs, generally set at night. To counteract this threat, dogs and their handlers were posted as teams along the length of the railway to act as sentries. They proved quite effective. Downey, in *History of Dogs for Defense* (1955), states that the fact that the Trans-Siberian Railroad was never cut during the course of the Russo-Japanese War is attributable, in part, to the fact that it was guarded by trained dogs.

By 1912, Russia had a number of regiments that used dogs for sentry work. One regiment, the Hussars of the Imperial Guard, at Tzarskoe Selo outside St. Petersburg, had 23 Airedales. They continued to train and use ambulance dogs, and as World War I loomed, the number being trained increased daily. When World War I began, Russia had a fair number of dogs ready for combat. They were mainly Airedales, German Shepherd Dogs and Doberman Pinschers. Many of the Airedales seem to have been imports from Britain.

Like the French, the Russians were quite innovative in their use of dogs. Among other tasks, they equipped them with lights on their backs to help illuminate "no man's land" during the night. They also delivered ammunition to men posted along extended lines. At this task, the dogs showed incredible ingenuity and diligence. Max von Stephanitz explained that

In Russia, dogs maintained faultless liaison between the forward detachments, the regiment itself, and the Higher Command over long distances. In cases where the distances were too long for one dog, stages were arranged, between which dogs ran to and fro. If any of these dispatch stages had to be moved, the dogs sought out the new place by tracing out the track of the handler or deputy handler. When a dispatch stage was organized permanently, the dogs would run over the accustomed route by sight only; they made short cuts and regular routes of their own.

According to Richardson, Airedales proved superior to German Shepherd Dogs and Dobermans at this and other types of messenger work for the Russian army. In fact, the trainers told him that they preferred the breed for such roles. The elite Russian regiments all had military dogs and one consisted of more than 30 Airedales. One estimate (Jager, 1917) places the number of military dogs in Russia in 1917 as high as 10 000.

Italy

Italy did not have a highly developed military dog program in place prior to the First World War, but it did make use of a couple of its traditional breeds, the Spinone and the Maremma. The former is a hunting dog, recognized for its tractability and keen powers of scent, while the latter is a renowned flock guardian that tips the scales at 40-45 kilograms and is renowned for its courage and, at times, its aggressiveness. The Spinone (which had a great many other breeds crossed with them) had been acquired from the Customs House and used by the army during the Turko-Italian war. They were normally kept to prevent smuggling along the Austrian border but soon proved effective as sentries, detecting the enemy and for finding hidden ammunition. The army, lacking any trained dog handlers, wisely used the customs agents as dog handlers.

During the Turko-Italian war, the Maremmas were sought when other dogs could not be found. Because they were untrained, they proved harder to handle, albeit they were formidable

An Italian coast guard on duty with his dog, on the Adriatic coast. (Courtesy of the Imperial War Museum, London, Neg. #Q19117)

An Italian postcard, with the tri-lingual caption "Turco-Italian [sic] War – Training wardogs to search for hidden arms." The dogs – or at least the one on the far left (partially hidden by the man) and the one on the far right – are Airedales. (Author's collection)

guards. During World War I, the Maremmas proved their worth in a more meaningful way, as guards and sentries. Hamer, in *Dogs at War* (2001), states that by 1918, Italy had trained about 3500 dogs for combat duty. Some of these functioned as pack dogs, carrying light munitions through conspicuous passes in the mountains.

Holland, Sweden and Bulgaria

Holland, Sweden and Bulgaria had all initiated military dog programs before the First World War. In Holland, the primary interest was in ambulance dogs, many of which had been supplied by Richardson. They were with the Grenadier Regiments whose headquarters were at The Hague. Shortly before the war, a training school was established under the presidency of the Prince Consort of the Netherlands at The Hague. Jager, in *Scout, Red Cross and Army Dogs* (1917), quotes a visitor to Holland during the First World War, who was permitted to view that country's war dogs and to report on them.

> *Through the courtesy of the army officer in charge of Holland's war dogs, I was allowed to see them work. They were truly wonderful. There are about 1000 dogs in the Holland army. The machine gun dogs are of a breed like the mastiff, strong, big chested, with enormous legs.[16] The ambulance dogs were almost all shepherds.[17] These latter ranged over a field of some hundreds of acres and very quickly found and reported the men, supposedly wounded, who were hidden in the brush or behind obstructions. These war dogs are bred and raised in government kennels. The soldiers in charge live right at the kennels. The effects of early train-*

ing were apparent, for when we walked through a yard in which there were numerous puppies of all ages, not one of the pups offered to jump on us. They showed all the lively interest a puppy does but no bad manners. I witnessed the turning out for exercise of at least 100 big fierce-looking dogs. Each dog as his or her door opened, dashed out, crossed two lots and went through two gates on the run, until he reached the lot he knew was his playground. Imagine this bunch of dogs playing frantically with never a fight. "We train our dogs", as the inspector said.

Sweden, by 1912, had a system in place for training both ambulance and sentry dogs and trials were periodically held in Stockholm. Similarly, Bulgaria had in place an excellent system for training military dogs and their entire frontier was guarded by sentries that were with the pickets and detached posts in the years prior to the war.

United States

Richardson, in one of his books, recounts meeting with an American official to discuss the use of war dogs. It was a couple of years before the First World War when the American army was in Mexico. Richardson was convinced of the value that well trained dogs might play in such an effort and, being aware of an American officer in his neighborhood on other business, sought him and arranged a meeting. There, he laid out some suggestions, explaining why he thought that dogs would prove useful to the American army with the war in Mexico. At the meeting's conclusion, the officer requested a full report. This Richardson sent, complete with maps and illustrations. He never received a reply. Consequently, the United States did not have a war dog program in place before or during the First World War. A single dog did play a significant role in the Spanish-American War at the close of the 19th century. A dog named Don was much heralded, for not a single patrol that he led was ever ambushed. Don lived and travelled with a US Cavalry troop led by Captain Steel. Aware of the role played by the dog, and perhaps several decades ahead of his time, Captain Steel astutely observed that "Dogs are the only scout that can secure a small detachment against ambuscade in these tropical jungles." Despite his successes, no other dogs were used by the Americans.

As has been noted many times in many accounts, the American troops were more than eager to get their hands on British and French dogs and avail themselves of their services whenever they could. A page from a US Army publication indicates American plans for developing a war dog program.

In the Spring [sic] of 1918, during World War I, a recommendation was made by G-5, General Headquarters, American Expeditionary Forces, that dogs be used as sentries, messengers, patrol aids and for special supply missions. It was proposed to procure 500 dogs from French training centers every three months to equip American Divisions with 228 each; training to extend to the United States, five kennels with 200 dog capacity each. However, the project was disapproved by G-3, General Headquarters, and the matter dropped. (National Archives, Ref. #4258)

This effort might have been what was alluded to in Jager's *Scout, Red Cross and Army Dogs* (1917) but never seems to have picked up on by historians of such matters. After a discussion of the French efforts to develop "ambulance dogs," Jager refers to the newsletter of The German Shepherd Dog Club of America in which it was observed that "Recently it became known that the United States War Department is arranging to buy and train dogs to be used for the same purpose." This very well might have been to what the above quotation referred.

That might not have been the end of American efforts, however. In *The New Country Life* (June, 1918), there was an article about concrete steps that were underway in the US to develop a war dog program. Walter Dyer, the author of the article, stated that at Camp Funston, in Kansas, nine Airedales were being trained by Lieutenant William L. Butler, an experienced dog and pigeon fancier. They had all been donated to the war effort. The effort was largely experimental, with no firm plans for the dogs, and only on completion of the training would it be determined for which branch of the services the dogs would be best suited. In general, the Americans were following the French example. The dogs, it was noted, "were taking to their training with pep."

Airedales had been selected for the same reasons that the Europeans admired the breed: their intelligence, strength, courage, endurance, trainability, size, coat color and texture, and their essential one-person character. At the same time, there was talk of crossbreeding the Airedales with Old English Sheepdogs to create an even better military dog. This plan faltered and disappeared. Had it materialized, it is unlikely it would have improved either breed.

As noted above, this article appeared five months before the war ended. It provides a contemporaneous account of a little-known effort to implement a war dog school. Few people are aware of these initial steps and there appears to be no other information available about the program or what eventually became of it. Indeed, in a private correspondence, the National Archives indicated that they searched the general correspondence for Camp Funston in the Records of US Army Continental Commands, but found no reference to dogs or the establishment of a dog training program. It is curious that such an endeavor was reported in a general magazine such as *Country Life*, but that no other records exist. The US did not embark upon a similar endeavor until the attack on Pearl Harbor in 1941.

PART TWO
Colonel Richardson's Airedales

CHAPTER THREE
Colonel Edwin Hautenville Richardson: A Brief Biography

When we consider that Richardson wrote five books, two of which are autobiographical and the remainder of which reflect his life's interest, it is remarkable that we really do not know that much about him. Searches of the conventional sources of material, such as The Imperial War Museum and Public Archives, reveal little about Richardson, other than his dates of birth and death, regimental attachments, his rank and that information related to his work with the War Dog School.

His two autobiographies, *Forty Years With Dogs* and *Fifty Years With Dogs*, reflect exactly that – his years spent breeding, raising and training canine allies. We learn little about Richardson the man. He divulges little about his domestic life other than that he was married to the same woman for decades and that he had two sons, one of whom was killed during World War I. Little passion for hobbies (other than his dogs) is evidenced, and of his military career prior to his development of the War Dog School, barely a sentence is written. We know next to nothing about his education and military training. It is telling, perhaps, that in one of his books the best he can tell us is that "one of us", i.e., either he or his wife, had an interest in exotic birds and, to that end, they had built a number of aviaries in their homes over the years. We don't learn who the bird fancier was, or what kinds of birds they had, or anything else pertaining to the matter. That alone speaks volumes about a man who, although he spent decades trying to get recognition for his work and who wrote nearly a half dozen books, sought to keep his private life very secure and away from the public. What we are left with, then, is what he told us in his own words and that appears to have been very selectively written.

To large extent, he was very much a product – admittedly, an upper middle class product – of the Victorian era and all that that implies: a sense of duty to Crown and country, a strong sense of right and wrong (defined by upper middle class British standards, of course), a latent adventurousness and yearning for a sense of accomplishment, and an awareness of the greatness of the British Empire which, at the dawn of the 20th century, was still extensive.

Ancestors

In *Forty Years With Dogs* Richardson provides the reader with a substantial chapter that deals with his "forebears." He does this, he says, because "it is sometimes useful to students of psychology to trace the sources from which the impulses of a person's life have sprung." How much a person is influenced by his ancestry is debatable, but the inclusion of Richardson's rationale for including the chapter is interesting in itself and hints at the complexity of the man. If Richardson wants us to find parallels with his ancestry and his own life accomplishments, perhaps they live in the religious and missionary zeal borne by his ancestors and a life devoted to the military. In his background may also be found a number of alleged cases where people saw the proverbial light and changed their views.

By Richardson's own estimation, the earliest reference to the Richardson family is to be found in 1602 when the will of the Reverend John Richardson, M.A., Rector of Warmington in Warwickshire, was proved. Through the ensuing three centuries, Richardson's ancestry comprised clergymen, soldiers and scholars. The "Hautenville" of his name comes compliments of an ancient Normandy family, originally seated at Hauteville (later Hauteville-la-Guichard) in France. The Seigneur de Hauteville had 12 sons whose combined impact was felt throughout Europe beginning in the 16th century. Political troubles in France during the reign of Louis XIV obliged many to emigrate to Ireland. Among these were his ancestors.

His grandfather, James Nicholson Richardson (1782-1847), was a landowner who turned his holdings to farming and commercial interests. He had seven sons, among whom was Joshua, Colonel Richardson's father. In *Forty Years With Dogs*, Richardson wrote that "In reading the family records of these seven brothers and their father…one gets the impression of a strong sense of living for a high purpose, supported by a distinct code of definite regulations to that end." It might be added that one gets the same sense when reading Colonel Richardson's own volumes. *Plus ca change*.

Joshua ran and farmed the estate of Brookhill, in County Antrim, Ireland, for a number of years. Typical of his social class, he was fond of hunting and, in addition to his own pack of hounds, was a member of the Killultagh Hounds. He was also, according to his son, a fine horseman and a fine judge of horse flesh. When the education of his growing family obliged him to move to Cheltenham, his opinion was still sought in both Ireland and England.

Richardson's ancestors on his mother's side closely parallel his father's. As he notes, his "mother's family also took root in the Church" when the Reverend William Nicholson, from Cumberland, moved to Ireland with Cromwell's army and became Rector of Derry-Brughas. Richardson relates a story, which he describes as "romantic," about the wife of one of the reverend's descendants, a Captain Nicholson. Allegedly, said Captain's wife was seen scouring a battle field with an infant in her arms, searching for the body of her husband. Cromwell, hearing of this sad state of affairs, arranged to have her properly safeguarded and subsequently bestowed a grant of land on her and her family.

The maternal side of his family had lived at Stramore, in County Down, for several hundred years. They were "absorbed in farming, hunting, and sports of all kinds." His maternal grandfather and great-grandfather had both been Masters of Hounds. Not unexpectedly, the family was well-connected through marriage with many of the influential and sporting families of Ireland.

Family lore maintained that Joshua Richardson met his wife, Charlotte Nicholson, when he went to purchase a horse from her father. The horse was a "fiery chestnut" which, it was alleged, could only be handled by young Charlotte, then only 17 years old. She was summoned from the classroom. Upon her arrival, Joshua decided then and there that not only was he going to follow through with the purchase of the horse, he was going to marry the young woman who could control it.

Charlotte, like other members of her family, felt the call of service. Members of her family had served with the army in India and elsewhere. In her case, rather than entering the military, she did social service among the "sick and ignorant" of London. While working in the docklands area she contracted smallpox, from which she never recovered. Joshua and Charlotte had three sons, of whom Edwin was the youngest. He was born August 25, 1863, in County Antrim. As was typical of the landed gentry during the Victorian era, one son entered the Church, another joined the navy and attained the rank of commander, and Edwin would go into the army.

Youth

Richardson's favorite subject in school in Cheltenham was "natural history," to which he devoted considerable energies outside of the class. He had a number of pets including a Spaniel, a Basset Hound and several "voracious hawks." In *Forty Years With Dogs*, he recalled being "deeply impressed by a fine old Bloodhound" that was the estate guardian, a rather unusual job for the normally mild-mannered breed. Regardless, Frigate, the Bloodhound of Richardson's youth, was believed to be from a long line of working and tracking Bloodhounds that were common throughout Ireland and England long before their work became formalized and institutionalized by police forces and the military. These dogs had been used for decades for tracking thieves and other nefarious types. Richardson himself speculated in his memoirs that it was this contact at an early age with a working Bloodhound that laid the seed for his subsequent work with working dogs. Undoubtedly, it did. It was also at this time that he first heard that dogs were being trained on the Continent for military purposes, an idea that he found quite intriguing.

Richardson's father was anxious for his youngest son to learn languages and so after his schooling in Cheltenham, he journeyed to Hanover and Dresden to learn German and later to Switzerland to learn French. He later claimed, in one of his books, to have become aware at this relatively early time that Germany was "tuning up" its military for some unforeseen purpose and he believed, even then, that there would be trouble ahead. Later, after the war broke out, he was able to capitalize on his experiences abroad in the training of military dogs.

While abroad, Richardson began his study of the historic use of military dogs beginning with the ancient Greeks and through to the 19th century. The training methods he read about, including having messenger dogs swallow written messages, necessitating the killing of the dog upon its arrival in order to extract the message, disgusted but intrigued him. As the century turned, he would begin his own informal training of military dogs, an effort that eventually culminated in the British war dog program.

Following his education at Cheltenham, Richardson continued through Sandhurst, the renowned military academy, and passed into the Sherwood Foresters. When he eventually retired from the regular army, he joined the West Yorkshire militia.

Blanche Richardson

In 1894, Richardson married Blanche, the younger daughter of Thomas Riley Bannon. Together they had two sons, both of whom passed through Harrow and Sandhurst and both of whom served in World War I. The younger son, Angus, died at the age of 18 at Loos.

The family would move a lot over the years. They would live in Scotland, London, on the Sussex coast, and Surrey, always moving, it would seem, to find ever larger and more spacious accommodations for the dogs.

Richardson was always eager to acknowledge the contributions of his wife, whom he called his "aide-de-camp." She seemed to be blessed with an almost uncanny gift with animals, as suggested by her remarkable work with Tweed, an Old English Sheepdog messenger (see Chapter Nine). An equally successful rehabilitative exercise was undertaken with a particularly difficult Bullmastiff, a big, powerful breed developed to assist gamekeepers with their work in apprehending poachers. They weigh between 45 and 60 kilograms (100-130 pounds). While not particularly sharp, i.e., easily forced into aggression, they were bred to run down and subdue poachers without mauling them. As evidence of how good they were at their jobs, contests were held in the 19th century between muzzled Bullmastiffs and men armed with small clubs. The latter would be given a head start and the dogs released. Despite the men being armed and the dogs muzzled, no man ever escaped from one of these dogs. It was one of these dogs that Blanche Richardson chose to work with rather than euthanize. Richardson related the story in *British War Dogs*. It is worth relating here in its entirety to demonstrate his wife's gifts.

> *I remember the case of a very large, fine bull mastiff [sic] which was offered to the School. It had not been off the chain for four years, as it was so savage that no one could approach it with safety. With great difficulty it was sent to the School and had to be taken out of the railway van with long poles. On arrival, it was fastened to a kennel but its behaviour was so outrageous, and as it seemed a risk of breaking away and attacking the staff, the opinion was formed that it would have to be destroyed. Preparations were made to this end, when Mrs. Richardson pleaded to have one more day for a final experiment.*
>
> *For two hours she stood near the dog, speaking to it softly. Gradually she edged nearer, still speaking, but never looking at the animal. She discerned that underneath the creature's savage behaviour there was a very highly-strung, sensitive nature, and that if confidence could be established, the ferocity, which was really due to soreness of mind and fear, would vanish.*
>
> *After a time she was able to lean against the kennel, and then very gently her hand was laid on the large brown head, and permission was given her to stroke the satin ears. With a very quiet movement she unfastened the chain, and led the poor beast away. Its gratitude and*

delight at being treated as an ordinary trustworthy dog was unbounded, and when I was making a round of inspection later in the day, I found the great beast at her feet, looking up with adoring eyes at his saviour. After that this dog was the great favourite with all the staff, and was absolutely reliable, while still retaining its guarding qualifications as regards strangers, and it did some very useful work for its country!

This story says a lot about not only Mrs. Richardson's unique talents with animals, but also her intrepid spirit and unwillingness to give in when she thought better of a situation. It also speaks to her innate compassion and kindness of spirit. We should also acknowledge what it says about Colonel Richardson and his acceptance of his wife's dissenting points of view. They were a dynamic team.

Colonel Richardson fitting an Airedale with a gas mask. (Courtesy of the Imperial War Museum, London, Neg. #D447)

The Richardson Dogs

A variety of dogs shared their lives with the Richardsons prior to the development of their training facility. The first was Johnny, a Dandie Dinmont Terrier purchased by Mrs. Richardson shortly before their marriage. He was found in a church in a Scottish village and relocated to live with his new owners in London. Johnny would live for 16 years with his new owners and was dearly loved. As Richardson recounts in *Forty Years With Dogs*, "a tear and a laugh still rise when we speak of him."

Johnny was to play a pivotal role in what was to become Richardson's life work. After London, the family moved to a house on the Sussex coast. The house was located at the foot of the downs some miles from Brighton, where the family did its shopping. One morning, they loaded Johnny into "a vehicle" and drove to Brighton via a road that completely bypassed the downs, taking a very circuitous route. Upon completing their errands, they entered a café for refreshments. At some point during this respite, Johnny disappeared. His worried owners scoured the streets and alerted the police, all to no avail. As the day drew to a close, they returned home with saddened hearts. As the sun was setting, they decided to go for a walk on the downs. As they walked towards the sinking sun, a little shadow raced towards them "hurrying without an instant pause or rest, and showing one steadfast purpose: to get *Home*!" As Richardson observed in *Fifty Years With Dogs*, how Johnny had found his way home through Brighton's streets, and over territory he had never seen, and in a totally different way of travel from that on which he had set out in the carriage that morning, no one knows. He surmises that Johnny "must have divined the direct crow's-flight route, which took no cognizance of paths and roads." In the end, Richardson observed, "this demonstration of homing instinct interested us very much and was of great help later on, when training hundreds of dogs for various Army and police duties, when a great part of the training was based on this instinct."[18]

He was followed by a number of Scottish Deerhounds, including Malcolm, Maida, Lady Ashton and Lorna. Bicycling was just becoming popular at this time and the Deerhounds had been acquired to keep the Richardsons company on their biking excursions. Wee Johnny could only keep pace for a short while before being placed in a basket and carried. The huge Deerhounds, however, could keep going for miles. Malcolm sired a number of litters, some of which produced fine show dogs. The first breeding was with Lorna, resulting in a litter of 11 puppies. Richardson acknowledges that while all matured and found good homes, the whole breeding experience was a novelty from which he and Mrs. Richardson learned a great deal. Following Lorna's initial brood, Maida whelped a litter of five.

Johnny and the Scottish Deerhounds were not to be the only dogs in the Richardson household. While visiting a dog show, they met a man with a number of Dogues de Bordeaux. These French Mastiffs are legendary for their ferocity and fighting prowess, having fought other dogs, bears, wolves, jaguars and lions in the barbaric days when animal combat was staged for entertainment of the masses. Aware of the breed's reputation with strangers, the Richardsons added Saida, a "mustard-coloured" Dogue bitch with cropped ears, to the household. They exercised caution when she was around strangers but found that, despite their reputation, "they nevertheless melt with affection towards their owners, in an almost pathetically contrasting degree, which is in itself attractive." Saida found herself loping along with the Richardsons as they cycled about, shedding excess weight as she did so.

The Irish Wolfhound, the close cousin of the Scottish Deerhound, was the next breed to find its way to the Richardsons' kennel. At the time they began adding the breed to the kennel, the Wolfhound had just passed the resurrection stage of its history. The original Wolfhound had been in existence probably for millennia, the first written record occurring in AD 391 when the Roman Consul Quintus Aurelius received seven of them as a gift. "All Rome viewed them with wonder," he wrote. Standing close to a metre in height, it is no surprise they evoked that reaction. However, with the extinction of wolves in Ireland (probably in the 18th century), with ownership of the great hounds restricted largely to the nobility, and with many exportations of the breed, its numbers dwindled. Indeed, some people still maintain that when the last wolf died in Ireland, so too did the last real Irish Wolfhound. Some people were unconvinced.

Captain George A. Graham, a Scot in the British army, had begun his work of reviving this ancient breed in 1862. He claimed to have found a couple of remaining specimens of the "real" Irish Wolfhound and began reviving the breed. Through the introduction of Deerhound and Great Dane blood, he re-introduced what he believed to be the Irish Wolfhound of old. In 1885, the Kennel Club adopted a breed standard for the Irish Wolfhound. The breed then began to rise quickly in popularity in the British Isles.

However, as Richardson observed in *Fifty Years With Dogs*, the effects of the introduction of Deerhound and Great Dane blood was still much in evidence, as throwbacks kept cropping up in the litters they bred. "Some very quaint specimens appeared, a mixture of Deerhound, Great Dane and various other unknowns of uncertified ingredients, all in the attempt to inaugurate the great size that was supposed to distinguish these hounds." Eventually, they succeeded in breeding a fine animal named Benny, who had the great size and conformation desired in the breed. Curiously, Richardson noted that Benny "for some unknown reason possessed an orange-yellow coat." Today, the Irish Wolfhound comes in a plethora of colors, including fawn, "red fawn," red, "sandy red" and yellow. Undoubtedly, poor old Benny was one of these now recognized colors, albeit he was probably a minority of one in the late 19th century.

While Benny's color might not have appealed to his owners, he apparently had an abundance of qualities that are treasured by the owners of these gigantic dogs. Richardson described him as having a "most affectionate and magnanimous disposition" and this he seems to have demonstrated. Breed fanciers claim that the Wolfhound is "gentle when stroked, fierce when provoked." Once, when Johnny got into an altercation with Malcolm and another Wolfhound, Benny intervened and saved the Dandie's life. On another occasion, towards the end of Johnny's life, when he was ill and ailing, he disappeared. After a long, frantic search, his owners found him, curled up and content in Benny's kennel, behind his huge friend.

At some time as the 19th century drew to a close, Richardson became interested in Bloodhounds, twigged, perhaps, by the memory of his childhood. As he recounts in one of his memoirs, he was interested in what a dog could do, as well as what it looked like. At times they would have as many as six of the big hounds in residence. He would work closely with the breed for the next 20 years or so, eventually sending some abroad to be used in warfare and police work. Other breeds – Collies, Newfoundlands and various smaller breeds of terrier – would also find their way into the Richardson home over the decades.

The Soul of the Dog

There is an aspect of Richardson that, surprisingly, he lets us experience. In both *Forty Years With Dogs* and *Fifty Years With Dogs,* he makes considerable digression into his spiritual beliefs (it is misleading to call them religious, which would place constraints on his beliefs) as he – somehow – weaves his spirituality into his views of dogs and their training. He writes, in the former volume, that "Those of us who train animals very soon trace the underlying soul – the golden thread which runs through all creation, from the individual person down to the smallest insect that creeps – that original thought of God, perfect and true." This is an interesting stance insofar as Judaeo-Christian tradition denies the existence of a soul to all but humankind. Richardson felt compelled to buttress his position by referring to two clergyman friends. Like Richardson, they believed that animals – or dogs, at least – had souls. One, however, confided that he would never voice such beliefs from the pulpit in his home parish, a wise move insofar as it would probably not only have labeled him eccentric, but probably would have had him defrocked. The other, Reverend Vivian Evans, was the chaplain of the English Church at Versailles. Richardson visited him at his home in 1915, the purpose of which was an interview. He came away greatly impressed, especially because the reverend held views "entirely [Richardson's] own." Upon his departure, Richardson was given a small book that Evans had written titled *The Soul of a Dog*, which he quotes at length. Passages are worth citing here, for Richardson concurred completely.

> *It cannot be proved that an animal has not a soul; and if it has, then in the nature of it it must be immortal. That animals have not souls is an assertion arrived at without any premises to warrant it – a philosophy of convenience, a form of argument often made use of by theologians when their mental evolutions have landed them in a hole – it would be more convenient so, therefore it is so. It is feared that if a dog were allowed a soul endless difficult questions would arise, therefore it is better to say; and to go on sincerely hoping that no one will ask us to explain what he has in its place to adequately account for his almost human actions. Personally I do not see where the difficult questions would arise....*
>
> *The breath, life, or spirit of God must always be immortal, and every creature that partakes of it partakes of immortality. It cannot be otherwise....*
>
> *If the story of the beginning of things is taken literally, and not distorted to suit theological theories, we can only infer from it that animals as well as man have a reasonable, conscious*

soul, but subject to limitations not put to man's; and, that they were not created for man's pleasure and use, but like him for themselves....

Why should man suffer from such a positive horror lest any other creature but himself should have a soul, and enjoy an after life in another world? Why shouldn't they? And why does man go out of his way, a long way from logic and obvious facts, to invent all sorts of lame excuses why they shouldn't? Personally, I am of the opinion of St. Paul that creatures expect an after life, and that they will have it.

Richardson, surprisingly, was unaware that Christianity denies souls to other beings, for he writes that "Until we talked together [with his clergyman friend] I do not think I had fully realized that the majority of people do not credit dogs or any other creature with souls." His attribution of souls to dogs is more in keeping with what used to be called "primitive" societies, i.e., hunting and gathering peoples. At times, his perception of the dog might be perceived by some as anthropomorphic. He writes, in *Fifty Years With Dogs*, that

The reason that the dog is more especially the friend of Man as above all other animals is, of course, because it approximates to the mentality of Man himself and exemplifies unselfish attachment apart from its own needs and desires. In some case, a dog actually has a higher concept of certain moral obligations than its own master. You may find a dog which under no circumstances will betray a trust, while its master may be continually doing so. A dog is frequently forgiving and loving, it is joyous and happy, and it can also die of grief. How many people can we describe thus? – and of those of which we can do so, are they not the best that we know, the salt of the earth?

There was yet another dimension to Richardson's spirituality that, today, might not seem that unusual but was probably looked upon askance in his time. He believed in certain telepathic and other paranormal qualities of dogs. He was convinced that some dogs have the power of communicating with human beings who are passing out of this life or when they (the dogs) are passing or have passed. As evidence, he presented a number of stories that he believed were irrefutable proof of his position. For those who doubted, the Richardsons suggested that the power of communication is necessarily more limited at present, perhaps, because we (humankind) have made a decree of separation once a soul has passed. In their co-written volume, the Richardsons state unequivocally that they believe that each dog has its own personality, distinct and eternal, and that "the tender love emanating from the soul…represents an unbreakable link between dog and master and will continue to hold through the rising stages of experience."

Incredibly, perhaps, Richardson was able to commingle this essentially animistic belief and paranormalism with more or less conventional Christianity. He states that the horrifying cruelties of our species is grinding down and

the inevitable evolution of all things is leading to that final solution wherein "The wolf shall also dwell with the lamb, and the leopard shall lie down with the kid; and the calf, the young lion and the fatling together; and a little child shall lead them.... They shall not hurt nor destroy in all my holy mountain; for the earth shall be full of the knowledge of the Lord as the waters cover the sea...."

Because of his religious beliefs, Richardson had no difficulty putting the dog to work for people. In *British War Dogs*, he addresses this issue head on. He acknowledges that some people might have difficulty putting the dog ("this dear friend") into war created by people. To this, Richardson relates the following:

> *There is a splendid story told that soon after the Creation, a great chasm began to open up in the ground, and man found himself on one side of it and all the animal creation was on the other. All the animals remained indifferent and acquiescent to the separation. The dog alone betrayed despair. With pitiful whining and imploring gestures, it strove to attract the man's attention across the widening chasm. The man gazed at the dog's wistful eyes and said "Come!"' The dog jumped, and just reached the other side with his front paws. "You shall be my comrade," said the man, and drew the dog up to safety beside him.*

While he might not have taken this story literally, Richardson extrapolated from it. The dog, he believed, had a very strongly developed moral sense, as well as an intelligence vastly superior to other non-human creatures. These qualities, coupled with a willingness to serve and a strong sense of right and wrong, characterize the dog. In Richardson's view then, "the trained dog considers himself highly honoured by his position as a servant of His Majesty." Thus, there was nothing exploitative in the human-dog relationship.

Richardson's religious beliefs were a remarkable blend of quasi-animism, Christianity and something approximating what we would call today New Age-ism. It is perhaps all the more striking given his military background and its emphasis upon empiricism and fact gathering. Regardless, it worked for him and more importantly it helped to shape his views of the proper care and handling of dogs. His belief in the existence of canine souls influenced his methods of training, which emphasized compassion, kindness, gentleness, reward and, most important, the dog's perspective in the process. In this sense, Richardson was light years ahead of his time. Ultimately, it was probably due to his spiritual beliefs, as eclectic and apparently irreconcilable as they might be.

Surprisingly, given his close-guardedness in almost all other matters, he was unabashed in his stating his religious views. In *Forty Years With Dogs* he writes that "I may seem to my readers to be unduly Biblical. I will make no apology as there is no other book in the world to which we can turn with a surety for a complete statement of creation in all its forms as we find there."

An Audience With Colonel Richardson

Dr. J. G. Horning wrote the following account of his visit to Richardson's kennel for the February 1, 1928, *American Kennel Gazette*. Richardson was, at this time, probably at the peak of his renown, having established the War Dog School and having trained and sent dogs worldwide. Horning's article provides a sense of immediacy.

Colonel Richardson and friends. (Courtesy of the Imperial War Museum, London, Neg. #D441)

The house itself is a long, rambling structure, its height varying from one to three stories.... The estate is a private park, covering several acres, and consisting of spacious lawns, a small lake and ample ground for carrying on the training of dogs.

When I arrived, Colonel Richardson was showing some other visitors through the kennels. So I was shown into the library and asked to wait. There I met his secretary, a very pleasant and charming young lady, and wandered around looking at the various pictures and other things of interest.

It was a large, commodious room, overlooking a beautiful lawn....

On the walls of the study were autographed pictures of various celebrities, and a letter from Czar Nicholas of Russia thanking Colonel Richardson for the dogs he had furnished the Army for services with the Russian troops. The letter was dated 1908.

After luncheon, Colonel Richardson showed me his kennels. I was at once impressed with their spaciousness and convenient arrangement. Originally, they were built for stables and carriage houses. It was Colonel Richardson who remodeled them into ideal living quarters for dogs. What had formerly been a box stall became a perfect apartment for a dog or a small *congenial group of dogs. This arrangement made proper sanitation a simple matter.*

The kennels, themselves, were well lighted and aired, and were of such dimensions that the dogs could have received all necessary exercise without leaving the building. However, in addition, spacious runways and exercise grounds were provided.

The Colonel had a splendid group of Airedale dogs on hand that, outside their trained guard service value, would have answered quite well for themselves in the show ring, regardless of where they were shown. Besides this group, he had a collection of [W]ire-haired [F]ox [T]erriers, Sealyhams and some Scotties that appeared to be a well-selected number, and in which his son was mostly interested.

The 1940s

Richardson continued raising and training his Airedales right up until his death. This should not surprise us, although an observation made by Gray in *Dogs of War* is intriguing. Despite his lifelong work, Richardson was never a member of The Kennel Club. On the other hand, on the title page of *War, Police and Watch Dogs*, he states that he was a Fellow of the Zoological Society. Perhaps his non-membership in The Kennel Club simply reflects the simple fact that national kennel clubs, generally speaking, cater to those people who show their dogs in dog shows and generally do not care about working animals. From this perspective, Richardson was probably forever an outsider. His fellowship in the Zoological Society merely reflects an interest that he had shown since boyhood.

By the 1940s, his reputation was solidified around the globe as a trainer *par excellence* of police, military, personal protection and security dogs for civilian purposes. When World War II began, he again offered his services, but by then he was well into his 70s (see Chapter 10). While his dogs did see action (they were trained at times by troops with the Toronto Scottish Regiment), Richardson was no longer the guiding force behind the War Dog School.

On May 30, 1944, the Richardsons celebrated their golden wedding anniversary. It had been a remarkable half century of living and working together. He had never failed to acknowledge the debt he owed to his wife. His last book, *Fifty Years With Dogs*, co-authored with Blanche, was published posthumously in 1950. In the "Introduction," he acknowledged the important contributions of his spouse.

> *The time covered [in the book] represents many years and I have always had the devoted assistance of my wife, who is an expert in the psychology of animals, and a clever trainer. She and I have passed through the "Golden" period and are now in the "Diamond", and we still enjoy life among our much-loved and loving dogs. I have asked her, seeing we have been partners in all our work and play, to assist me in writing this new book, and to allow me to include her name as part author.*

Beneath his introduction, Blanche penned her own thoughts and tribute to her late husband.

The above introduction was written by my dear husband a year ago. He has since passed away. I have brought up to date this book which we wrote together and publish it as a loving memorial to the work of over half a century we did together in our study of animals, and of dogs in particular.

Richardson died on August 4, 1948, three weeks shy of his 85th birthday.

CHAPTER FOUR
An Uphill Battle

On Friday, March 15, 1889, E. E. Bennett, Veterinary Surgeon for the Army Veterinary Department, presented a talk to the Royal United Service Institution at Whitehall. He began his talk by noting that the utility of the dog was "being fully recognized and taken advantage of by most Continental [a]rmies," the implication being that Britain should do the same.

After a lengthy summation of the role of the military dog during the last several thousand years, Bennett suggested five possible uses for the contemporary war dog: 1) as auxiliary sentries for outposts and to the advanced rear and flank guards in general; 2) as scouts on the march for reconnaissance and patrol duties; 3) as "despatch" carriers; 4) as ammunition carriers; and 5) as searchers for the wounded and killed after an engagement. He cited the breeds used for service on the Continent, and then suggested potential breeds that might serve usefully as military dogs, foremost among them the Shepherd's dog or what we now know as the Border Collie, followed by Lurchers and Retrievers (Airedales had only been extant for a few years at this date and were virtually unknown, even in Britain). Discussion then followed with personal observations about the sagacity and faithfulness of the dog.

What is notable about Bennett's talk at the Royal United Service Institution in 1889 is that Richardson would deliver almost the same talk nearly a quarter century later.

In the interim, Britain had progressed no further in developing a war dog program.

Beginnings

Richardson often stated that he became inspired to breed and train military dogs after an experience he had in Scotland. He had been in Scotland hunting on a friend's moor when he witnessed a "foreigner" trying to buy a sheep dog from one of the local shepherds. Curious, he investigated further and discovered that the man was an "agent of a foreign government" sent over to buy suitable dogs for use in his government's army. The "foreigner" was a German and his assignment was to buy as many suitable Collies (which may mean any variety of sheep dog, including Border Collies and Rough Collies) as he could and to that end, he was travelling widely in his search. Richardson was later informed that the German had found working sheep dogs to be excellent for the work demanded of them by the German army. From that point on, he alleged, he began a systematic study of the use of dogs in police and military services.

While the story is undoubtedly true, in reality, Richardson's interest was already piqued by his childhood experiences with his father's tracking Bloodhound and his own interest in natural history. Furthermore, he had begun experimenting with Bloodhounds and Collies even prior to the encounter on the moors.

At some point in the late 19th century, Richardson saw, in an English magazine, a picture of a German war dog. Intrigued by what he had heard about the Continental – especially German – training of war dogs, he made a trip to Germany to see for himself what was going on. He quickly noted that the Germans had a strong preference for British breeds, at that particular time, Collies. Richardson spent a fair amount of time at a training school in Lechernich, where he discovered that most of the dogs were being trained for sentry and ambulance work with the German troops and the Red Cross. He found the Germans to be most accommodating and made a visit to a war dog training facility and received a number of invitations to witness war dog trials, which he viewed with strong interest. They freely demonstrated their training techniques to their English visitor. The Germans were using primarily Collies for Red Cross work and Richardson would soon copy much of the German training practices, although he would later find much to criticize in terms of their harshness. He returned home with "a very nice Collie bitch," a tricolor named Sanita, who turned out to be "very well trained and unusually intelligent." He would eventually train her as a messenger, in addition to the Red Cross work for which she had already been well educated. On his return home, Richardson made a trip to the French war dog training facility, again paying strict attention to training methods and techniques. He arrived home convinced that Britain had breeds that were better suited than any he saw on the Continent.

Back home, he began training Collies and, later, Retrievers. (Richardson's own accounting of when he began training varies, but it was at the end of the 19th or the beginning of the 20th century). His training was quite unlike the serious work that he would undertake years later, as he and his wife used games to bring out the best in their charges. In *Forty Years With Dogs*, he recounts how this initial foray into the serious work of training war dogs began.

> *My wife and I used to amuse ourselves playing various games with Collie dogs, teaching them to find us when hidden, to run with messages, to lie down and guard objects, etc. This systematic study taught us a great deal about the dog mind and the wonderful results which could be obtained by steady routine training along the lines of least resistance according to the intelligence of each particular breed.*
>
> *The Collies we found were useful in any teaching which entailed a seeking out and return to a given spot. .....*
>
> *In Retrievers the instinct, was, of course, the same in the sense of going out and returning, but in their case they like to bring something back in their mouths. We tried them for ambulance training, where they were supposed to search underwood for hidden persons representing the wounded and return to me, bringing some article away. ....*
>
> *This training was extremely interesting, and we found that very fine results could be obtained both with messenger dogs and ambulance dogs.*

Serious Training Begins

The training became more serious as time passed, with Sanita being the nucleus around which Richardson developed a "team of fine Collies like herself." The training took place mainly among the sand dunes that were found on the seashore by the Richardson home. He concentrated initially on "ambulance" or Red Cross training, outfitting the dogs with a coat or saddle bearing the Red Cross insignia. Within the pockets of the saddle were bandages, food of some kind, and a bottle of brandy. The "wounded" would be in concealed places where, had there been an actual battle, they would have dragged themselves for shelter. The dogs were trained to go ahead and scour the area looking for victims, to locate the person, and to lie down beside him while he revived himself from the supplies contained in the dog's saddlebags. The dog would then return to the stretcher-bearers and lead them to the wounded man.

At this time, of course, Richardson was working without official sanction or backing. In the early stages, training was conducted using Richardson's own family, the kennel-help, school children "who were delighted to earn some pocket money," friends, "various unemployed" and "anyone else who could be roped in." He would soon have all the extras he could use.

The Richardsons were living on the east coast of Scotland at the time, and various and sundry of his military friends would spend their summers, with their regiments, practicing maneuvers nearby. Richardson, with the full blessing and compliance of these friends, would

A remarkable testimonial to Richardson's work, this 1902 cigarette card is captioned "Rendering First Aid." On the back, it says "Major Richardson and his War Dogs. Our illustration represents Ambulance [sic] dog rendering first aid to wounded man." (Author's collection)

Another very early acknowledgement of Richardson's work, this postcard from 1906 is captioned "Major Richardson's War Dogs." (Author's collection)

work and try his dogs under simulated real life conditions as the men trained. The men, from all accounts, enjoyed working with the dogs. If nothing else, it would have been a novel experience and an interesting diversion from conventional battle training. Furthermore, as Richardson noted, once word got around that he was using brandy bottles as part of the training exercise, there was much competition to take part in the show as a mock wounded casualty. To the extent possible, he worked his dogs at night and under other adverse, but realistic, war time conditions. Through this trial and error approach to training, Richardson was able to detect flaws and weaknesses and adjust and make alterations where necessary.

It became apparent that only the very best and most intelligent and trainable of dogs could be trained completely in the work with which Richardson was involved. He discovered, for example, that all of the dogs he had could be trained to seek out the wounded, a relatively easy task as it simply involved the dog using its nose. As he noted, this in itself was a useful task. However, not all could be trained to lie down beside the wounded and then return to the stretcher-bearers and lead them back to the victim. He cites as an example a clever Collie that easily found the victims and could be counted upon to return to the base. But, because of his particular nature, he could never be relied upon to lie down beside the victim. Because of his sensitive disposition, upon finding his man and returning to the handler, he clearly demonstrated by his furtive gait, flattened ears and "conscience-stricken glance" that he hadn't completely fulfilled his duties.

Support

It is remarkable, perhaps, given the official non-response to Richardson's endeavors, that some military commanders saw merit in his work. Some of them were sufficiently impressed that they sent letters, of their own volition, to the War Office recommending that an inquiry be held into the wisdom of the official recognition of war dogs. Nothing came of these requests, of course. In the meantime, Richardson was being invited to attend maneuvers, invitations that he always accepted, although it meant doing so at his own expense. For his part, he viewed these costly excursions as experience gained for his training and an investment in what he viewed as the inevitable time when there would be a need for trained war dogs. And, all along, he was receiving media attention. Articles appeared in various newspapers, magazines and elsewhere about Major Richardson's "war dogs."

It was about this time that Richardson also started working with Bloodhounds in a serious way. In his memoirs, he suggests that Bloodhounds had been employed primarily in the realm of "sport" (a dubious claim) and that he wished to raise it to a more practical level, especially in the realm of police and military service. Again, as word got around that he was working with dogs in this field, he and his dogs were put to work in finding lost people. As he notes, in many cases the people he was asked to find were not "lost," but had simply boarded a train and left town without bothering to say farewell to their loved ones. Nonetheless, the legitimate cases provided opportunities to train and work his dogs.

Throughout all of this, Richardson kept in touch with trainers of police and military dogs on the Continent. Being able to speak and write German and French fluently, he was able to keep in touch with the commandants of the schools in France, Germany, Holland and Belgium. Among those he visited, and whose experiences with war dogs he studied, was Lt. Dupin of the 32nd French Infantry, who had started experimenting and testing military dogs at approximately the same time as Richardson.

In 1904, the Russo-Japanese War broke out. In addition to its political implications, it would also have significant impact upon Richardson. He had been following the developments of the war with the keen interest of a retired military officer, but with no intention of getting involved, when he received an urgent wire from the Russian Embassy in London, asking if he could supply ambulance dogs for the Russian troops. He soon had two dogs ready. One, named Carlo, was a Collie type with "a strain of Northern Sheepdog" in him, while the other, Robbie, was a tricolor Collie. The dogs left for Russia from Dundee with Richardson's fervent hopes that they would do him proud. He heard nothing for the longest time, and when he finally did, it was through an English newspaper. One of the paper's correspondents, who had visited the front, reported – *inter alia* – on the dogs' performances. The report had been written by an officer of Count Keller's staff and said, in part, that "For searching out the wounded, with which the millet fields are strewn, nothing has succeeded like our ambulance dogs. The English ones are especially intelligent." Subsequent reports confirmed the initial feedback about the dogs' performance.

Richardson must have been euphoric. With perhaps typical British understatement, he wrote in *Forty Years With Dogs* that "The report gave me great pleasure, and I felt that my labours had not been wasted. Even if the dogs had only saved one life, I should have felt repaid, but they did much more than that." He was undoubtedly even more pleased to learn that the dogs survived the war and were brought back to St. Petersburg where they lived for many years in the Czar's private kennels. For his work, the Dowager Empress Marie, who took a personal interest in the life-saving and hospital work of the war, sent him the Red Cross medal and an appreciative letter. The Czar presented him with a gold and diamond repeater watch embossed with the Royal Coat of Arms in diamonds and a heavy gold chain.

In an interesting twist of fate, years later Richardson would make the acquaintance of somebody who had been involved – albeit peripherally – with the work of his dogs. He was in the south of France some years after the war when he was advised that a Russian woman wished to consult him regarding the purchase of one of his dogs for personal protection. The woman was running a laundry and struggling to make ends meet. She told him that her name was Keller and Richardson, recalling that his dogs had been attached to the staff of the Russian general of that name, asked if she were any relation to Count Keller. Indeed, she was his widow.

It was shortly after this that Richardson received an additional boost of support. It came from his old friend Major-General (later Sir) Charles Tucker. Tucker was in charge of the forces in Scotland and he invited Richardson to include his ambulance dogs as part of an immense review of troops that was held in 1905 before King Edward in Edinburgh on the plain beneath Arthur's seat. Richardson took four Collies with him, which, by his account, "excited great interest." The Collies were adorned with their Red Cross jackets.

Tucker, according to Richardson, was a man respected for his ruling and judgment and was perceived as being a person of vision and action. After seeing the Collies at work, Tucker felt compelled to voice his views in a letter to the War Office. In support of the use of dogs in war time, he sent the following report (cited in Richardson, 1950)

> *Forwarded and strongly recommended. Seeing that every foreign Government has already recognized the use of dogs either for ambulance purposes or sentry work, or both, I am of opinion that advantage should be taken without delay of Major E. H. Richardson's knowledge and expertise in the matter of breeding and training them, and some military training selected for the purpose. It seems likely that Salisbury Plain might offer greater facilities in this respect than Aldershot; but on this point, as on other matters of detail, I would suggest that Major Richardson be consulted.*

The endorsement by Tucker was but one of many that were to follow. Richardson had begun broadening his training to include sentry dogs (in addition to Red Cross and messenger dogs) and he would test them using soldiers. Tucker was one of a number of senior military men who began to see the potential in a military dog program in Britain. Among other concerns, Tucker was convinced that sentry dogs would heighten a sense of alertness and provide a greater sense of security for soldiers on duty.

Sir Evelyn Wood was another prominent soldier who was convinced of their usefulness. Richardson had met him while attending maneuvers one summer at Colchester with his Collies. Wood was enjoying retirement in the area, but expressed a wish to meet Richardson and discuss his work. He went out of his way to establish contact with him and to encourage him in his work. Sitting with Richardson in his tent, Wood emphatically stated his position that dogs could be employed in many useful ways during war time.

Others of influence also lent their support in these early years, some of whom had never met Richardson personally but had nonetheless heard of his work and offered their support. Lord Breadalbane was a frequent summer visitor to the army camp near his home. Being a Collie fancier, he was keen to assist Richardson with his experiments in military dog training. Richardson respected him for his insights and directness and, although he was invited to Lord's Breadalbane's Taymouth Castle to conduct further work, the opportunity never presented itself.

The Duke of Abercorn, who resided in Baronscourt, Ireland, wrote Richardson a "most sympathetic and encouraging letter" although the two had never met. Nonetheless, he had heard of Richardson's work and the difficulties and rebuffs he had encountered. The Duke recommended that Richardson press on, as he was certain that great good would come out of it in the end.

More Foreign Assignments

In 1907, Richardson was living in Aldershot, where he had received permission from the commanding officer of the district to train his dogs on the military grounds. He was asked one day to go to the Turkish embassy in London where he was interviewed and advised that the Sultan Abdul Hamid was greatly concerned about unauthorized persons entering the grounds of his palace, Yildid Kiosk. The intruders would enter and remain hidden on the grounds so that the palace guards could not find them. It was a situation made especially difficult under the cover of darkness. In his memoirs, Richardson speculates that the sultan was concerned that the trespassers might have had designs on the women of his harem, of whom there were 700. Regardless of the sultan's motivations for concern, Richardson was asked if he would travel to Constantinople with some of his dogs and instruct the servants and guards in their proper use. Richardson was "quite pleased and amused to go," not only because all his expenses were paid in a very generous manner, including a room in a luxury hotel, but it was also early summer in Europe when travel was most enjoyable. He selected three dogs that had been well trained in tracking and had just come off some hard work: Laddie, a "beautiful" and "sagacious" Collie, Warrior, a black and tan Bloodhound that had been imported from the United States and that came from a long line of penitentiary dogs (Warrior himself had once trailed an escaped convict for two full days, resulting in his re-apprehension) and another Collie.

Richardson travelled in style aboard the Orient Express, a journey that took nearly a week. Two military officers, a naval commander and an infantry colonel, accompanied him. Upon his arrival, 20 men were assigned to work with the dogs. Every day, the dogs and their escorts were taken to the palace and put through various tests and exercises, preparing them for their eventual work. They were trained to seek out, especially by scent, any hidden persons and to give voice when having found them. It was a relatively easy matter for the dogs in the morning when dew was on the ground and scent thereby retained, but considerably more difficult when the sun rose and the scent dissipated with the heart of the day. The Collies compensated by using their wits when the scent failed, while the Bloodhound, by breeding and training, never failed to miss the slightest bit of scent if any were to be found. One day, as the sultan was returning from one of his functions, he stopped and watched as Richardson was working the dogs. He was most pleased with the performance and gratified with what the dogs were capable of doing.

His stay was three weeks and, at the end, the sultan requested that Richardson stay and oversee the policing and guarding of the palace and its grounds. To sweeten the offer, the sultan offered handsome remuneration and every possible facility. It must have been tempting, for the sultan was devoted to dogs and owned a most impressive kennel of various breeds that he had brought from all over Europe. They were housed in a fine kennel under the supervision of an expert German kennel manager. Not only that, during his stay, Richardson had been allowed use of the royal yacht. In the end, he turned down the offer and returned home, his reputation further established and recognized abroad, if still shunned in his homeland. As he left the sultan and his palace, the two officers who had been assigned to him approached to say good-bye and to show him the latest court circular, indicating that they had been made "Masters of Hounds."

There ensued a number of other assignments and travels as they pertained to his dogs. Upon his return from Turkey, he was invited to give demonstrations of his dogs at the Naval and Military exhibition held at the Crystal Palace. The invitation came from a colleague, Captain Sinclair (later Lord Pentland), who was one of the directors. He also happened to be Member of Parliament for East Forfarshire, where Richardson was residing at the time. Richardson would lecture every afternoon and then give demonstrations of his dogs seeking out the "wounded," acting as sentries, and carrying messages. All of this was wonderful publicity, but also very demanding of the dogs. The fair grounds were inevitably littered with the remains of lunches and picnics, all of which were tempting to the dogs as they worked. Nevertheless, they performed well, entertained the crowds and garnered publicity. Two people who paid special attention were Sir George Beatson, a well known physician in Glasgow, and Sir James Cantlie. They were both keenly interested in any developments in Red Cross work and so paid close attention to the ambulance training.

In 1908, Richardson received a telegram from the Empress Eugenie, stating that she wished to present a tracking dog for ambulance purposes to the Spanish army which, at the time, was engaged in war in Morocco. The request was politically charged, of course: the Queen of Spain was the Empress's god-daughter. That, and possibly other reasons, spurred the interest in the campaign that was being waged. Richardson was asked to accompany the dog and to report to Her Majesty at San Sebastian. He took a bitch named Boadicea and arrived at the palace, where he was warmly received. He was thence directed to report to Madrid and present himself to the

"Captain General" of Madrid. He was duly informed that he was to proceed to Melilla, on the Moroccan sea coast, where he would work while receiving the rank and salary of an officer.

Boadicea was promptly renamed "Perra de la Reine" or "The Queen's dog." She worked under very difficult circumstances, as the hot, dry, windy climate and the stationary nature of warfare worked against her. However, she proved her worth. When the troops returned victorious at the end of the campaign, she was awarded a position of honor, marching with them through the streets of Madrid, her neck wreathed with flowers. For Richardson's contribution, King Alfonso presented him with the Order of Military Merit. Upon his return, the press carried an account of Richardson's work in Morocco. It said, in part, the following (cited in Richardson, 1929).

When Major Richardson reached Melilla the Spaniards were practically besieged within it and fighting was proceeding each day. He took the bloodhound out to the firing lines and gave the ambulance drivers instructions on how to utilize it. The dog was with the first division in the advance on Nador and saw a good deal of the fighting. It soon became very popular with the soldiers, who named it Perra de la Reine – "the Queen's dog." Everyone took the greatest interest in Perra and it soon justified its character as one of the best trackers Major Richardson possessed.

After the ground had been gone over by the search parties, at the end of an engagement, the ambulance dogs are sent out to see if anyone has been overlooked. They work better at night than in the daytime, and have the additional vantage that they avoid the use of lanterns, which invariably draw the enemy's fire.

The English Army is the only army which ignores the use of dogs. They are employed in the German, French, Austrian and other Continental armies, and if the German Army were mobilized to-morrow they could put four million men into the field within a fortnight and four thousand ambulance sentry dogs. The dogs used by the German police would also be immediately mobilized with those in the Army. [Richardson adds parenthetically that "This statement proved to be correct."]

The Moors understand the use of dogs in warfare pretty well. They have a cross between a deerhound and a mastiff. At night they would go down near the Spanish lines and put out their dogs to detect the enemy's sentries. When the dogs barked they were able to locate the sentries and fire on them. They also dressed up their dogs in their own turbans and chelabas, in which they would run up the mountains and draw the Spanish fire on them. Sometimes they would send their dogs in the camps, and the Spaniards would rush out and fire upon the dogs, and the Moors would fire on the Spaniards.

In 1910, Richardson undertook another major expedition. The Balkan War had broken out and he was anxious to see the potential for the use of war dogs in the mountainous terrain. He travelled to Cattaro, the port on the shores of the Adriatic Sea, and then took the road into the mountains to Montenegro. He finally arrived at Cettinje, the capital. With the judicious exchange of currency, he was able to rent a pair of horses and travelled throughout the mountainous region, making detailed observations of everything he witnessed. He discovered on his journey that the Bulgarians used their indigenous sheepdogs as sentries at their outposts and found them to be most effective. Again, upon his return he was interviewed by the press.

He was not to rest long upon his laurels. A year later, in 1911, there came another call for his dogs, this time from far-off India. An English naturalist had been killed that March by the Abor, a people who lived on the China/India border. The Abor had lived in relative isolation from other peoples, due to their remote Himalayan homeland. The Indian Government thought it wise to send a punitive expedition into Abor territory. They were aware, however, that the prospect of ambushes was very real and thought that one or two good, well-trained scout and sentry dogs were advisable. Richardson was asked to supply the troops with suitably prepared canine assistance. He soon had two "very alert intelligent dogs" ready, one a purebred Airedale and the other an Airedale cross. They were to accompany a force of 2000 Gurkha soldiers. The press stated that this relatively small contingent was going up against 30 000 Abor. Richardson, in *Forty Years With Dogs*, includes a detailed press account of the expedition's launch. In it, the reporter states that "Although Major Richardson is sending out his scent-hunting dogs, it is doubtful whether they will come up to expectations." They were wrong, as Richardson relates in a number of reports. The first stated that

> *Before the encounter of November 7th, one of the dogs accompanying the advance guard gave timely warning of the presence of Abor. The dogs are also employed at night time, being used by the Gurkha sentries who keep them on a chain to supplement their own vigilance.*

The second report also confirmed the usefulness of the dogs:

> *Expedition has now reached Rotung, a gathering place of the Abors which was found to have been burned. After marching unopposed to the limit of the made road, the striking force began the ascent of the rising ground beyond the Lelek river, through a thick bamboo forest. Information had been received to the effect that a stockade might be met with and the Gurkha scouts who were accompanied by Major Richardson's war dogs were accordingly ordered to keep a sharp look out. The dogs again proved their efficiency as they gave warning to the outposts of the presence of the enemy's scouts before they were seen....*

That same year, Richardson journeyed yet again to see for himself the use of war dogs in Tripoli, which was the scene of conflict between the Italians and the Turks. He travelled first to Genoa, and then boarded a steamer bound for Syracuse. From there, he boarded another steamer that took him to Tripoli, arriving the day after the Italians had bombarded the site and taken occupation. He studied the use of dogs that were used as sentries and for patrol work. They were at the outpost line, about three miles outside the town in the desert, picketed in small dug-outs in the sand about 400 yards ahead of the sentries, where they proved their worth by giving warning much in advance of any human. They were particularly effective at night. Richardson, in *Fifty Years With Dogs*, cites a newspaper account of how they proved their value:

> *In the early part of the evening of February 11, 1912, the Turks, under cover of darkness, advanced in two columns against the Italian position at Derna, one column of 500 men on*

the right, the other consisting of about 1000 Bedouins, with a stiffening of Turkish officers. The whole of the country is difficult in the extreme, without roads, and crossed by a series of tracks, for the most part known to the Natives only, running on the edges of precipices. This force took every advantage of the sinuosities of the ground, and practically crawled undisturbed to the Italian position. The alarm, however, was given by the dogs chained to the entanglements, and at 8:30 began an engagement at this point which lasted the whole night.

The dogs used were Maremmas, large, shaggy white livestock guarding dogs. During the daylight hours, the Italians would patrol the desert with dogs, looking for potential enemies. In *Forty Years With Dogs*, Richardson includes three historically interesting photographs of Italian soldiers with their Maremmas. As a rare breed outside their homeland, the photos provide wonderful evidence of the historic use of this breed.

Back in England, Richardson began – unofficially, but by request – to supply sentry dogs for his own country's armed forces, among them the Gordon Highlanders, the Norfolk regiment and the King's Durham Light Infantry. They were well received by the commanding officers and the troops. An officer reported on the dog provided to the Gordon Highlanders:

Soon after midnight,…I decided to visit the outposts of both forces, and suggested that the attached officers should accompany me. We did not know in the least with which group we should find Jo and in the course of our rounds came upon him. The sentry in charge of him reported that he had been aware of our approach for some time, and that the dog had been more than unusually uneasy.

I had gone forward alone close up to the group, and was questioning the sentry in low tones, when a cyclist officer who had halted with the other a short distance away, came to join me. Without the least warning, Jo sprang forward and fixed his teeth in the 'British warm' coat of the officer. Luckily the chain was short and the sentry strong, while the officer sprang back instinctively, so the dog only just reached the coat, which was unbuttoned, and no real harm was done.

The incident served to show that the dog could distinguish between those with whom he was accustomed to serve and strangers, and tends to prove that a sentry accompanied by a dog would run no risk of being surprised and overpowered by a single assailant. Owing to the exigencies of the service my personal dealings with Jo ended that night, but I have lately heard that while he remains most friendly with men of his own regiment he is exceedingly fierce with all others.

The next major excursion was to Russia, where Richardson was invited to judge the military and police dog trials. The invitation had come from the Head of the Criminal Investigation Services at St. Petersburg, a Mr. Lebedeff, who had visited Richardson at his home in Harrow. There were two other judges, both German, befitting the status of the military and police dog in that country.

In May, 1914, Richardson left for Russia, where he was warmly and generously received by authorities. He was then taken to Tsarskoe Selo, which is where the working dogs were trained.

The trials involved nearly 300 dogs that were employed by the army, police, railway companies and other institutions. The breeds comprised primarily Airedales, "sheepdogs" and Doberman Pinschers. The press carried an article about the trials, specifically mentioning Richardson as "the English expert." Dogs of the army contingent demonstrated their skills, leaving the firing line on command and racing away to receive fresh ammunition that they carried back to their handlers. Each carried 100 or more rounds of ammunition in their backpacks. They also demonstrated their abilities as ambulance dogs, scouring the battlefields and returning with the cap of the wounded men to their handlers. Other dogs drew miniature Maxims. Many of the exercises were performed under fire and only a few – mainly younger dogs – showed any fear or nervousness.

The Guard regiments had a number of messenger dogs, almost exclusively German "Sheepdogs," i.e., German Shepherd Dogs, and Airedales. These, too, demonstrated their skills through a variety of tests, with Richardson receiving messages that had been dispatched from all over the countryside. The dogs had to travel over marsh, fields and woodlands in order to complete their tasks. Richardson relates that the records of the Airedales were, in his words, certainly greatly superior to those of the German Shepherds and, in conversations with the trainers and handlers, the Airedale was much preferred for the work. Many of the Russian Airedales, not surprisingly, were imported from England.

Richardson was less impressed with the tracking trials that he judged. The dogs, the breeds of which he did not identify, did not perform as well as he expected. In part, this was due to the trainers, who lacked the skills needed to bring about the best in their animals. He also inspected the chief police dog kennels and was able to offer constructive advice. In all, Richardson was royally treated and well received, to the point where, upon his arrival at the train station, his host displaced three German travellers in order to allow Richardson to complete his journey in comfort.

Upon his return home in June of that same year, he received yet another invitation to take some of his war dogs for inspection by Queen Alexandra and her sister, the Dowager Empress of Russia, who was visiting her at Marlborough House. The latter remembered fondly the work that Richardson's dogs had done for Russia in 1905.

A Growing Reputation

Richardson's reputation was firmly established and he was selling dogs all over the world, but in particular in Europe. They were in use by police forces as well as private citizens who perceived the need for a guard dog or personal protector. The extent of his reputation was such that he could write, in *British War Dogs* (1920), that prior to the First World War "There [were] very few parts of the world from which I did not receive either visitors or letters in connection with [trained dogs]. Owners of tea and coffee estates, sugar plantations, poultry farms and animal farms in all parts of the world, penitentiaries in North and South America, rubber estates, large rambling mansions, factories, docks, etc." In brief, Richardson was supplying both dogs and expertise to people around the globe in terms of how "to provide the necessary guarantee of security." He assessed each situation and worked accordingly. In his words, "Each case was treated separately, according to the circumstances, climate, personnel and environment." In a sense, he was a pioneer in the field of institutional and industrial security. But despite the fact that some military personnel had made significant, albeit unofficial, use of his dogs, the armed forces still failed to recognize their value.

Richardson's reputation as a trainer and as an advocate of working dogs, for both the military and the police, had reached North America early in the 20th century. Robert Gersbach and Theo. F. Jager, writing in *The Police Dog* (1910), observed that "England has in Major Hautonville [sic] Richardson a staunch friend for the Police dog. He is leaning especially towards Red-Cross dogs and makes this sub-branch at Panbride in Scotland his main study." They went on to state that "his favorite" was the Bloodhound, but that he was planning to look very soon into the potential use of other breeds for similar purposes. It would seem, however, that by this date Richardson had discovered the Airedale and was working actively with the breed.

Enter Richardson's Airedales

It is unclear exactly when Richardson turned his attention to the Airedale, the breed that he would consider the finest of working dogs and would help make world famous. In *Fifty Years With Dogs* he relates that he had heard from a friend in the Midlands that all the Airedales in

The Airedale's reputation as a guard dog is duly noted in this early postcard captioned "Watchdog. Airedale Terrier." (Author's collection)

In this early photograph, an Airedale guards the entrance to his house. (Author's collection)

that part of the country were being bought by German agents for training as sentry dogs with that country's army. At the same time, Collies and Sheepdogs were also being purchased in the Highlands. It seems that it was at this point that Richardson began greatly expanding his kennel and diversifying his training and the breeds with which he worked. In *Forty Years With Dogs*, he provides us with more information. Following his return from Constantinople, he began working more closely with sentry dogs and running tests with various breeds, essentially doing what he could with any dog that showed potential for the work. He found, though, that Airedales and Airedale crosses were particularly suited for the work by virtue of their size, hardiness and temperament. He also states that following his 1910 trip, when the Balkan War erupted, he returned home and began studying the various breeds with an eye to determining which would prove the most suitable in terms of being a house dog, a guardian and a companion for children. He writes that "It was for this reason that I formed my kennel of Airedales, as I found that in this dog all these requirements could as a rule be safely counted upon if properly used." In an uncharacteristically immodest moment, Richardson writes that "Of course, others had known this, and for several generations now, Airedales have been one of the most useful guard-dogs, but I claim to have caused this fine breed to have become more widely known, and it would be difficult to find many places in the world where one will not come across an Airedale which will be found generally 'doing its bit' in a steady matter-of-fact fashion." Airedales rapidly became his preferred breed while the Bloodhounds, Collies and Retrievers – still much appreciated – were accorded secondary status.

Richardson's Police Dogs

Evidence that Richardson was working seriously with Airedales by 1910 comes from an article in *The Kennel* from that very year called "Hull Police Dogs." While Richardson is never cited by name, the article states that Hull was the first city in Great Britain to use police patrol dogs. They were engaged at the Third Port after having been established three years earlier by the

North Eastern Railway Company Police. The railway police had grown tired of the thefts, arsons and assaults on officers and armed themselves with the dogs, which had contributed greatly to a decrease in these and other crimes.

While the use of dogs by police forces had been the norm for some years on the Continent, the author, Walter Watson, states that the practice had never caught on in Britain because of the belief that the criminal, no matter how bad, should not suffer undue physical or mental pain in the process of arrest. Inspector Dobson made the journey to Ghent and witnessed the use of police dogs in Ghent, where the "Flemish sheepdog" was most commonly used.[19] After observing training methods on the Continent, Dobson returned home, convinced that he could do even better than his Continental counterparts. He decided that the Airedale was the ideal breed for the English situation and established a kennel on the Albert dockside, next to the North Eastern Company's police station.

Watson's article does not state where the Airedales came from, simply that "a number of the hardiest young Airedales that could be found was got together." Given the time (1907), the breed and the fact that no other institutions, i.e., police or military, in Britain were breeding and training service dogs, there is little doubt that they came from Richardson. In his various memoirs, he explicitly refers to training and providing Airedale patrol dogs for municipal, railway and dock police. Furthermore, in *British War Dogs,* he wrote that "In England, before the war, I was the sole person who took any interest in trained dogs for the army and the police, and the outflow from my kennels constituted the only source of supply." Similarly, in *Forty Years With Dogs*, he stated clearly that "Hull was one of the first towns to start police dogs. These are found useful in the dock area where hidden persons at night are very difficult to dislodge unless with the aid of good hearing and scenting dogs." It would seem, then, that while the provenance of the dogs is unstated, they were Richardson's.

The dogs were well provided for in the kennels, with each dog having a pen to itself, equipped with a sleeping compartment furnished with straw. They were fed a diet of meat, bones, bread and rice, all of which was prepared twice daily. In the three years that the dogs had been in service at the time of writing, none had ever been sick or unable to work.

The training of the dogs was extensive, albeit in one respect, somewhat primitive by today's standards. In brief, they were trained to recognize everyone in a police uniform as a friend, and anybody who wasn't as an enemy. Following this, the dogs were taught to obey a police whistle. Then, criminal apprehension was taught. They were trained to pursue and apprehend fleeing felons, and to guard prisoners when caught until the arrival of the police officer. To ensure gameness in the face of battle, they were trained to fight in the face of a club or a revolver. The dogs would not be discouraged or dissuaded by obstacles, as they were taught to leap over or scale walls and to jump through windows of shops and houses in pursuit of thieves.

The officers helped in the training of the dogs, which, as a rule, took place among the huge dockside warehouses at Hull. An officer would dress in plain clothes, presenting himself as a fleeing criminal while the uniformed handler would release the dog, which would then apprehend and hold the "felon" until his partner arrived. In other instances, an officer would disguise himself and hide in one of the massive warehouses. The dog would then be told to search and inevitably would find the hidden constable, whereupon the dog would reveal his presence by constant barking. They were able to detect a hidden person up to 20 feet above in the rafters of the warehouses. Concealment in boxcars was not an option for thieves or vagrants, as the dogs inevitably detected their presence.

Every night, from 10 p.m. until 6 a.m., the Airedales patrolled the dockyards with their handlers. On wet nights, the dogs were provided with a waterproof coat. The dogs always worked muzzled, because of the British belief that even criminals should not be unduly harmed. Regardless, nobody ever escaped from one of the Hull police dogs and, more often not, they were brought to the ground by the dogs that would hurl themselves on to the fleeing suspect's back.[20] Once down, the dogs would, if need be, stand guard for hours. Such was the extent of their training, that they would, if need be, throw themselves against a moving bicycle if a suspect attempted to escape by that means.

The effectiveness of the dogs, both in terms of detecting criminals and apprehending them, was demonstrated by an Airedale named Jim. While on patrol one night, he alerted his handler to the presence of people in a locked coffee shop. While the officer blew his whistle for assis-

An English postcard celebrating Airedale police dogs. (Author's collection)

tance, Jim circled the building, found the open window through which the thieves had entered, leaped through and cornered and held two men until the officers arrived and made the arrest. It turned out the two were notorious dock thieves and "shopbreakers" and subsequently received long sentences.

At the time when the article was written, the number of Airedales had recently been increased. Their training had also been developed further, so that the dogs were trained to follow the beam of the police officer's "lamp." The consensus was that the breed's "unrivalled hardiness," endurance and "extraordinary gameness" made it the ideal breed for the job.

These were not the only police dogs that were making a name for Richardson. Among other cities, Glasgow, Liverpool and Nottingham all found them to be most effective in preventing crime and assisting in the apprehension of wrongdoers. In *Forty Years With Dogs*, Richardson related some of the successes the police forces enjoyed with their dogs. Glasgow was one of the first to have canine cops, and they were used extensively to provide additional support for officers walking isolated and dangerous beats alone at night. We must bear in mind that the constables were unarmed except for a nightstick and, although lawbreakers were also typically unarmed (this being Britain), the police officer was often outnumbered, sometimes considerably so, when attempting to make arrests. It was in situations like that where a police dog was of immense value. Richardson wrote:

In the Queen's Park Division where they have two splendid Airedales, marked success has attended the introduction of these four-footed officers, one of them, Bob by name, showing particular aptitude for police work. The constables who have charge of the animals patrol the extensive and quiet district of Pollockshields at night, and it is worthy of note that no house burglaries have occurred since the dogs took up duty.

Liverpool at one point had 20 of Richardson's Airedales on duty and the Chief Constable was pleased to report that no innocent person had ever been harmed or threatened by the animals. However, their effectiveness as deterrents and as tools for arrest was never in doubt. The Chief Constable in one report stated that, in the Mersey seaport, one constable and one dog were able to effect the arrest of six men who were attempting to commit a crime.

In Nottingham, the Chief Constable reported that

The police dogs are a distinct acquisition to the force, particularly in connection with the patrolling of outside districts. They are powerful, sensible animals, and are regularly exercised and trained for police duties. They have proved most useful in finding persons secreted in out-of-the-way places and followed and stopped others at some distance away when the police were desirous of overhauling, but would have failed to get in touch with without the dogs' assistance. They are valuable companions to constables patrolling lonely beats.

As he expanded his kennel and his areas of expertise, people began to turn to him for advice about training and employing service dogs. At the same time, he began to receive even more invitations from foreign militaries and police forces to visit and to exchange information. On one occasion, he journeyed to Holland, spending a summer there studying training methods and visiting trainers. He assisted the Dutch as they worked their dogs on the sand dunes under conditions that very much resembled those under which he trained at home. On another, he journeyed to Brussels, where he trained with the Grenadier Regiment. One spring was spent in Albania, studying the Sheepdogs of that country as they were employed for guarding purposes throughout that country.

The Struggle For Recognition Continues

With his ever-growing reputation at home and abroad, one would think that the military would have capitalized on Richardson's expertise. Britain steadfastly remained the only major European nation without a war dog program as World War I loomed. There is a telling passage in *British War Dogs* that exemplifies much of the attitude with which Richardson had to contend in his struggle to establish a war dog program. He writes:

> *I well remember meeting a distinguished general, some years before the war, who had a good deal of power to bring progressive measure to the notice of the highest military authorities of the time. I ventured to suggest it might be worthwhile to devote some study to the question of Army dogs. He replied that he was not only not interested in the subject, but strongly disapproved of such measures. "My own action as commanding officer would be to prohibit, under all circumstances, the use of dogs, in any connection, with a regiment in the field."*

Richardson added that the general's only son was later killed in the war under circumstances that could have been prevented had his regiment been serviced by a couple of trained dogs.

On Wednesday, October 30, 1912, Major Richardson gave a talk to the Royal United Service Institution. It was called "The Employment of War Dogs, With Special Reference to Tripoli and Other Recent Campaigns." (Ironically, perhaps, in light of how he would be ignored by the powers that be over the next half decade, he was identified as "Major C. H. Richardson" in *The Journal of the Royal United Service Institution*, December, 1912. Perhaps they really weren't paying him much attention at this time). Chairing the gathering was Brigadier-General R. C. B. Haking, C. B.

His talk was interesting for a number of reasons, not the least of which that he acknowledged the pleasure with which he received "the invitation of the Royal United Service Institution to speak on a subject which ha[d] been [his] especial study for close on 20 years." It would seem, then, that while Richardson's efforts to have a war dog program established within the military were rebuffed for decades, it is apparent that at least some factions were willing to listen to him. Whether or not he solicited the invitation is unknown.

It is also interesting to note his somewhat romanticized (and ethnocentric) treatment of non-Western peoples. In his opening remarks, he observed how we have become dependent on our vision (as a result of being bipedal), while our olfactory organs have deteriorated except that "certain primitive tribes, such as the Puongs of Cambodia, the Ainus of Japan, and the Aborigines of Peru, still possess the sense of scent, and can distinguish in the thickest woods between the approach of one of their own race, a white man or a negro." Similarly, he said, because of his position near to the ground and the increased size of the tympanum of the ear, the dog "can hear sounds unheard by civilized man." While a superb dog trainer, Richardson was not the most astute of anthropologists.

Following this ethnographic foray, Richardson briefly outlined some of the historic uses of dogs in warfare, beginning with Julius Caesar and concluding with the Russo-Turkish War of 1878. Over the centuries, and in various places, they had primarily served as guards, sentries and – to a lesser extent – as trackers. But, he observed, recent changes in the development of warfare had brought about a more "scientific" approach to the use of military canines. He identified three categories of use to which military dogs could be put (in his perceived order of importance): 1) as a scout or sentry (a dubious combination of two distinct military dog roles); 2) "as an aid to the ambulance in looking for the wounded"; and 3) as a messenger and ammunition carrier.

He rationalized his perception of the needs of these dogs by observing how warfare had changed in the recent past. Scout and sentry dogs, he argued, were essential in light of the development of modern firearms and an increasing tendency for battle to take place under cover of darkness. The greater acuity of the sense of hearing and scent made the dog invaluable for detecting the enemy at great distances or in the darkest night. Furthermore, the major maintained, under conditions in which the human soldier is fatigued or subject to nervousness and therefore prone to imagining sounds or sights in the darkness, "the dog will be found tirelessly wakeful and alert, and acutely sensitive to all scents and sounds." To make his point, Richardson submitted that "after hundreds of experiments" he had "proved that a dog can hear 200 to 400 yards further than a man" and that when wind and atmosphere are especially favorable for scenting, the distance at which detection can be made was even further. As incredible as it must have seemed at the time, the use of scout dogs in a number of subsequent wars would eventually prove Richardson to be correct.

Being not only a dog fancier and trainer but also a military officer, Richardson was able to make logical and practical suggestions for the use of dogs in combat. He suggested that the presence of dogs would make the human sentries more alert and vigilant in their own duties, thereby reducing the "appalling results due to rushes and ambuscades." He further suggested that, in addition to having sentry dogs used in front, they were also beneficial for guarding bridges, tunnels and columns bringing up provisions. In his view, a regiment should have a minimum of 12 dogs to be properly safeguarded, with at least double that number when in "very enclosed dangerous country." When marching, the major advised, the advance and flank guards should have dogs and at the bivouac they should be distributed among the sentries and placed on guard in the trenches and in front of the wire entanglements.

The use of sentry and guard dogs had an ancient history when Richardson gave his talk in 1912. One of the more recent developments was the use of "ambulance dogs," perhaps more commonly known as "Red Cross dogs." Their task was to seek out the wounded on the battlefield and identify their location so that their comrades in arms could aid them. Unfortunately, while their intended use seemed noble and needed, they would not see much action.

Richardson presented the case for ambulance dogs by first citing a case where their use would have been of inestimable value.

The Medical-Inspector Czernicki, of the French Army, wrote these lines:

"On August 19th, 1870, I found in searching the battlefield of Rezonville, Gravelotte, two of the Lepasset Mixed Brigade who had fallen wounded on August 16th, that is three days previously – hidden at about a distance of 300 metres from each other in some excavations at the edge of the wood in the Gorze ravine. They had not seen a living person from the moment they fell, though the field had been overrun by the belligerents and searched by ambulance men."

He then noted how, during the Russo-Japanese War, battles lasted from eight to ten days, during which time it was possible to seek the wounded only at night. At such times, of course, searches had to be done without the benefit of light for fear of drawing the enemy's fire. Richardson stated, in plaintive terms, the situation of the wounded. "…it is appalling to think of the sufferings of the unfortunate wounded men, driven by raking shell fire to take every possible cover, lying sometimes quite close to their would-be rescuers and quite unable to cry out while hearing the footsteps of the succoring party recede into the distance." During the Russo-Japanese War, he noted, "For want of removal many died where they lay of haemorrhage [sic], exhaustion and cold." If more evidence were needed, he cited the case of a Russian soldier brought in by two Japanese ambulance men, who had spent 36 hours, unconscious, in a ditch while enduring -10 degree temperatures.

Germany and England had sent trained dogs to the Russian Red Cross that had proven extremely useful. It would not go unstated by Richardson that his dogs had performed beyond the norm. He quoted Count Persidsky, who wrote that "In finding the missing and wounded, with which the millet fields are strewn, nothing succeeded like our pack of seven dogs. The English ones are exceptionally intelligent. In our last engagement 23 men were found in unsuspected places."

While perhaps not as valuable as scout and sentry dogs, whose work was constantly in demand, Richardson believed that ambulance dogs, as he called them, were of "immense service." Ideally, they would go out ahead or on long leads with the searchers and stretcher-bearers to identify the wounded. Under certain conditions, such as under the cover of darkness or when there was increased moisture in the air which aided scenting, dogs were of particular value. And, of course, under normal circumstances, the blood of the unfortunate wounded quickly led dogs to their location, which might otherwise be missed by a human search party.

Richardson, when prioritizing the importance of his three types of military canines, listed the messenger (and ammunition carrier) dogs last. History, on the other hand, seems to have paid greater attention to the messengers than to the other two. In part, this is because the "ambulance dogs" were quickly removed from battle and partly because the scout and sentry dogs are left unnamed in the historical record.

The training of the messenger dog was much more technical and difficult than that of the scout or sentry dog, he maintained, for in the case of the latter it was merely a question of cultivating the inherent qualities found in most animals. The former, however, required a much longer time to bring about the desired results. While the First World War, which was just two years away, would clearly demonstrate that Richardson was more than capable of bringing dogs to that high level of training, he was obliged to fall back on a German case to make his point. He cited a case from the Boxer Rebellion, in which the order was given to shell a Chinese patrol. A dog delivered the order over a distance of five miles in a matter of minutes.

If one were cynical, it could be argued that Richardson was more than a little self-serving in his presentation that day. He "emphatically denied" that it was possible to obtain a suitable number of dogs for military service during times of war. Based on his experience, he maintained, out of 20 likely candidates only one would prove suitable. Furthermore, greater success had been achieved with those dogs that had been trained carefully during peace times than with those hastily obtained, hurriedly trained and pressed into service during a war. He emphasized the needed qualities for a military dog: intelligence, acute hearing and scenting, biddability and a serviceable coat, i.e., one that was adaptable to extremes of climate. When large numbers of dogs were needed, he cautioned, the cost could not afford to be high and expensive breeds were "useless." (What exactly he meant here is unclear). At that point in his talk, Richardson made the case for his favorite breed, the Airedale. Noting the breed's abundant qualities, he added that "Former inmates of my kennel are serving with troops or police in all parts of the world, and from both cold and tropical climates I hear good accounts of their health. There are few breeds of which this could be said. I frequently use various crosses, but the Airedale is the basis of my breed."

He went on to provide descriptions and accounts of war dogs used in Cuba, South Africa and elsewhere, as well as the policies and measures taken by other nations. In his conclusion, he wisely advised caution against expecting too much from the use of military dogs, "as great harm can be done by expecting impossibilities." Nonetheless, he reiterated his point that scouting, sentry and ambulance work fell within the innate capabilities of the dog.

Richardson also emphasized again the danger of waiting until "the eleventh hour" to develop a war dog program. Such hesitancy, he advised, was no answer and would result only in waste and expense. The only option was to provide regiments in peace time with properly selected and trained animals. He suggested that this be done at training establishments built for that purpose and from which the dogs could be drafted to the various regiments. When not engaged in actual combat conditions, the dogs could be used, as was done with the continental armies, as sentries for forts, hangars, magazines and so on and thereby reduce the number of human sentries required.

At the conclusion of his talk, Richardson presented a series of slides illustrating the types of dogs used by various armies on the Continent and also presented two of his own trained Airedales. The floor was then opened up for questions.

The Chairman, Brigadier General Haking, initiated the discussion by suggesting that the use of sentry dogs could prove detrimental. His argument was that the sentry would come to rely on the dog, thereby relaxing his own vigil. If the dog failed to provide any security, it may be more of a source of danger than an advantage. He then asked whether or not a dog could be trained to go to a locality on command, search the area, and if it were to find an enemy, provide a signal or bark, or return again to its handler.

The ensuing exchange between Richardson and the Chairman is illustrative of much of the attitude with which Richardson had to contend.

Richardson: Yes, I think it could be done, but it is extremely difficult.

Haking: You always find that the thing you want most is the most difficult thing to do. But if dogs could do that they would be invaluable.

Richardson: Yes, but in dealing with dogs one has to avoid overstating one's case. These things are possible, *but one must not expect too much.*

Brigadier General Haking, as Chair of the meeting, set the tone for the question and answer session by suggesting potential dangers of the use of dogs and by delineating the limitations of their use and establishing the extent of the capabilities of the trainer.

Much of the subsequent discussion focussed on the difficulties of using dogs in specific situations, e.g., issues of color for sentry work (dark dogs for sentry work at night, white dogs in arctic climates, the need for silent guard dogs and so on). Brigadier-General Haking inquired about the usefulness of the Irish Terrier as a military dog, to which Richardson replied that they were "magnificent" watchdogs but more excitable than Airedales.

Major Richardson had a brief dispute with a Major General J. B. Richardson regarding the viability of messenger dogs when the latter had witnessed dogs used for smuggling that went on through the lines between Gibraltar and Spain. One hundred and fifty to 200 dogs a night were used to smuggle tobacco across the line with upwards of 40-50 being killed a night. The Major General seemed to fail to recognize the point the Major was making regarding messenger dogs not always travelling between two fixed points.

One final point, a significant one, was made by Major General Richardson. He observed that there were St. John Ambulance and Red Cross detachments throughout Britain and he did not see "why each of these detachments should not be requested to keep a dog and train it." If that system were to be adopted, he stated, there would be a number of trained dogs available in the eventuality of war. Major Richardson replied that it was a "very good idea" and was "exceedingly obliged" to the Major General for the idea.

A surprise endorsement came from Captain A. C. Temperley of the Norfolk regiment. It was to Captain Temperley that Richardson had sent, on the Captain's request, a fully trained Airedale sentry. He admitted that he had been opposed to the idea, because the dogs he had seen previously were "barracks dogs," animals that served little purpose and became camp scavengers. His men persisted, however, and he had written to Richardson who supplied him with "a very fine specimen of an Airedale Terrier" that worked with the men while on maneuvers during the summer. As a sentry, he detected the approach of a human being two to three minutes before his handler. His signal was a low growl and stiffening of his body. The dog worked either at night with a sentry or went on patrol. He was found to be no expense as he was not allowed to run loose, and was fed (scraps from the men's meals) only by his handler. He also reinforced Richardson's demand that the country be ready with trained military dogs before the onset of war, rather than trying to improvise at the last moment.

In brief, Richardson's presentation at Whitehall on October 30, 1912, reflected a pattern that would characterize his mission for years: unqualified support from men in the field who had experience with military dogs, and feigned interest and disdain from the army brass. It would be another four years before the military lent him their full support.

Even after the dogs had been officially accepted and shipped to the Front, there was resentment and a certain reluctance on the part of some commanding officers. Richardson, in *Forty Years With Dogs*, recounts a visit to some handlers shortly after the first lot had been sent across the channel.

> *The keepers whom I had trained at the school in Shoeburyness were glad to see me and my visit encouraged them in their difficult task. Many of them had, when the first drafts went out, great obstructions to contend with in the management of their charges. The important nature, which later on was recognized, of the work the dogs were able to do, was not immediately recognized. Commanding officers of those battalions to whom they were first sent very often made light of the dogs or else ignored them, or worse still cynically set them to tasks under impossible conditions. I feel deeply grateful to those officers who had sufficient perspicacity to grant the man [sic] and dogs a fair trial wherever they were and to make allowances for difficulties in working which later were overcome. Definite orders from Headquarters were after a time formulated, governing the reception and disposal of these valuable animals and the men who were responsible for them, so that respect was soon inculcated and was retained when it was found what could be accomplished by their aid.*

One cannot help when reading this passage but to recall Richardson's cautionary note to General Haking when he gave his talk in 1912 (above). Then, too, he had warned of the dangers of placing too high demands on the dogs. The degree of lack of respect is suggested by the fact that initially it was virtually impossible to keep the men – other than their handlers – from treating the dogs as "pets." In brief, the discipline to which the men were subject did not seem to apply to the dogs, although they, too, were soldiers at the front lines. In Richardson's words, "It was only when the importance of the work which the dogs were able to do began to be realized and it was lifted out of the rut of a rather amused and condescending tolerance, that general officers, officers and men combined to observe in every way, in their own interest, the rules which governed these canine soldiers in their arduous work." With this realization, Richardson's long uphill battle was, for all and intents and purposes, finished for this war.

CHAPTER FIVE
The British War Dog School is Born

In his opening to the twelfth chapter of *Forty Years With Dogs*, Richardson states eloquently, in a manner reminiscent of the Victorian era, that "I feel this book would not be complete were I not to mention that period of my life for which all the previous years seemed to have been a time of preparation." Chapter Twelve is simply called "The War," so we may forgive him for discussing, in a relatively brief 50 pages, the culmination of his life's work.

When the horrors of the First World War broke out, a mere three weeks after his trip to Russia, he recognized that his kennel of trained dogs had an important role to play. He believed that they could serve as sentries and guards for sensitive installations such as factories, bridgeheads and magazines. Through his years of experience supplying dogs for such purposes for the civilian sector, he realized their effectiveness not only in deterring crime and apprehending perpetrators, but also the extent to which they freed up men for other duties. With these thoughts in mind, he offered his entire kennel of trained dogs to be used on an experimental basis immediately by the army. Remarkably, he writes in *British War Dogs* that "My ideas were, however, not in any way understood at the time, and I could make no headway." He is more generous in *Forty Years With Dogs*, suggesting that when the war broke out "those in authority were wrestling with gigantic problems, the moving of vast bodies of troops, the preparation of equipment, food, etc., etc. The lesser aspects of war – the trimmings, so to speak, could not receive any attention, and one hesitated to add to the exigencies…"

With his offer of sentry and guard dogs rejected, Richardson then offered his services to the Red Cross, suggesting that he take some ambulance dogs to the Continent to aid the troops. At this point, as he states in his memoirs, the British believed in the inviolability of the sacred symbol of the Red Cross. He offered his services to the British Red Cross Society and, with some trained ambulance dogs, was sent by the society to Belgium in August, 1914. He made his way to Brussels only to find the Germans entering the city from the east, the Belgians in retreat, and the British not yet arrived. He managed to get back to Ostend with his dogs. Shortly thereafter, the use of Red Cross dogs, i.e., those bearing the international symbol, greatly declined. The French discovered very early on in the war that the Germans would shoot both the men and dogs as they went about their work. The French War Office entirely forbade their use with their army after the first few weeks of the war. Richardson states that the only ambulance dogs that were used with any success were those with the German army when the Russians were retreating on the Eastern Front.

There is an irony in this history of the early stages of the war. Despite the fact that ambulance dogs, bearing the Red Cross insignia, served for a very brief period of time, images of these dogs are fairly common. Their work, and the perceived nobility of it and the valor displayed by the dogs, captured the imagination of artists and writers. These depictions, in turn, found their way onto postcards, magazine covers and other forms of mass distribution. One of the results is that, for the general public, there is the misguided perception that during the First World War the exclusive (or, perhaps, primary) role of military dogs was as Red Cross dogs. One of the iconic images of the military Airedale, for example, is Charles Bull's depiction of a Red Cross dog crawling under the barbed wire, carrying a wounded soldier's helmet (see illustration p. 108). The dog is equipped with the Red Cross blanket, and a collar and dog tag, both also emblazoned with the international symbol of aid. It matters little, perhaps, that the dogs worked in such a manner for only a brief time.

Although Richardson's initial plans were thwarted by the realities of the new war, it was not long before he began receiving requests from officers for sentry and patrol dogs. He did his best to meet these requests and found that Airedales met these needs best. He also sent dogs to the Belgian army. He also discovered, to his pleasure, that officers were submitting requests to the War Office, asking that dogs be *officially* supplied for a number of different military purposes.

In the midst of this, Richardson made two visits to France in 1915, one in April and another in December, as he was interested in seeing how his French contemporaries were faring with their war dogs. During his first journey, he visited the French 6th Army at Villers Cotterets. Dogs were being used as sentries to a fair extent, but he also observed how there was considerable loss of life to dispatch bearers due to the intensive bombardments. The high toll, as well as the difficulties of maintaining communications, was causing considerable anxiety among both the troops and the brass.

During his second trip of 1915, he arrived in Paris and received permission to travel to Vosges sector, where most of the dogs (sentries) were concentrated. He was warmly received by his colleague, Monsieur Paul Megnin, who had been at the very forefront of the French war dog movement. Richardson concluded that the dogs were invaluable and were a great safeguard for the sentries and, in *Fifty Years With Dogs*, provides just a couple of examples. In one case, it was believed that the enemy had approached the French line, but the exact location could not be determined. At night, the sentry dog evidently heard something and started growling. By following the dog's lead, the sentry sent word as to the likely location, which was determined to be correct, and the situation was taken care of. In another instance, the enemy seized seven French sentries in one week. The men were then given sentry dogs to accompany them, and never again were the sentries surprised, as the dogs gave advance warning of the approach of the enemy. In a third case, at which Richardson was a witness, warning was given by a sentry dog. A spotlight was turned on, following the lead of the dog's "point" to reveal the enemy cutting the wire in front of a blockhouse. Richardson's last stop was at a training facility in Chantilly. He returned home, more convinced than ever of the value that could be had from a good, well-trained dog.

In the winter of 1916, he received a letter from an officer in the Royal Artillery expressing an interest in trained dogs to keep up communications between his outpost and the battery during bombardments when telephones were useless and the risk to human runners incalculable. Richardson went to work right away and trained two Airedales named Wolf and Prince. They were educated to the point where each would carry a message for two miles without a hitch. They left for France on December 31, 1916, going to one Colonel Winter. He would later provide Richardson with some very useful observations and advice on the training and deployment of messenger dogs.

In *British War Dogs*, Richardson provides us with the first report on Wolf and Prince.

...during the operations against Wytschaete Ridge, two messenger dogs attached to this brigade were sent forward at one a.m. One was attached to the forward liaison officer and one with the group forward observation officer.

After being led up through communication trenches during darkness, they went forward as soon as the attack was launched, passing through the smoke barrage... One was dispatched at 10:45 a.m. and the other at 12:45 p.m.

Both dogs reached brigade headquarters, travelling a distance as the crow flies of 4,000 yards over ground they had never seen before and over an exceptionally difficult terrain. The dog dispatched at 12:45 p.m. reached his destination under the hour, bringing in an important message, and this was the first message which was received, all visual communication having failed.

A second report was also supportive of the work of the dogs.

When the Germans withdrew their line in the spring of 1917, the dogs were taken up the night before to a wood east of Bucquoy. They were then sent up to a forward observation post, 4000 yards to the east of the wood, and were released with important messages. They found their way back through masses of troops on the march, to the wood, although they had only arrived there the night previous, and the ground was quite unknown to them.

However encouraging these reports were, it was the next that would be pivotal, for it forever changed the life of then Major Richardson and his efforts. It was the Battle of Vimy Ridge, and the performance of Wolf and Prince convinced the British authorities – finally – to develop a war dog program (see Chapter 8 "The Heroes"). As Richardson writes in *British War Dogs*, "The definite results obtained through these two dogs and through Colonel Winter's initiative, led the authorities to inquire into the question of establishing some means whereby supplies of these messenger dogs could be provided for the army." To that end, he was summoned to the War Office to discuss the matter. He was more than happy to propose a definite plan for the creation of a training school for military dogs and all of his suggestions were met with approval by the authorities. It was decided that the school should be established at Shoeburyness so that the dogs could get accustomed to the constant firing of heavy guns. It was also determined that his wife would accompany him in the project. Richardson often acknowledged his wife's skill with animals, and in particular her adeptness at training, and he credits her with much of the success that came with the War Dog School.

Major Richardson's Sentry and Ambulance Dogs at Earl's Court. (Author's collection)

Within a week of being asked to establish the school, Colonel (then Major) and Blanche Richardson had sold their home, stored their furniture and moved to Shoeburyness. Richardson also quickly turned his kennels, which consisted mostly of Airedales by this time, over to the government. The Richardsons had two sons at the front, one of whom was killed, and they found the next several months of intensive organization and training an outlet for their grief. Amidst the sounds of the guns, they delved into their work with increasing success. The location of the school was a closely guarded secret, but there was always the fear that they or their dogs would be bombed from the air. In *Fifty Years With Dogs*, they relate the details of one of the first raids. Twenty planes flew over "in the formation of a spearhead," passing over their kennels. As they did so, "the anti-aircraft guns began barking from the town. With a sudden shudder one of the planes began turning over and over, gradually sinking, while two black specks fell headlong down into that awful abyss far below." The raids were fairly constant from that day forward, but although bombs fell in close proximity to the school, they were never hit.

The school was underway with the full blessing of the military. A certain number of men were to be sent each month to the school for instruction in handling the dogs and, at the end of the course (which took approximately five weeks), they would take the dogs overseas. The program was beset with growing pains in the early days. The first keepers/handlers were recruited from battalions in France whose commanding officers had expressed an interest in having messenger dogs. This initial policy was carried on for a number of months, but it was realized that the maximum potential was not being made of the dogs. The utility of the dogs was clearly demonstrated, but there was inadequate supervision over their working and management in the field. Furthermore, in some regiments, Richardson felt that the full measure of their usefulness was not being brought out. The failure of some people to recognize that the dogs were capable of useful work was a major stumbling block in the early days and Richardson was soon receiving feedback that the capabilities of the dogs were being inadequately recognized. Likewise, the handlers were often not receiving sufficient attention from their commanding officers. On the other hand, certain battalion commanders, who had – in Richardson's words – "sympathy" for dogs and an appreciation for what could be obtained from them in the field, arranged so that full use could be made of them and, in turn, kept records that were then forwarded to General Headquarters (G.H.Q.) in France.

The system was in need of revamping, a job that was undertaken by Major Waley (see Chapter Six: "British War Dogs in France"), who built the messenger dog service around a central kennel and sectional kennels. To ensure its success, very strict and carefully monitored regulations for the management of the dogs and their keepers were drawn up and issued. This system soon began to bring about much better results. However, it is clear that through mismanagement or simple apathy on the part of some commanding officers, there were some dogs that did not meet expectations (see Appendix B). In many cases, these expectations were not, in any sense, realistic. To be fair, given the brief amount of time that Richardson had to prepare both animals and their handlers, the results were more than satisfactory.

While the dogs were being sent to France and working there, Richardson continued training men and dogs at Shoeburyness, turning out class after class. Upon completion of training, they were sent initially to the central kennels and thence to the sectional kennels. Meanwhile, as the war escalated and there was ever greater demand for fighting men, soldiers who had been doing guard duty all over Britain found themselves being shipped to the Continent. The result was that there was a great concern on the part of the government over the security of munitions factories, magazines and other vulnerable installations. Richardson was summoned and questioned as to whether dogs could help fill the void, serving as guards and thereby freeing up even more men for combat duty. He must have wondered why they had turned him away months earlier when he had approached them with the very same idea.

He responded enthusiastically and emphatically that, yes, they could, but with some caveats. Drawing on his years of experience training guard dogs for civilian purposes, he knew that they would need careful management in order to be effective. To ensure the best results, he drew up guidelines for their use and management, which were issued to each centre where the dogs were to be employed. Once this branch of the school was established and running, applications for dogs began to come in from all over Britain. In *Fifty Years With Dogs*, Richardson states that during the First World War 2000 guard dogs were trained at the War Dog School. Given that conventional wisdom holds that such an animal frees up five or six men, their contribution to the war effort was considerable.

A third branch of training was initiated when Richardson received a request for sentry dogs to be used with the troops at Salonika. The request specifically asked for Airedales, which were to be used at posts in the front line to provide early warning of an enemy approach. These were sent to that mountainous region and, although they had their uses and were well reported on, Richardson felt that they weren't used to their full potential because there was no officer there fully trained and authorized to oversee their management and proper use. He was more pleased with Airedale sentries that were sent to the Italian Front. These were in the hands of an officer who was personally and keenly interested in seeing that full use was made of the dogs' services and every condition supplied for their proper working. In this instance, the result was completely satisfactory.

Richardson contends, in *Forty Years With Dogs*, that sentry dogs were "not given a very full trial." The reason for this, he suggests, is that where the front line becomes more or less consolidated during the whole of the period of operation and where the presence of the enemy is more or less always known, the usefulness of such dogs was discounted. He had seen the value of such

Major Richardson's dogs. (Author's collection)

dogs at Vosges and elsewhere and was convinced of their value, but he felt that they were quickly discredited in many cases by the British army. Regardless, a new type of service was thus developed and with it came a very large demand for suitable dogs.

When he began his official work with the government, Richardson probably never anticipated how quickly and how large the school would become. At times, there were as many as 500 dogs on the site. With the establishment of a division in the field and expansion to include the training of guard and sentry dogs, it was soon found that the training grounds at Shoeburyness were becoming crowded. Most notably, there was the sea on one side, the firing ranges on another and swamp on a third. The result was that there was only one bottleneck through which the dogs could be sent for their return journey. This meant that, as the numbers increased, too many dogs were encountering each other as they underwent training. For the more fully trained dogs, this did not present a problem as they went about their assigned tasks, but for the tyros, there inevitably would be "greetings" en route which delayed and frustrated training and sometimes resulted in injured dogs.

To accommodate the growing demands of the War Dog School, a new site was selected at Matley Ridge, above Lyndhurst, in The New Forest. The departure from the original site was bittersweet for most involved. As Richardson writes, it was part of the background where the school was first created. That, and the physical environment, with the fresh sea air, the marshland and the booming of the great guns, had become home. And, Richardson notes, for the men who had come from the Front to work with the dogs, it was a place of rest and peace. In November, a train carrying about 100 men, 250 dogs, and all their gear and luggage left Shoeburyness for The New Forest. The school would stay at Matley Ridge until May, 1919, when it was moved again to Bulford, on Salisbury Plain.

Richardson would eventually be acknowledged, if perhaps not as directly as he might have liked. Many distinguished visitors paid their respects by making the journey to the War Dog School. Among them was Field-Marshall French, who inspected the establishment whilst accompanied by General Lowther. This happened in the early days, before the school had truly demonstrated its usefulness and effectiveness, but Richardson's spirits were buoyed by the tribute. As he wrote in *British War Dogs*, "the genuine interest Lord French showed in the dogs, and the few words of helpful encouragement he gave me, at a time when very great difficulties were being overcome, will always be remembered with gratitude." Officers from the Allied and neutral countries also visited, as did writers and editors of various media from the Allied nations. The number of visitors became so great that during the summer of 1917 one day a week had to be set aside to accommodate them, so that the training of the dogs would not be affected.

Perhaps the ultimate vindication for Richardson came in two forms. It is perhaps best if it is related in his own words, as he penned them in *British War Dogs*:

In November, 1918, the armistice came, but just before that event the latest instructions for divisional attack were issued. In these it was ordered that infantry battalions in the attack were to be provided with messenger dogs. This seemed to set a seal on the work. The long uphill struggle, the open sneers, the active obstruction, the grudging assistance, all was forgotten, in the knowledge that countless men's lives had been saved and that this fact had now been realized and acknowledged.

Field-Marshall Haig, in his final dispatch on the war, pays a tribute to the work the messenger dogs did in the field. This, perhaps, pleased Richardson as much as anything else could have.

CHAPTER SIX
British War Dogs in France

That the British War Dog School was successful is beyond question. Having received official permission to train war dogs was but one part of the battle, however. Despite the individual officers who had requested dogs prior to the government's blessing, and their success with them once put into service, others still balked at the idea and, in some cases, flatly rejected their use even when supplied with dogs. That, coupled with a general ignorance of their purpose, value and management, presented difficulties for the handlers and for Richardson. In the passage below, from *British War Dogs*, Richardson suggests the degree of prejudice that still existed nine months after the dogs had been officially put into service by the military. It is in reference to a report from a keeper whose dogs were covering, in some cases, 3.5 to four kilometres in 10 and 11 minutes and which, in other instances, were covering distances in 11 and 15 minutes that human runners were completing in an hour and five minutes.

Conditions were, by now, getting much easier for the keepers, as the work of the dogs was understood by the officers under whom they had to work. At the same time it is extraordinary the amount of prejudice there has been to overcome. I have come across officers with a pile of official reports on successful dog work in front of them, and who have never themselves, tested them, [sic] who blandly remarked that they did not believe in dogs. It is this unreceptive attitude to new ideas, that has been at the bottom in many mistakes of the war.

It is clear that there were problems with the organization and management of the dogs when they were first shipped across the

The Red Cross Magazine, August, 1918, featuring the painting "The Wounded Comrade" by J.O. Todahl, an interesting switch on the heroic dog saving the soldier. (Author's collection)

Life Magazine, March 14, 1918. The cover is titled "Pass, Friend." (Author's collection)

Channel. As Waley wrote in his assessment of the program (IWM 69/75/1), in most cases the utility of the dogs depended entirely upon the battalion commander to whom they were assigned. In many cases, after a few weeks, the dogs, rather than being an asset to the troops, became nothing more than a regimental mascot. The dogs were often indulged by the men, who fed them and indiscriminately treated them as pets, rather than working dogs. To overcome these difficulties, and to make the most efficient use of the dogs, there was a need to reorganize the system.

The first step was to gain feedback from those who were handling and in charge of dogs in the field. The General Staff called for reports from all commanders who had messenger dogs in their service. Reports were received from the First, Third, and Fifth Armies and from XV Corps. The reports were favorable, but all agreed that the service was in need of better supervision. Note some of the responses received from the commanding officers. From the First Army it was reported that

> *Divisions in this Army to whom Messenger Dogs have been supplied, speak highly of their value. Results in the majority of cases, have been satisfactory, the dogs have made good time, and messages have been received considerably quicker than was usual by runners. I am of opinion that Messenger Dogs will prove of value to supplement existing means of communication.*

The Third Army submitted reports from various regiments. The 14th A. & S. Highlanders and the 12 S.W. Borderers reported that the dogs were found useful during normal trench warfare with messages failing to be delivered only twice and in both cases the same dog was at fault. The dogs also showed strong dislike for trenches, especially those that had been floored with duckboard. At the time of the report, there had been no opportunities to test them in "active operations."

The 13th King Liverpool Regiment found that the dogs carried messages "very successfully." The response from units within the XVII Corps were somewhat less enthusiastic, although there was support for the service. At that early stage, the dogs ran in considerably less time than a man, but the dogs were not that reliable and some tended to go off hunting.

The Fifth Army perhaps provided the most realistic assessment of the service. It reported that the dogs were useful and with good training promised to be of great value. There were sufficient satisfactory reports of the dogs to warrant the continued provision of dogs. Tellingly, the Fifth Army reported that "Everything depends on the strict observance of the G. H. Q. Instructions to their treatment."

XV Corps reported that messenger dogs had been used successfully and worked quickly, averaging a mile (1.6 kilometres) in under seven minutes in some instances. However, it was found that under heavy shell fire they were not always reliable. But there was an even more significant problem. The dogs sometimes worked for five months at a time with only three days' rest. Lt. General J. du Cane of the XV Corps acknowledged that the dogs had proven useful but value could not be derived because the dogs and their handlers were in need of rest. Gas affected the dogs and also rendered them unfit for service. Having said that, it was the opinion that under some circumstances they were "undoubtedly useful."

Based on the feedback from those who responded, it was concluded that there was unanimous support for the continuation of messenger dogs. To that end, on November 27, 1917, Captain (later Major) Alec Waley of the Carrier Pigeon Service was designated to reorganize the service. His first task was to go to France and make a round of the messenger dog service of the French army. He left on

Life Magazine, May, 1917, featuring a Red Cross Airedale by Robert Dickey. It is called "Count on Me." (Author's collection.

November 28, 1917, and on his tour visited the kennels in Paris and the kennels of the 4th, 6th and 3rd French Armies and filed a report upon his return.

The French dogs were under the control of the Minister of War, not the army, and the service was, in comparison to Britain's at the time, well organized. Dogs were either "presented" or lent for military service and any breed considered suitable was considered. Dogs were received in Paris, cleaned and disinfected and then sent to one of eight training kennels in and around the city for a month of training as either guard dogs or messengers. From there, they were sent – semi-trained – to one of the armies. At the time of Waley's visit, France was in the process of building a huge training facility near Versailles that could house 500 dogs for training. It was near a bombing school and it was hoped that, in addition to the training received there, the dogs would become accustomed to continual shelling. It was expected that most of the eight existing facilities would be closed down upon its completion.

He next visited the kennels of the 4th Army, which housed 150 dogs. These were received from Paris and underwent another six weeks of thorough training. While there, he witnessed some trials that he found quite impressive. In one instance, twenty dogs were sent 2000 yards away and returned under a heavy barrage of grenades. The dogs averaged about seven minutes in making the run, with only one dog being disinclined to face the grenade barrage. In another

The illustration from the well-known Saturday Evening Post cover from November 23, 1918, featuring Charles Livingston Bull's famous Red Cross Airedale. (Author's collection, courtesy of Nancy Nieset)

Another famous Robert Dickey illustration from "Dogs from Life" called "Reminiscences." An Airedale and a German Shepherd Dog share war stories. The Airedale says "And right there, comrade, is where I swam the river with the dispatches and got this bullet in my shoulder." The art is accompanied by a poem called "The War Dog." (Author's collection)

trial, two sets of dogs were released, one from the trenches 1500 yards away and the other from battalion headquarters, 800 yards away. The former took 13 minutes and the latter seven minutes, both sets of dogs travelling over heavily entrenched ground. The Brigadier and the Major in charge at the battalion headquarters told him that the messenger dog service had proved of real utility, a position corroborated by the army commander who said that he believed that the dogs had proven their usefulness and that he would like to see the service extended.

Waley heard familiar reports when he visited the 6th Army. The messenger dog service there was undergoing reorganization. Until just prior to his visit, the dogs had been allotted to regiments and a large number of them had, because of lack of supervision, become lost or "useless" owing to the fact that they had been made into "pets." Consequently, it had been arranged that

Three Airedales equipped with gas masks. (Author's collection)

all of the dogs had been recalled and retrained. In spite of this setback, the officers were pleased with the work that the dogs did when under proper care and supervision.

At the 3rd Army kennels at St. Sauveur, Waley witnessed some "exceptionally fine trials" of liaison dogs. Liaison dogs, whereby the messenger dog is trained to run between two handlers, were not extensively used by the British in World War One. Richardson states that there were two reasons for this. One had to do with the amount of training involved, which was roughly double that of the messenger dog. By the time the War Office had decided to bestow its blessing on the use of military dogs, "the order was for unlimited output with the utmost celerity," in Richardson's words. In other words, they needed as many dogs as possible and they needed them yesterday, precluding the possibility of extensive training if a one-way messenger dog would suffice. Furthermore, many dogs that could be trained for the one-direction method, and prove very successful at it, could not be trained for the liaison system.

The second reason, according to Richardson, was that unidirectional messenger dogs necessitated only one keeper or handler, as opposed to two. The keeper or handler stayed behind at battalion headquarters while other soldiers took his dogs away to the front line trenches. When it was time to send a message, the dogs were slipped and they returned to where they had last been with their handler. The liaison system, however, required two handlers, one of whom went out to the trenches with the dogs and the other who remained behind. The handler in the trenches would slip a dog with the message. The dog would return to its other handler, who would take the message and, if need be, attach a reply and release the dog, which would then return to the trenches and its other handler. Richardson maintained that this system took up valuable manpower, with its need for two handlers. Furthermore, it exacerbated the risk to both men and dogs, to the former because of the need to have an additional handler in the trenches and to the latter because of the necessity of having the dog run in both directions, often under gunfire. Writing in 1920, Richardson argued that with the shortage of manpower in the early days, and the increasing shortage as the war dragged on, the simpler method proved more advisable. Regardless, he also suggested that if the program were to be maintained through peacetime, a certain number of liaison dogs should be always available.

Upon his return from visiting the French war dog facilities, Waley submitted his suggestions for revision of the British program. On the 8th of January, 1918, the suggestions were adopted with some modifications. The old system was done away with and a new central kennel established near Etaples, France. The location had a number of advantages, one of which was that it included a stretch of land that had originally been used as live bombing school. It was intersected with trenches and bomb craters and consisted mainly of sand dunes. Consequently, the dogs

Blue jackets with War Dogs. (Courtesy of Phyllis Wayne)

Officers of the Suffolkshire Regiment with their Airedale. (Author's collection)

Sailor with Airedale. (Author's collection)

An interesting postcard titled "The War – a guard dog of the English trenches." The dog appears to be an Irish Wolfhound. (Author's collection)

could not return by sight to their handlers and had to rely instead on their intelligence and instinct.

All the personnel and dogs from the front line, as well as those arriving from England, would be withdrawn to this central kennel. Each dog was given its own kennel, carefully constructed to give the animal maximum comfort, given the conditions. From the central kennel, the dogs and their handlers would proceed to sectional kennels housing 50 dogs, which supplied messenger dog sections continually in the front line for 15 days. The work of training the dogs already in the country, and organizing the sectional kennels, was started on February 15.

Waley set and prioritized himself a number of tasks. The first was to transfer all the men to the Royal Engineers. The messenger dog service became a branch of the signals service, and all personnel were transferred to the Messenger Dog Service Royal Engineers. The next step was to get rid of what he called the "dud" dogs. Exactly how this was accomplished is left unsaid, but one assumes that it was determined, in large part, by testing their reaction to heavy gunfire. Poor performance records undoubtedly helped cull the field.

Task number three was to organize the dogs into teams. They were put into teams of three and whenever possible, it comprised dogs of the same breed, e.g., three Lurchers, three Collies, three Airedales.[21] A team was then allotted to a man whose sole duty it became was to look after and train his dogs. Each dog was registered (see Appendix A) and given a name and number that were stamped on its collar. Pertinent observations and comments about the dogs were duly noted in a book by the OC (Officer Commanding) of the battalion to which the dogs were assigned.

The fourth task was getting the dogs used to bombing and heavy shell fire. This was accomplished in a relatively simple, yet effective, manner. Bomb-pits were dug round three sides of the central kennel and four bomb-pits inside the kennel area. The British borrowed from the French something called an O.F. Grenade, which contained a large amount of powder in a thin, tin cover and which was extremely noisy. In Pavlovian fashion, three minutes before the dogs were to be fed (which was once daily), bombs were thrown into the prepared pits. The noise, Waley reports, was "sufficient to recall a heavy barrage."

With very few exceptions, for the first few days after their arrival at the central kennels, nothing could induce the dogs to come out of their kennels after the bombing. This is not surprising, given that they had no possibility of retreat other than into whatever their houses provided. As their food was removed after the bombing, the dogs were forced to go hungry. Inevitably, hunger would overcome fear for the majority of the dogs, and within a week, Waley states, all the dogs that were going to be of any value were straining against their chains in anticipation of being fed as soon as the bombs went off. The method proved to be very effective in meeting its objectives of acclimatizing the dogs to the bombs and, by default, eliminating those animals that would never be of any use.

Buglers of the 71 Field Ambulance R.A.M.C. and their Airedale. (Author's collection)

A postcard captioned "One of Major Richardson's Sentry Dogs on the Western Front. This dog was gassed by the Germans, but recovered. He has been with the troops at Loos and in Egypt and is now on duty once more in France." (Author's collection)

The actual training of the dogs was the next step. This followed the essential pattern that Richardson had developed. The handler (or keeper) would take his three charges out to the training ground. The handler would stay in one spot while the dogs were led away by a stranger. The dogs were then let go, or slipped, separately, out of sight of their handler, to whom they returned at full speed. The distance was gradually increased until the dogs were covering 3500 yards. Meanwhile, the handler was continually changing his post, so that the dogs, too, had to learn to find their way to where he was waiting. Training was conducted both at night and during the day. In a qualification that strikes one today as somewhat dangerous, before a team was deemed acceptable, the dogs had to run three miles (4.8 kilometres) along the Etaples-Boulogne Road which, Waley states, always had much traffic. He asserts that this was "really a hard test of the dogs' intelligence" but one would think that luck played as much a part in keeping them alive as did intelligence. Very few dogs ever become truly traffic wise.

The dogs also had to learn to co-operate without fighting. The messenger dog service was also organized into what was called "Messenger Dog Groups," each group comprising two teams of three dogs. The groups always worked together at the front, so it was essential that the six dogs get along without fighting. The six dogs that constituted a group were always kenneled next to each other so that the dogs would grow familiar with and accept each other.

Waley's final task was to establish sectional kennels. These included one sergeant, 16 other ranks with their eight messenger dog groups of six dogs each. There were three such sectional kennels, with the first being allotted on February 19, 1918. The second followed on April 6. During the nine months that followed this reorganization of the messenger dog service, the sectional kennels were moved 13 times as fortunes in the war shifted.

The first dogs to see action under the new system were employed on April 14, 1918, when the Germans were attacking heavily in front of Hazebrouk. XV Corps asked that some dogs be provided for use in the Forest of Nieppe. The dogs performed exceptionally well, which aroused considerable interest in the use of dogs. Two dogs out of 12 were badly injured and all were gassed, although they ultimately recovered.

On the 17th of April, during the German attack on Kemmel Hill, three messenger dog groups were sent to XXII Corps and immediately re-allocated to 9th Division. The dogs assigned did "sterling work" during the whole of the German attack on Kemmel Hill. From then until the close of the war, the dogs proved themselves time and time again.

After one month in the field, reports were requested from the commanding officers of the corps to which dogs had been assigned. Waley, in his summary comments of the reports submitted, writes that "From the...reports it will be seen that the concensus [sic] of opinion was that the dogs were undoubtedly a useful additional means of communication. Most of the faults in the dogs' running were assuredly caused through the rules laid down not being adhered to." Interestingly, the Australians who had use of the dogs were the main dissenting voice. Indeed, in the report submitted by the Fourth Army, it is unequivocally stated that "The 1st Australian Division did not take the same interest in the dogs. After the first day or two, they were kept fastened up for too lengthy periods. It would appear that they do not wish to have messenger dogs." In this regard, Richardson himself wrote, in *British War Dogs*, that "The keepers found considerable difficulty at first in working the dogs with the Australian troops, as the latter were somewhat indifferent in observing the regulations with regard to the dogs in the field." The problem, however, seems to have resolved itself when a commanding officer recognized the benefits to be gained through their proper employment and use. In contrast to the Australians, Canadian troops who worked with the dogs appeared to recognize their benefit. American troops, as well, admired the messenger dogs and, in fact, often tried to buy, borrow or steal them.

Not surprisingly, the casualties among dogs (and their handlers) were high. Many dogs were gassed and/or shot in the line of duty. Richardson, in his guidelines for the use of messenger dogs (guidelines that were quite extensive, touching on everything from feeding to treating mustard gas attacks), stated that the dogs should spend seven days at a time at the front, being on duty for 12 hours at a stretch. However, in actuality, the dogs were serving fortnight tours of duty, in twelve hour shifts, according to Waley's reports. The near-ceaseless firing of the guns and pounding of the cannon must have wrought havoc for man and dog alike. Of the first 21 dogs listed in Appendix A, two were gassed and returned to duty, four were listed as "missing" or "lost" (of these four, one was found and returned to work and another was found, returned and subse-

Left: British artilleryman with Airedale. (Author's collection)

Below: Bandaging a dispatch dog wounded in the head, at a dog hospital behind the lines. (Courtesy of the Imperial War Museum, London, Neg. #Q56508)

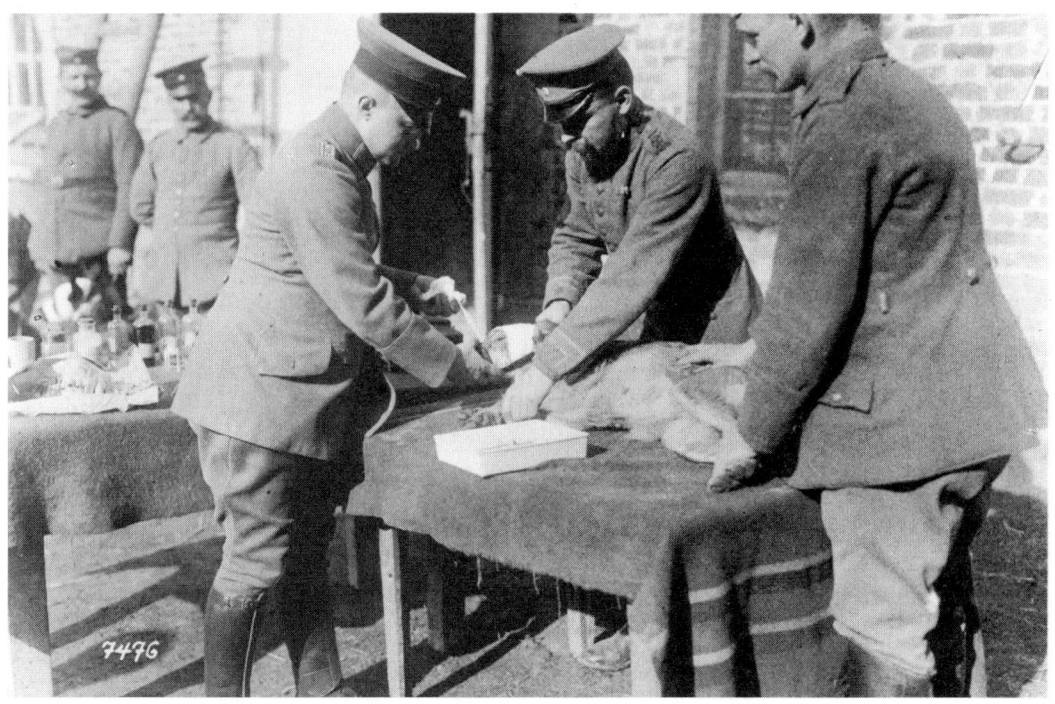

quently killed in the line of duty), and two were shot. Of the two dogs shot, one was killed by the order of the OC. The good news, if there is any good news in all of this, is that Waley reports that although the dogs suffered badly from mustard gas, all but four eventually recovered.

Waley admits to "fairly high casualties" among the dogs, adding that it was necessary to continually send up fresh groups. He cites one officer's diary from May 21, 1918. "Visited No 2. Sectional kennel. Whilst I was there 4 Messenger Dog Groups returned from the front line. 3 dogs had been badly wounded and 4 gassed during the last two days."

As evidence of the tremendous physical punishment the dogs had to endure, Richardson, in *British War Dogs*, cites the case of Paddy, an Irish Terrier of heroic proportions. He was gassed at Nieppe and spent three weeks recovering in a veterinary hospital and then returned to duty. He was gassed a second time in an advance in the Nieppe Forest in the front line and returned a distance of 17 kilometres to the section kennel. Unbelievably, though he was completely blind, he made his way directly to his own kennel where he remained until his keeper went to his assistance. In three hours, his eyes were open and he was as lively as ever. When he returned to action, it was at Passchendaele. There, he was shot by a German officer who left him for dead on the battlefield. He lay there a long time before he revived, and then made his way to brigade headquarters where his keeper was summoned to fetch him. Irish Terriers are known to be among the toughest and most durable of all dogs, but Paddy's story is almost beyond belief. It is also indicative of the horrors that the messenger dogs had to endure.

The messenger dogs faced other hazards and impediments to their work. Among these were the numerous dogs that ran loose all over the countryside. Some of these were farm dogs that had owners while others were strays whose families had been killed or dislocated by the war. A report from XV Corps, for example, a month after the dogs had first been assigned, noted that, as a rule, the dogs ran well and the times were fairly good. However, they observed, "One difficulty was the large number of stray civilian dogs at deserted farm-houses…that tended to make the dogs tarry." Other obstacles with which the dogs had to contend were double lines of barbed wire and canals. In terms of the latter obstacle, most dogs simply swam across.

The dogs were also sometimes led astray by bitches in heat. At the outset, bitches were occasionally used as messengers, but soon afterwards they were eliminated from the service because of the distraction they posed to males when in heat. As for male dogs, it became apparent that no matter how trustworthy a dog might be, it could never be counted on if there was a bitch in heat anywhere within the vicinity.[22] It is alleged by Waley that the Germans "undoubtedly had trained bitches to draw all stray dogs to their lines" and that on two occasions German bitches in heat, wearing German collars, were captured by the Allies. From records maintained in the archives at The Imperial War Museum, it is clear that many commanding officers also ordered that all stray dogs be shot, so that the messenger dogs could do their work without hindrance.

And, as noted before, the dogs' own allies, the soldiers in the trenches, posed a threat to their profitable service. At first, it was nearly impossible to keep the men from making pets out of the dogs. They had to be admonished constantly and reminded not to pet or feed them as they were

A British messenger dog with feet bandaged as a result of injuries caused by mustard gas, at the Corps H.Q. Kennel near Nieppe Wood, 19 May, 1918. (Courtesy of the Imperial War Museum, London, Neg. #Q10957)

waiting to be put to work. Many good dogs were spoilt in the early days because of this (understandable) tendency. Little by little, it was recognized that they were working dogs and could, in a pinch, save lives and the promiscuous feeding and indulgence of the dogs was overcome. With all of these distractions, it is remarkable that the dogs performed as well as they did.

As the appendices in this volume indicate, many dogs were shot by orders of the commanding officers of the battalions in which they served. As Gray implies, in *Dogs of War*, there are a "suspicious number of executions" recorded in the messenger dog record book. As he tactfully puts it, "They can't all have been justified, surely?" He lays the blame squarely at the feet of the commanding officers who, it is agreed here, were only too quick to "cast" (a euphemism for "shoot") the messenger (literally). Gray pulls no punches: "Those who signed the register [detailing the messenger dogs] are convicted of arrogance and ignorant prejudice by the death sentences they passed on those who were only too anxious to please."

Gray is equally quick to condemn Waley, who seems ambivalent at best about Richardson's contributions to the War Dog School. Waley, in his summary comments about messenger dog service (IWM 69/75/1), writes that

these dogs were put through a preliminary course of training in England before being sent to France; this training, although superficial, was sufficient to assure that all dogs surviving were intelligent enough for the work which they would be required. The percentage of dogs which had to be cast was extremely low, and shows how thoroughly the Commandant of the War Dog School, Shoeburyness, sifted out the wheat from the chaff.

As Gray states, the number – with decades of hindsight – does not appear extremely low. Nor, from other accounts, does Richardson's training in Shoeburyness appear to be "superficial." Richardson had, by this time, decades of experience in the breeding, selection and training of service dogs for the military, the police and civilians. They had proven themselves worldwide, from Russia to South Africa, Morocco to Italy, North America to India. The War Office had appointed him, because of his expertise, to head up the War Dog School. To suggest that he would send dogs off to the trenches when they had only "preliminary" or "superficial" training is mind-boggling. The film footage of Richardson's training of the dogs suggests otherwise, as do the many accounts of the dogs he sent to other nations. Rather, as Waley's own report attests, it

The Dominion journalists visit the Messenger Dog Service Central Depot at Etaples, 6 September, 1918. The dog appears to be a Scottish Deerhound. (Courtesy of the Imperial War Museum, London, Neg. #Q11311)

was the mishandling of the dogs that – more often than not – resulted in their failure to perform. The British, it must be recalled, had never before worked with military dogs in any meaningful way, so to a large extent the concept was foreign. That, and perhaps Waley's own desire for recognition for having re-organized the service, explains his position. In the end, there is something disconcerting to read in the register that a dog was "deemed useless, shot by O.C.'s orders." To reiterate, the allegation of uselessness inevitably came from an officer who, in all likelihood, had a prejudice towards the idea of messenger dogs to begin with and, beyond the shadow of a doubt, had no experience with them. In such cases, the declaration of "useless" was probably inevitable.

Other Forms of Training in France

Richardson, of course, had trained guard dogs, sentry dogs and Bloodhounds before the war broke out. Sentry and guard dogs had found employment in England protecting sensitive installations such as factories and munitions depots. In Major Waley's report on the Messenger Dog Service – France (IWM 69/75/1), he includes as an appendix a brief report about "sentry dogs." He reports that in March, 1918, the demand for every available man "in the firing line" rendered it difficult to find a sufficient number of men to guard such things as stores, depots and prisoner-of-war camps. To help remedy the situation, Waley writes, a plan was put forward to use what Waley calls "watch dogs" to guard these places. The initial proposal was made September 25, 1918. Eighteen dogs from the central kennel and forward area that were "specially savage" were trained for guarding purposes, but the program was only in the process of being implemented when the Armistice was signed.

A similar proposal was made for the use of Bloodhounds. It was suggested that a number of dogs be brought over from England to help in the capture of escaped prisoners. A couple of Bloodhounds were used with good results at Rouen but, as was the case with the sentry dogs, the plan never fully crystallized.

Waley also mentions that 30 dogs (ten teams) were trained as liaison dogs at the central kennel at Etaples. However, as Richardson had suggested, no use was made of them because of the fear that if one handler were killed in the line, the whole system would be rendered *hors de combat*. Thus, although the dogs and handlers were trained in this capacity, no use was ever made of them. Dogs were also trained, after the French fashion, to carry supplies on their backs. While the French dogs carried small arms ammunition, the British at Etaples had specially made harnesses that were meant to carry two large water bottles, each of which held four pints. The idea was that the dogs could carry hot soup or other food to men in isolated places such as pill boxes. Twelve dogs had been trained to follow a keeper, whom they followed single file, at a distance of about eight yards between each dog. Again, with the cessation of hostilities, the scheme was never put into effect.

A Corps H.Q. messenger dog kennel near Nieppe Forest, 19 May, 1918. (Courtesy of the Imperial War Museum, London, Neg. #Q10964

November 11, 1918

Hamer, in *Dogs at War*, states that more dogs were killed after the war than during it. The French, it is claimed, killed all 15 000 of their dogs at the conclusion of World War I. As well, it is contended, the British, Germans, Italians and Russians killed most of their military dogs. Richardson begs to differ with this version of the fate of British dogs. In *Fifty Years With Dogs*, he writes that "The war came to an end, and all the dogs were either returned to their owners or were found good homes." Patmore, in *Your Obedient Servant*, elaborates, stating that "Despite the work of the British dogs and the concern of their handlers, it was left to the RSPCA to bring them back from Europe in 1918."

The story is quite complex. From a North American perspective (and, indeed, probably from a Continental stance, as well), Britain is virtually paranoid about rabies. The disease had been eradicated from the British Isles since 1902 and, in their frenzied attempt to keep rabies out, dogs entering Britain from abroad were quarantined for no fewer than six months. Needless to say, at the end of the war, the sudden influx of several hundred dogs (including pets as well as service animals) represented a considerable investment in money and facilities.

So, what *did* become of the British war dogs? According to the files housed at The Imperial War Museum, by December, 1918, all dogs and personnel were again centralized at the central kennel. The training of the dogs continued, but as the men were increasingly demobilized, it became ever more apparent that something had to be done regarding the future of the service. One plan, which did not materialize, was that one section kennel should be transferred – dogs and personnel – to England and that the remainder of the dogs be auctioned in Paris. When this suggestion was not accepted, it was finally decided, in March 1919, that the Messenger Dog Service was to be liquidated and the dogs given to any officer or other rank remaining with the Army of the Rhine. A notice was circulated stating that upon receipt of 20 francs to be applied to the cost of muzzle, message-carrier, collar and chains, dogs could be purchased. Over 800 applications were received, making it necessary to draw lots for the dogs. Fifty percent of the demands "from all other ranks" were first met. All dogs were dispatched to their new owners by April 4th, with the closure of the central kennel two days later. The official record, as related by Major Waley, ends there. However, there still remained the issue of rabies and the notorious British quarantine laws.

Gray, in *Dogs of War*, explains the fine details that abound regarding the return of the British war dogs. To begin with, it cost 14 British pounds to quarantine a dog, roughly a month's wages for a farm worker, and an amount beyond that of most military personnel. In 1917, the Royal Society for the Prevention of Cruelty to Animals (RSPCA) undertook to defray in whole or part the expense of renewing 542 dogs' licenses for those who were incapable of finding the money themselves, especially soldiers and sailors. This they did with the blessing of the Army Council.

There was also the difficulty of accommodation for the dogs. By arrangement with the Battersea Dogs Home, special kennels for 500 dogs were established at Hackbridge, the quarantine station of the home. Four hundred and fifty of these kennels were for dogs returning from France, 25 for those from Salonika, 15 for those from Egypt and 10 for those returning from Italy. To help meet the expense and to ensure that each dog would be claimed at the end of the lengthy quarantine period, owners were asked to pay two pounds, upon receipt of which a special license was granted by the soldier's commanding officer who, in turn, had made special and careful inquiries into the genuineness of each case. There was a proviso, however: the RSPCA insisted on the humane destruction of any dog that could not be brought back. The authorities also issued definite statements to the same effect. Further funds were obtained from the Charity Commissioners of the War Charities Act, which permitted 15 000 pounds to be transferred to the dog fund from the RSPCA sick and wounded horses fund, and a further 10 000 pounds were invested, with the interim interest available to the society.

Also aiding the cause was a fund for soldiers' dogs established at the request of the Army Council. This was well supported by the public. *The Evening News* helped by arranging a sale of cartoons by its popular caricaturist "Poy." If further motivation to contribute were needed, it was found in the true story of Prince, an Irish Terrier that mysteriously found his way from Hammersmith, in London, to his owner fighting in the trenches of Armentieres. Such a story, especially once proven to be factual, would warm the cockles of anybody's heart and almost certainly loosen the purse strings.

The story sounds apocryphal but it was well researched and proved to be factual. Private James Brown went to France in September, 1914, leaving his wife and Prince behind in Ireland. Mrs. Brown and Prince shortly thereafter visited her in-laws in Stafford. Following a few weeks

Two British messenger dogs with feet bandaged as a result of mustard gas. At a Corps H.Q. near Nieppe Wood, 19 May, 1918. (Courtesy of the Imperial War Museum, London, Neg. #Q10965)

there, the two went to her home in Hammersmith. From the time his master left for France, Prince had moped and proved inconsolable. About a month after settling in London, the dog disappeared. Mrs. Brown wrote two letters to her husband, informing him of the sad news. In response to her second message, she received a reply saying that Prince was safely with his master in France. Somehow, through the streets of London, down to the coast, across the Channel, and through the battlefields of France, the intrepid Irish Terrier found his master and, the story goes, leaped into the trenches and into his master's arms with the greatest of joy. He was eventually brought home by the RSPCA and lived with his beloved master until 1921, when he ate some poisoned meat on the street and died.

The soldiers' dogs were again centralized at a veterinary hospital near Boulogne that had been set up especially for their care. The dogs underwent a physical exam upon their arrival and each day that they were there, with each dog staying a minimum of five days under care and supervision. The dogs were taken back to England in groups, escorted by a sergeant and a number of men from the Royal Army Veterinary Corps. Upon arrival at Southampton, they were met by an inspector from the RSPCA and taken immediately to the facilities at Hackbridge. There, they were again examined and placed into their six month quarantine. Five hundred eighty dogs were thus conveyed from France to England. In December, 1919, the last dog was released from quarantine, the system, generally speaking, having proven successful in ensuring the return of the war dogs and in helping to prevent rabies from entering the country.[23] Over a period of two years, only ten animals died from unavoidable causes. As a bonus, Gray notes in his discussion of this Herculean effort, the scheme was a financial success due to the good will of the public and the various agencies involved. A surplus of 5300 pounds was made and invested in the resuscitation of the late Sick and Wounded Horses Fund in the eventuality of another war.

Britain's war dogs had returned home.

CHAPTER SEVEN
The Dogs

Following the creation of the War Dog School, the demand for trained dogs quickly became apparent. Initially, the only supply came from the Home for Lost Dogs at Battersea. Later, the Birmingham, Liverpool, Bristol and Manchester Dogs' Homes were asked to participate by sending potentially suitable dogs. Following that, the Home Office ordered the police around the country to send all stray dogs of certain breeds to the school. By these means, many a stray or otherwise unwanted dog was saved from the gas chamber and given a new leash on life, albeit not one without its own risks.

As the war progressed, however, even these means of recruiting dogs were found insufficient. In response, the War Office appealed to the public for donations of dogs. The timing, in some respects, could not have been better. Britain, as was the case with much of the world, was going through hard times and many people were happy to oblige by donating their family pet. Food shortages were acute and there was the prevailing awareness that, even though the family might not be able to afford to feed the dog, the army would provide him with good food and proper care. The response was overwhelming, with dozens being received every day. Purebreds with distinguished pedigrees and show championships, along with mongrels of varying descriptions, found their way to the War Dog School.

In *Watch-Dogs: Their Training and Management*, Richardson provides us with an example of the number and breeds of dogs that passed through the War Dog School, trained as messenger dogs, in a typical month. It is a remarkable example of what can be accomplished with diverse breeds. The list is as follows:

Breed	Count	Breed	Count
Collies	74	Greyhounds	2
Lurchers	70	Eskimos	2
Airedales	66	Bedlington Terriers	2
Sheep Dogs	36	Dalmatians	2
Retrievers	33	Pointers	2
Irish Terriers	18	Bulldogs	1
Spaniels	11	Whippets	1
Deerhounds	6	Total	340
Welsh Terriers	5		
Bull Terriers	5		
Setters	4		

While this is revealing, it is also somewhat vague. Amongst working Border Collie people, for example, "Collie" means Border Collie, not the Rough Collie (or its Smooth Collie brother) of "Lassie" fame. However, there is evidence that Rough Collies were used. Thus, we are left wondering exactly which breed Richardson was referring to here. Certainly, when we look at some of the photos in his memoirs, and others found in archives, we are led to believe that the Border Collie was intended. Similarly, the term "Sheep Dog" is vague. Again, the heroic Tweed (see below) was, in fact, an Old English Sheepdog. But, once again, the term has a vastly different meaning to herding dog fanciers and workers. "Retrievers" and "Spaniels" likewise imply a number of breeds. We may assume that the former represented, in most cases, the Flat-Coated Retriever (then the most popular of the Retriever breeds) and in the latter case, the Springer Spaniel. "Bull Terrier" is the proper name of the down-faced breed known to Canadians as "Spuds Mackenzie" of beer commercial renown. On the other hand, among many dog people in Great Britain, the name refers properly to the Staffordshire Bull Terrier, the original pit fighting dog. Both are English creations, known by these names, but amongst a certain segment of the population only the latter is entitled to the name "Bull Terrier." Which did Richardson mean in this instance? In all likelihood, he meant the Bull Terrier per se, but we can never be certain. Finally, one can only wonder about the "Bulldog" that served as a messenger dog. Today's Bulldog, largely a caricature of what was once an athletic and powerful animal, does not resemble the dogs of the early 19th century and earlier. By 1914, the Bulldog was on the rapid and slippery slope to becoming obsolete as a working dog. We must assume that the Bulldog indicated in Richardson's inventory was one of the last remaining athletic Bulldogs of the early 20th century, or else a crossbreed.

The astute reader will observe that Richardson had clearly defined notions about what constituted fine working dogs: quite simply, they had to be British breeds. It is fair to say that he had an almost paranoiac xenophobia on the subject. In particular, he found the German breeds particularly offensive, despite the fact that he includes photographs of German officers with German Shepherds and Dobermans in *War, Police and Watch Dogs* (1910), in addition to Belgian, Dutch and French officers and their dogs. Indeed, there are almost as many photographs of German Shepherds and other breeds as there are of Airedales in this, the first of his five books. That would never happen in the subsequent volumes.

Given that Richardson had spent time in Germany, and keeping in mind the early publication date of *War, Police and Watch Dogs*, one is tempted to believe that Richardson's anti-German bias was the product of the First World War, in which he had served. The British Empire lost over 900 000 men, had over two million wounded and another 190 000 either taken prisoner or missing in action. It is clear, when reading his five books in order of their publication, that Richardson's inflexible political biases were shaped by his war-time experiences.

In *Watchdogs: Their Training and Management* (1923), he stated in unequivocal terms his view of homegrown dogs when he wrote that "For intelligence, reliability of character, courage, humour, and fidelity, there are no other dogs in the world which can touch the British breeds." Of foreign breeds, he was critical, contending that "foreign breeds,…are aliens, and as in the

Above: A British messenger dog swimming a canal during training at a Corps H.Q. kennel near Nieppe Wood, 19 May, 1918. (Courtesy of the Imperial War Museum, London, Neg. #Q10959)

Below: A Royal Engineer reading a message delivered by the messenger dog. (Courtesy of the Imperial War Museum, London, Neg. #Q10960)

human family, so in the dog – the national and racial characteristics of each country are inevitably reflected, and not less so in their most intimate associations with man."

He was particularly upset with the growing popularity of the German Shepherd Dog following the cessation of World War I. The breed had been called the "Alsatian Wolfdog" in an attempt to overcome lingering hostility towards Germany and all things German after the war. Many people, including Richardson, believed (or chose to believe) that the breed was, in fact, part wolf – which, of course, it wasn't. The "Wolfdog" was dropped, but Richardson did his utmost to convince his readers that the dog was a wolf hybrid and therefore completely at odds with everything British. So deeply did he feel about the encroachment of "foreign breeds" on British soil, especially the German Shepherd Dog, that he devoted a complete chapter in *Watchdogs: Their Training and Management* to "British V. German Police Dogs."

His views are again blatantly apparent in the following passages:

The characteristics which have made and will conserve the British race for what it is are mirrored in the minds of many of the native breeds of dogs. Some of these are the most wonderful animals in the world, and cannot be approached by the dogs of any other nation.

There is a movement, in certain directions, to decry our British dogs, and to attribute extraordinary virtues to foreign dogs, which have been used abroad especially in Germany for police purposes.

A common form of such advertisement is a statement, frequently met with in connection with these German "Alsatians", that they were the dogs which helped our soldiers in the war. Of course this not the case. Many hundreds of dogs helped the soldiers of the British army, but they were all of our native breeds.

It was exclusively with "native breeds" that Richardson would work (although, as we shall see, there was at least one notable exception – see Appendix A # 278). His choice of breeds (and crossbreeds and mongrels) would likely make many trainers today wince. National kennel clubs, such as The Canadian Kennel Club, The American Kennel Club and The Kennel Club (UK) classify breeds according to their original use and purpose. To this end, in Canada and the United States, breeds belong to one of the sporting, hounds, working, herding, terrier, toy or non-sporting groups. (The last named is a catch-all group for breeds that were bred specifically for companionship or whose function no longer exists, such as the Dalmatian and Chow). Thus, it is to be expected that the hounds, such as the Beagle, Greyhound and Whippet, are specialists at hunting game by either scent or sight, and the sporting dogs are used for pointing, flushing and retrieving birds. Traditionally, military and police dogs have come from the working and herding groups (until fairly recently, all of the herding breeds belonged to the working group – that group was split in two in order to make a group specifically for dogs that herd). For example, Doberman Pinschers, Rottweilers, Boxers, Giant Schnauzers are all guarding/police/war dogs that are categorized as "working dogs."

The German Shepherd Dog, Belgian Sheepdog (of which there are four varieties – the all-black Groenendael, the wire-haired Laekenois, the Tervuren, which resembles a German

Shepherd Dog, and the increasingly popular Malinois) and the Bouvier des Flandres are all herding dogs that are very common as military and police dogs because, in addition to their role as herders, they were all expected to protect their charges against predators and human thieves. They combine their traditional herding instinct with a strong sense of property and territoriality. These traits, as well as an innate intelligence and trainability, make superior working animals for the army and police forces. In recent decades, the Malinois has started to replace the German Shepherd Dog as the service dog of choice worldwide.

Today, the Labrador and Golden Retrievers, the Springer Spaniel and – in some rare cases – the Weimaraner, are occasionally used by police forces and the military for specialist tasks such as narcotics detection, bomb detection and other work that does not involve aggression and fighting. The reason is that temperamentally, these breeds are unsuited for this type of work (in addition to the relatively small size of the Springer). There is nothing in the history and development of these breeds that predisposes them to being territorial, protective and easily agitated and aggressive to people. Instead, tasks that involve these types of traits have been left to the breeds discussed above. Stated briefly, trainers today focus on the latent instincts and ability of specific breeds and match the tasks demanded with the breed's innate abilities. Dobermans

Demonstration at the Central Depot of the messenger dog service at Etaples, 6 September, 1918. (Courtesy of the Imperial War Museum, London, Neg. 11312

guard, Irish Setters hunt birds and Malamutes haul heavily loaded sleds. These can be capitalized on so that the little scent hound, the Beagle, can be trained to sniff out illegal substances at immigration points, but we would not expect a Beagle to act as a sentry dog or to consistently perform as a circus dog.

None of this seemed to matter to Richardson. Virtually any breed, or combination of breeds, was used and tried during the Great War, from 20-pound (9 kg) Welsh Terriers to 150-pound (68 kg) Newfoundlands. The only criterion was that they had to have been a "native breed." (Their breed names notwithstanding, the Labrador Retriever and Newfoundland have, since the 19th century, been perceived as "English breeds"). Most trainers today would balk at the idea of using a retriever or a Newfoundland for guard work, as this type of endeavor runs completely counter to the breeds' disposition and instincts. Such was not the case with Richardson. If the individual animal showed tendencies in that area, the dog would find his future guarding. Indeed, in *British War Dogs*, there is a picture of a group of guard dogs, the majority of them Airedales but also a number of retrievers. In another, a sentry stands guard with a magnificent Newfoundland. In yet another photograph from *British War Dogs*, showing a morning parade of guard dogs, there is an eclectic mix of a Mastiff, a Great Dane and – incredibly – what appear to be Irish Wolfhounds or Scottish Deerhounds or perhaps Lurchers. Elsewhere, in *Forty Years With Dogs*, he recounts using Saint Bernards, Newfoundlands and Great Danes for guard work. While Mastiffs and Great Danes are traditional guard dogs, most contemporary trainers hesitate to use them, for a variety of reasons. Being giant breeds, they lack the agility often needed for serious training. More important, with their huge size they can easily kill a man if provoked. The idea of training Saint Bernards, Newfoundlands, Wolfhounds, Deerhounds or Lurchers for guard work is anathema to 99% of contemporary trainers. In fact, the traits needed for guard work run in direct opposition to those inherent in the shaggy, lifesaving Saint and Newf. But, as noted, with Richardson, it was the individual dog, not the breed or its heritage, that was of consequence. (One cannot help but notice that not all of the breeds used by Richardson were native to Britain, despite his protestations otherwise. The Great Dane is German – the name notwithstanding – and Saint Bernards are Swiss in origin.)

So what breeds did Richardson favor for war work? He used a variety of breeds and crossbreeds, but seemed to prefer Airedales, Collies, Lurchers, Retrievers (primarily Flat-coated and Curly Coated), Bloodhounds and Old English Sheepdogs. Added to this were Irish Terriers, Bullmastiffs, Bull Terriers and various and sundry others. One is truly taken aback at the range of breeds that saw service under Richardson during World War I. Incredibly, one breed that he singles out for praise as a messenger dog is the Welsh Terrier, a black and tan tyke that resembles an Airedale put through a compactor.

Richardson made it abundantly clear that his preferred breed for any and all purposes was the Airedale Terrier. On October 30, 1912, when he gave his talk to The Royal United Service Institution, he stated that fewer than one in 20 dogs recruited for training would, in the end, prove suitable. He then added that "After years of experiments with every sort of breed, I have found that the Airedale proves about the best of all those we have in this country." He then itemized the qualities that made the breed superior: fidelity, intelligence and trainability, weather resistant coat, highly developed senses, size and strength, and extreme hardiness under any and all conditions. These would be the same qualities that he would find to be true throughout the war, when dogs had to work under the most trying of conditions.

In *Watchdogs: Their Training and Management*, he provides statistics for one month's output from the War Dog School. While Collies and Lurchers slightly outnumber Airedales, it is probably a reflection of the relative availability of the breeds. In a number of his books, Richardson makes his case for the superiority of the Airedale as a service dog. In *Forty Years With Dogs*, he writes concerning the breed as a police patrol dog.

> *I have found as a whole that Airedales are very good, especially for this sort of work if they are properly selected and trained. They have the necessary weight and power and besides, in their nature, are essentially honest and intelligent. They take a great interest in people and are good at discrimination. When under orders they are extremely determined and courageous, so that one does not feel, as it were, that there is a broken reed on which to lean.*

A British messenger dog with the tube in which the message was carried around its neck. At a Corps H.Q. near Nieppe Wood, 19 May, 1918. (Courtesy of Imperial War Museum, Neg. #Q10958)

He added, in *British War Dogs* (1920), that as messenger dogs Airedales were "remarkably hardy dogs and not inclined to be nervous under fire." This view was echoed by Keeper Fergusson, a handler of messenger dogs. He submitted that he considered "the most useful dogs for the work are Airedales, pure or crossbred. They have not great speed, but they are sure, and soon find their way on strange ground."

In *Watchdogs*, Richardson sums up the qualities of the Airedale for general guarding and watchdog duties.

> *I have owned and trained at one time or another, nearly every kind of dog suitable for guarding work...as the result of all my work of years it is my considered judgment, that for all-round watching and guarding work, the most reliable dog in size and character is the Airedale Terrier. This conclusion has been reached, not only from experience in my private kennels, but also from that gained during the time I was Commandant of the War Dog School, during which time hundreds of dogs of all breeds passed through my hands for training.*

One final note must be made. In *War, Police and Watchdogs* (1910), Richardson made it plain that there was a distinction between the show specimens and real working Airedales. He wrote that "Lastly, they are of a very good size – but by this I do not mean the specimen which the modern show-bench has evolved. I have found that the old-fashioned heavy type, with a good wiry coat, is a particularly useful dog…" Four decades later, in his last book, *Fifty Years With Dogs*, he hadn't changed his mind. He wrote, "The reason that [the Airedale] *is* our favourite breed is that, after supreme tests over many years, we found it the best dog for the work we took up."

The Collies and related Sheepdog breeds proved superior messenger dogs during the First World War, and Richardson had great respect for them as working dogs. Their innate qualities, he found, were the result of the hundreds of generations of dogs that had served as companions and workers with people. He noted that, in many cases, crossbred dogs often had a dash of Collie blood, which proved an advantageous mix. As sentries and guard dogs, though, he found them wanting. Generally, they were quick and alert at giving warning, but also high strung, nervous and "apt to retire in the attack."

The Lurcher has the reputation of being the poacher's dog of choice. It is, strictly defined, a sight hound (typically a Greyhound) crossed with some other breed (typically a Border Collie or some sort of terrier). The intent was to get the intelligence of the Border Collie or other breed and the fleetness and hunting instinct of the Greyhound. Being a poacher's ally, the dog also had to be a mute hunter. Interestingly, Richardson claims that in most cases the Lurchers with which he worked were either Collie (presumably Border Collie) or Airedale crosses.

The Lurchers excelled as messenger dogs, as might be expected. Their great speed, derived from their Greyhound ancestry, allowed them to cover distances much faster than many of the other breeds. One such dog was Major, a Lurcher/Deerhound cross, who once covered 17 kilometres in under an hour, a phenomenal rate of speed under war time conditions. For other service work, such as police, sentry and guard work, Richardson found Lurchers too easily distracted.

A man of the Royal Engineers leading two messenger dogs. (Courtesy of the Imperial War Museum, London, Neg. #Q26534)

Retrievers, especially Flat-coated and Curly-coated, were commonly employed by the War Dog School. Again, contemporary breeders and trainers must read with incredulity what Richardson was able to accomplish with these typically mellow-mannered dogs. He observed that retrievers were often met with as guard dogs, and found the Curly-coated Retriever to be well-suited for this task, but were sometimes not quite reliable in character "especially as they increase in years," while the Flat-coated were usually not sharp enough. (At this time, Labrador and Golden Retrievers were not that well known).

In *Animal Heroes of the Great War* (1926), Ernest Baynes relates visiting Richardson's training facilities at Lyndhurst in the New Forest. He was skeptical about the real effectiveness of the trained guard dogs he saw, an unimaginable crew of Setters, Retrievers, Great Danes, Scottish Deerhounds and "at least one gigantic Irish Wolfhound." He asked Richardson if he might try to make friends with one of the dogs. After receiving permission, he approached a retriever.

I strode boldly forward, smiling and speaking in tones which were meant to be "kind but firm." The dog, a black retriever, did nothing but watch me until I was just within the radius of his chain. Then I stepped back suddenly as the brute hurled itself, a living thunderbolt, and a set of white and very willing teeth bit a chunk out of the air where my throat had been but a moment before. I simply cannot tell you how glad I was that the chain was not made of anything that stretched.

Richardson admired the Mastiff, a breed that some cynologists and historians view as being British in origin. The animals with which he was familiar in the early decades of the twentieth century he viewed as being far removed from their glory days of centuries past. He described them as "curiosities, mostly of a lazy and sluggish temperament" albeit "their great weight and size renders them a serious menace in attack." With all of their ferocious appearance, however, he considered them to be too sluggish and lazy to be efficient guardians, and when one of his friends bought a "a very ancient baronial castle" and a Mastiff to guard it, he also took the precaution of providing himself with an Airedale as well for security purposes.

Incredible as it may seem, Irish, Welsh and Bedlington Terriers served in World War I, primarily as messenger dogs but, in the case of the Irish, also as sentries. These three breeds, all exceptionally rugged and durable animals, only weigh between nine and 12.25 kilograms (20 to 27 pounds). Despite their diminutive size (and in the case of the Bedlington, a lamb-like appearance), they are athletic and working dogs to the core. Both the Bedlington and the Irish have a partial heritage as fighting dogs, a history that undoubtedly contributed to their steadfastness under war time conditions.

Richardson's assessment of the Irish Terrier, as he related in *British War Dogs*, is well known to fanciers of this fine breed.

I can say with decided emphasis that the Irish Terriers of the service more than did their part. Many a soldier is alive today through the effort of one of these very Terriers. Isolated with his unit in some advanced position, entirely cut off from the main body by a wall of shells, and thus prevented communicating his position or circumstance by telephone or runner so that help might follow, this messenger dog was often the only means his officers had of carrying the dispatch which would eventually bring relief. My opinion of this breed is indeed a high one. They are highly sensitive, spirited dogs of fine mettle, and those of us who respect and admire the finer qualities of mind will find them amply reflected in these Terriers. They are extraordinarily intelligent, faithful and honest, and a man who has one of them as a companion will never lack a true friend.

In *British War Dogs*, Richardson singles out the little Welsh Terrier as a messenger dog, observing that the only thing that kept more of them from being used was their scarcity. He also provides a most vivid description of a Welsh Terrier doing his work. We can do no better than to again quote directly from *British War Dogs*.

Another Australian officer told me that one of the sights that impressed him most was his first sight of a messenger dog. He saw it first coming from the direction of the front-line trenches – a little Welsh Terrier. The ground it was going over was in a terrible condition and was absolutely waterlogged. The little creature was running along hopping, jumping, plunging, and with the most obvious concentration of purpose. He could not imagine what it was doing until it came near, and he saw the message on its neck. As the dog sped past him he noticed the earnest expression in its face.

The charm of the Welsh was evident among some of the military brass during the war. One handler, Keeper Errington, had three messenger dogs, Jack, Whitefoot and Lloyd. Jack was an Airedale, the other two Welsh terriers "of a large size" (which probably meant that they weighed about eleven kilograms or 25 pounds). At Nieppe Forest, the dogs were averaging five kilometres in 45 minutes, under conditions that included mud, vehicular traffic, cattle, sheep, poultry and carcasses, in addition to the bombardment. Whitefoot acted as a runner for Brigadier General Taylor, who personally took the wee fellow to visit his battalions in the line. All three dogs were badly affected by the gas, which particularly wrought havoc on their feet, especially during wet or damp conditions. Jack was eventually killed doing his work, but the Welshes survived.

To briefly summarize Richardson's views of the Irish and Welsh Terriers, we may quote him from *British War Dogs*. "It must be admitted, however, that many of our best dogs were Irish terriers and Welsh terriers. These little fellows were remarkably easily taught, and were tremendously keen on their work."

Bedlingtons are especially fast terriers. One of them, Blue Boy, served at a number of battle sites, including Mount Kemmel. His keeper described him as a very reliable dog who did very good work. While at Nieppe Forest, he was released with an important message while under a barrage of machine-gun fire. He was sent to deliver a message from an outpost to the headquarters. Two human runners had been tried and were killed. He, too, was killed.

Richardson's selection of dogs for training was interesting, to say the least. By conventional standards, he went completely against the grain, using breeds for work for which they were never intended. Nonetheless, he was successful. He is recognized today as a pioneer in the working dog movement, even if contemporary trainers would strongly disagree with some of his ideas.

CHAPTER EIGHT
The Training

Richardson was no novice trainer when he began the War Dog School. He had been training dogs on his own, experimenting with techniques, uses and breeds, for nearly 20 years by the time he finally got official approval to supply trained dogs for the military. Nonetheless, he faced some initial barriers.

He had difficulty finding suitable trainers and handlers for the dogs during the early months of the War Dog School. He had hoped to train handlers who would then return to the battlefield with the dogs. Many potential trainers came from the army and, while some of them were good and well intentioned, others lacked any real interest in or potential for the work. To his disappointment and dismay, Richardson soon found that some of the men had applied for the position in order to avoid potentially dangerous service on the front lines. In *British War Dogs* he describes the ideal handler and trainer for messenger dogs, the backbone of the British War Dog program during World War I. It is an interesting set of observations and dispels some stereotypes.

> *The training of the messenger dog requires a decidedly special gift in the instructor. Without a long, intimate and practical working experience among dogs on a large scale, no one need attempt to train messenger dogs in war-time. It must be understood that training includes the instruction of the men who are to act as keepers to the dogs, as well as the dogs themselves.*
>
> *In organizing the school in the first place, I recommended that gamekeepers, shepherds and hunt servants should be especially asked for, and this may be said to be a fair working basis on which to start, but my experience goes to show that many of the men who had actually worked among dogs all their lives were not necessarily the best for this particular branch.... The men comprising the personnel require to be of an honest, conscientious character, with sympathetic understanding for animals.... This must be accompanied by a fondness for, and a gentleness, with dogs. Complete confidence and affection must exist between dogs and keeper, and the man whose only idea of control is by coercion and fear is quite useless. I have found that many men, who are supposedly dog experts, are not sufficiently sympathetic, and are apt to regard the dog too much as a machine. They do not study the psychology of their charges sufficiently....Some of the most successful keepers, that is to say, those who obtained the best results from the dogs in the field, and were also the most helpful when under instruction at the school, were those who, having a natural love of animals, had had no previous experience of a particular nature with dogs.*

One of his laments, which he relates in *Fifty Years With Dogs*, is that had the government recognized the need for military dogs earlier, considerable difficulties would have been averted by having in place carefully selected personnel. As it was, he had to sift through what he called "the good, the bad, and the middling."

The training of war dogs took a minimum of five weeks and, at that, very few left that early. The majority spent six weeks to two months in training before being shipped to France. The standards Richardson held for the dogs were high, with only one in 15 making the grade. Those that did not measure up were returned to their owners if they had been donated, or given a lethal injection if they had come from a humane society.

In addition to the training for specific tasks, the dogs had to be brought up to peak physical condition. Health, endurance and muscularity had to be enhanced. Most of the dogs came from homes in which they were kept mainly indoors, fed table scraps and were not exposed to great physical exertion. Once at the War Dog School, they were expected to live outdoors, run several kilometres and negotiate all types of obstacles and barriers without showing discomfort or fatigue. It took weeks to get the dogs in top physical condition and weather resistant. A major concern was feet, the pads of which were seldom tough enough for the work the dogs were expected to do. In fact, in one of the field reports housed at The Imperial War Museum there is a reference to an Airedale bitch that showed great potential except for two failings: she had come into season and her feet were badly damaged after even slight marching. Despite this, she was going to be kept in service. One wonders how she made it to France with her paws so suspect.

Messenger Dogs

Messenger dogs were considered so important in the War Dog Program that the school was unofficially called the Messenger Dog Service (or School). The messenger dogs were speedy, strong, equipped with great endurance and had a host of mental attributes. They underwent the most rigorous training and, compared to sentry and guard dogs, the dogs had to work on their own initiative, often kilometres from their handler, had to figure out what to do and how to do it, often under the most trying of circumstances. Richardson believed that in order to bring about the finest messengers, it was essential to appeal to the dog's sense of love and duty. Coercion would never work, he argued. Furthermore, if a dog were two or three kilometres away, and had been trained by coercive methods, how would the handler bring about compliance if he were not there to coerce the dog into performing? Thus, the dog was gently taught to associate pleasant experiences with its working hours and under no conditions were the dogs to be roughly handled or roughly spoken to.[24] Dogs that made a mistake while being trained, or were slack, were shown how to do it properly. They were never chastised. Richardson had clearly stipulated that if anybody were caught violating this fundamental rule, they were to be immediately dismissed from the school.

At the time when the messenger dogs were brought into the war, the army had often been relying on human dispatch bearers, or runners. The dogs, once put into service, did the same work as a human runner in at least one half to one third the time and often very much faster. More important, they worked just as efficiently at night as during the day. Human runners often arrived cut and bleeding from barbed wire, after being lost for hours, while a dog could do the same trip without injury or delay. And, the dogs proved a much smaller target for enemy riflemen.

The dogs were brought up gradually until they were capable of travelling 3.5 to four miles (4.8-6.4 kilometres) without difficulty. They were trained over every possible type of terrain and learned how to negotiate vehicular traffic, how to find their way through towns and villages, and how to ignore cook houses and camp sites with their myriad odors and temptations. They were taught how to navigate water and to leap ditches. To make the situations as realistic as possible, every conceivable type of obstacle and obstruction was introduced to the training. The dog was left to learn how to negotiate its way through these on its own, but it was imperative that the dog succeed. Somehow, the dog had to find its way over, through or under all of these difficulties.

Of course, the dogs had to get used to the sound of weapons. To do this, canine recruits were exposed first to rifle fire during their daily practices, generally one or two rifles at a time. As the dogs got accustomed to them, the number of rifles was increased. Afterwards, thunder-flash bombs were used at varying distances. The dogs were also taken daily to the battery range, where they were exposed to 18 pound guns and then finally to 12 inch guns. The whole process was very gradual and entered into with much gentleness and kindness. Especially timid dogs were fed tid-bits while undergoing exposure to weapons fire. This helped to more quickly accustom the dog to weapons fire and to help the dog associate the noise with positive things.

Dogs developed at different rates. It was Richardson's custom to divide the messenger dogs into classes according to their progress. These were first, second and third class. At times, one class would be left behind while the others were taken out to work. Richardson maintained that this engendered even greater feelings of competition and thus a willingness to work, especially among those of the first class, or most highly trained.

Richardson discovered that competition was a great motivator. There are remarkable archival photographs of numerous dogs undergoing training, racing with their messages across fields and ditches and leaping obstacles. One cannot help but believe that each dog was motivated to keep pace with the others as they raced to their handlers. Given Richardson's stance on training, whereby dogs grew to perform through the expectation of praise as opposed to performing out of fear of chastisement, it is to be expected that the dogs would be anxious to work.

This view is corroborated by a remarkable 13 minute silent film, taken in 1918, that shows Richardson's messenger dogs in training (Imperial War Museum Film and Video Archive IWM 235). One is struck by a number of observations during this incredible footage. The first is that the dogs all appear remarkably happy. Contemporary trainers who trial their dogs in competition can always immediately identify those dogs that are not happy in their work: they move slowly, their ears and tails are down, and they often look as if they are expecting a reprimand. In many, not necessarily all cases, those dogs have been "trained" by coercive methods.[25]

Another somewhat surprising observation is that Richardson clearly did not train his charges in the fundamentals of basic obedience. The dogs do not heel, sit in the proper position (if at all) or demonstrate any of the basics we associate with trained dogs today. This should not come as a surprise when we consider that some of the dogs were finished their training in five to six weeks. Service dogs today invariably spend the first couple of months learning basic obedience before beginning their advanced training, whether it be protection, narcotics detection, search and rescue, guide dog work or any other form of service training. It is apparent that Richardson did not subscribe to this. In the film, trainers and their pupils line up for inspection, the dogs milling about at the end of their leads, unrestrained.

In the Richardson film, the dogs are shown learning their messenger work and it is clear that the animals were given the most rigorous training available. In one dramatic scene, a score or so of dogs run down a road, leaping a succession of fences – some of them 1.5 to two metres in height, barely missing a stride. They race through a thick and extensive wall of smoke, completely obliterated by it, to emerge the other side, clearly undeterred by their sudden inability to see. In the same sequence, we see puffs of smoke as the men fire blanks at the dogs as they race past. It is clear, as Richardson expressed in his books, that competition fueled the dogs' drive to perform. Those dogs that are slower, or that were perhaps released later, appear to be racing all the harder to catch up to those in the lead. One dog, a Collie type, literally turned a somersault as he clambered over a gate, as he raced to complete his task. Other dogs – incredible athletes that they were – leaped the same barriers and landed two metres beyond on the other side. It is mesmerizing footage. Watching this, one gets the impression that Richardson could easily be the father of modern agility dog training.

Another interesting point is the sheer diversity of breeds and crossbreeds that Richardson used. The Airedales are there, of course, but Collie, Border Collies, Bearded Collies and Old English Sheepdogs (as well as crosses of all of the above) are there in abundance. Richardson gave lie to the belief that only certain breeds are suitable for such serious work.

Individual dogs are shown being released and delivering their messages, racing down roads, leaping or swimming rivers and streams, and scaling or leaping fences. Upon reaching their destinations, the dogs wriggle in excitement at completing their tasks and receiving their reward – pets and praise and, sometimes, liver pieces. (Sometimes, jealousy raised its ugly head. In the Richardson film, an arriving Collie is being rewarded and an Airedale, resentful, perhaps, of the attention the Collie is receiving, tries to sneak in a bite). Other scenes show dogs receiving veterinary care (a Welsh Terrier is treated for sore paws), the residents in the dog town chained to their kennels, and being taught to swim (an Airedale is shown entering a river and delivering his message). It is a remarkable early film and we should be grateful that it has survived and that it has been made available through the IWM.

Training followed a regular pattern. Dogs that had been there a while were taken out each morning for the firing drill. They were led to a large shed where they were exposed to trainers firing rifles loaded with blanks. Great care was taken with any dog that showed timidity. Those that were completely unnerved were removed and very slowly re-introduced to gunfire under less stressful circumstances. This was followed by a system of bomb-firing, which demanded even more of the dogs. This particular acclimatization often had to be undergone for some time, to ensure that the dogs were ready for real war.

The dogs were then trained to run among the keepers, who were lying down across the road over which the dogs were forced to travel. The dogs, in other words, were trained to run into the face of gunfire without flinching. Those that had mastered this test were then taken to the larger weaponry, including the 18 pound and 12 inch guns. Obstacle training followed, in which the dogs were expected to navigate through smoke (caused by harmless smoke bombs or bales of hay that were set alight) and through water. In the latter case, the dog had to leap, swim or wade through a stream.

Through all of this, the dog had to work voluntarily. Richardson's strict guidelines forbade any coercion or compulsion. If a dog failed, it was given an easier task of the same type, e.g., leaping a metre stream instead of a two metre stream, until it had mastered what was required and was doing it joyfully and competently. The dogs had to *want* to do the work. Finally, through gentleness and patience, the dog was brought not only to the point where it had balked or failed, but was beyond that point.

The dogs were then trained in running, taking on shorter or longer distances based on their capabilities. Each dog was usually run twice per day, except for those in the highest class which, because they ran four miles in each direction, ran eight miles a day in training. The dogs were led out by a handler and slipped back, gradually increasing the distance as the dog became more competent, confident and experienced. The soldier/handlers enclosed a piece of paper (indicating the time) in the leather pouch attached to each dog's collar, and then released the dogs. The dogs then raced back to the camp as fast as they could. The officer in charge of training watched closely from an elevated platform. From there he surveyed the landscape, studying the dogs individually, noting their progress, their levels of distraction, confidence and ease with which they navigated the terrain.

Richardson himself would be waiting with the other officers, noting the time at which each dog arrived and praising, petting and slipping a liver tid-bit to each dog as it arrived.[26] Thus, the development of each dog was carefully observed and noted. He claimed that the combination of two "instincts" – to return to their master and the prospect of reward – were gratified as the dogs completed their run. By the end of a month or so, most dogs were completing two to three mile (3.2 to 4.8 kilometre) runs accurately and well, while a little later they were travelling four miles (6.4 kilometres).

Richardson relates a telling story in *Fifty Years With Dogs*. The school started in early summer and, he says, it was difficult to train under completely dark nights. After being in operation for only two or three months, he received notice that the camp was to be inspected and that part of the inspection was a series of tests in which the dogs worked at night. The notice he received did not allow him to train under cover of total darkness. He had no time to conduct any trials himself and, he admits, he felt that the two to three months of training that had been taken since the school opened did not justify, in his view, so harsh a test.

When the day came, the dogs performed satisfactorily during the daylight hours. As the men took their leave for dinner and waited to conduct the night-time trials, a heavy mist set in. They set out at 10 pm. The dogs were to be released from distances of a half mile (.8 kilometres) to two miles (3.2 kilometres), at various points surrounding the camp. As per usual, the dogs would be slipped, carrying a note indicating the time and location of release. Richardson admits that with the combination of complete darkness and heavy mist, he expected, at best, only a couple of dogs would perform well, albeit with perhaps some difficulty. He was relieved to see, in quick succession, the 35 or so dogs come running in. He was standing at the camp's entrance with the other officers when they arrived, virtually all of them within 10 to 15 minutes, an appreciable time given that they had to navigate streams and negotiate fences and other barriers in darkness and mist. After that, Richardson states, he began training seriously under heavy fog conditions and in complete darkness and found that the times were generally much faster and the messages more reliably carried than in daylight or on clear nights.

An interesting observation needs to be made about the role of messenger dogs. In July, 1918, Richardson paid a visit to France to visit the troops and to see how his dogs were doing. He also visited the French army where he spoke with a General Gouraud. The officer informed Richardson that "If only two out of six dogs come back, with their messages, I am satisfied."[27] This says much about the French and their experience with military dogs and their expectations of them, and of the British who, in the early days, had no experience and either dismissed the idea completely or held out too lofty expectations. On the one hand, the statement implies that the expectations, given the nature of their task and the conditions under which it must be performed, were demanding. On the other hand, it suggests that the French were willing to pay a horrific price with their dogs.

Sentry Dogs

There is a clear distinction between guard dogs and sentry dogs. According to Richardson, the latter require more intelligence, and better auditory and olfactory development. While the guard dog is expected to defend a specified area, the sentry is expected to take up duty with any soldier at any spot. Their training was thus much more difficult and sophisticated.

Richardson had supplied a number of sentry dogs in an unofficial capacity before finally winning approval for a War Dog School. He had sent dogs to the Western Front and to the expeditionary forces in Egypt and Mesopotamia. One of these, an Airedale supplied to the Berkshire Regiment, facilitated the capture of an enemy patrol. The dog alerted its handler by a low growl. The party heard and saw nothing, but the officer, believing the dog, ordered his men to take cover. They did so, and shortly after an enemy patrol passed closely by them. They rose and captured all of the enemy, thanks to the dog. Eighteen Airedales were with the South-West Africa Force, where they also did good work. In one case, a dog warned of a large ambush, which not only saved the lives of the troops but also resulted in the capture of a large number of the enemy.

Richardson believed that there was a future for sentry dogs, especially under conditions of open warfare. At the same time, he realized that there was not much interest taken in them for use on the Western Front as time passed and the position of the enemy became more entrenched. He also had to fight biases on the part of some officers against the general principle of sentry dogs. The arguments fell into two broad categories: 1) the belief that a sentry, having a dog to rely on, would be tempted to be careless in his work and 2) that the dog's barking would reveal the position and draw the enemy's fire. These, of course, were proven to be unwarranted and the success of sentry dogs then and since is beyond challenge.

As was the case with the guard dogs, training began late in the day. The handlers took the dogs out at dusk, to pre-determined posts, each dog to a different location. Men, representing the enemy, were instructed to approach the post from various directions and under different types of cover. The dogs were expected to alert the handler, obviously the earlier the better. Detection and alerting the handler brought praise and it was expected that the dog would learn to be on the alert for trespassers and respond more quickly when they were detected. Meticulous records were maintained for each dog, noting the time and distance at which the dog first took notice and, perhaps more important, how much ahead he was of the human sentry in detecting the enemy.

Such training was slow. The dogs were not tested by the "enemy" more than two or three times a night, for to do so made the exercise redundant and the dogs grew to expect someone, thereby lessening its alertness. It is comparable to an owner who takes his dog to work every day. The dog watches – without blinking – scores of people pass by. After some time, the sentry dog-in-training not only learns that it is expected to alert at the approach of strangers, but that it is supposed to *be* on the alert for the approach of strangers. Furthermore, the dog learns that it can sense the approach of the enemy before the handler – it, in fact, assumes the role of sentry. Richardson maintained that the dogs' senses "developed in a remarkable way." Whether this is literally true is debatable; rather, the dog simply learned to be more alert and suspicious. Regardless, the training was effective, as the records show that the dogs proved their worth in combat.

Guard Dogs

When the War Office came around to realize that guard dogs could provide a useful service, Richardson added a number of other breeds to the existing list of Airedales, Collies, Lurchers and others that were employed as messenger dogs. Specifically, he sought Great Danes, Mastiffs, Bullmastiffs, Bulldogs, Bull Terriers, Retrievers and crossbreeds of these breeds. Dogs that were brought in were initially tested for work as messengers. Those that did not meet the standard were then tested for guard work and, if successful, were then taken to a separate part of the school where they underwent training. At one training location, an entire valley had been set aside for this type of work.

Guard dog duty was the last option for the dogs that found their way to Richardson's War Dog School. If they failed to make the grade as messengers, they were tested as sentry dogs. Those that failed at both messenger and sentry dog work were then tested as guards. A dog that failed at all three was either returned to its owner (if donated) or euthanized.

The dogs were trained at night, as this was when it was expected that they would be most often employed. Therefore, both dogs and trainers – men who had been especially selected for training of guard dogs – rested during the day. The dogs were staked out on running chains attached to long wires, 45 to 90 metres long. Each dog also had a kennel to which it could retreat in inclement weather. The trainer's job was to develop heightened awareness in the dogs, and to help develop acumen in them. The trainers observed and maintained records of the dogs' senses of sight, hearing, smell and general alertness.

When a dog had demonstrated its ability to work efficiently and was to be placed, an N.C.O. was required to visit the War Dog School and to spend two or three days familiarizing himself with the proper care and handling of the dog. Among other things, he had to learn about proper placement of the dog in terms of what the animal was to be guarding. Richardson cites one case in which dogs were requested to guard a building. He discovered that the building in question housed machinery that was in constant operation. The dogs were rendered virtually useless, because the noise from the machinery completely drowned out all other sounds, including potential trespassers. He was also surprised to discover that the expectation was that the dogs could work 24 hours a day, without rest. It was found necessary to instruct the handlers that the dogs, like people, needed rest and that this should occur during the day well away from any noise and disruption (and when human sentries can best work alone). Upon beginning their work, the dogs were to be given a brisk walk and then fed when their shifts were over at dawn. To ensure the best possible results from the dogs, Richardson issued detailed guidelines for their proper care and maintenance.

That the guard dogs were effective is beyond dispute. Richardson requested feedback from every facility in which they were placed and the evidence is impressive. The deterrent effect alone made the dogs worthwhile. For example, stores in Buford had been broken into nightly until Richardson's guard dogs were put in place. Two months after their arrival, all breaking and entering had ceased.

Not only did they prevent illegal entry, the dogs released, on average, three to five men from sentry duty. In some cases, it was even more. One dog in West Beckham, for instance, enabled the authorities to reduce the guard from 15 men to seven men. In Hayle, human guards were reduced from 14 to eight where a dog was posted. As noted above, the call for the animals came in when the man-power shortage for the war was very serious. Given that Richardson turned out 2000 such dogs, the number of men freed for other duties is impressive. Richardson notes, gratefully, that when the dogs were de-mobilized from active duty and returned to the War Dog School, they came back in "first class condition," a testimonial to how much they were appreciated by the officers and men.

Richardson claims that at the end of the first month he shipped out 30 dogs[28] to France, mostly Airedales, Collies, Retrievers and Lurchers. It was, perhaps, a bit premature, for a few of the dogs, once arrived, proved fearful around gunfire. Richardson himself admits that he should've taken longer in this regard to prepare for the real-life conditions of the battlefield. After a while, though, they became inured to the sounds and performed well. Meanwhile, fuelled by the generally enthusiastic reports from the battlefield, he carried on, training more dogs.

CHAPTER NINE
The Heroes

There are several of Richardson's war dogs – messengers, Red Cross, sentry and patrol dogs – that achieved considerable fame and acknowledgement for their efforts. More often not, it was the messenger dogs that garnered the most attention because of the nature of their work. The sentries, guards and patrol dogs essentially had preventative tasks: keeping the enemy away or warning their handlers if danger threatened. Consequently, most of the fame fell to the messengers. Their stories are truly heroic. Not surprisingly, many dogs lost their lives doing their duty. The following are just a sampling of the many dogs that did their part during World War I.

The Mystery of Jack

Undoubtedly the most oft-cited story told about Colonel Richardson's war dogs is that of Jack, the Airedale messenger dog that saved an entire battalion. Over the years, there has been some rewriting of history, but the story, in its essence, has continued. The problem with this story, however, is that it has taken on a life of its own and is repeated in Airedale monographs and general dog books without, it would seem, anybody ever bothering to check the origins of this canine legend. And that is where the difficulty begins. How much of it is verifiable? Before looking at the questions surrounding this near-mythical hero, it is worth retelling the story, in its various incarnations. What follows is the story of Jack, as it has been told over the years, with all of the "facts" given as gospel.

Like so many of the Richardson war dogs, Jack had been acquired from the Battersea Dogs Home in London, a shelter for stray dogs. After his training, he was sent to serve in France where he worked as a messenger with the Sherwood Foresters under the handling of a Lieutenant Hunter.

In 1918, the Sherwood Foresters were at an advanced post at the front, waging intense battle with the enemy. The Germans had succeeded in cutting off every line of communication with headquarters, four miles behind the lines. It seemed inevitable that the entire battalion would be killed if help were not received quickly.

It was apparent that the only hope rested with Jack. His handler, Lieutenant Hunter, affixed a message to his collar and sent him on his way. During their training, the messenger dogs were taught to take advantage of every piece of shelter available to them, from shrubbery to crater holes caused by artillery. In this case, cover was sadly lacking and the troops watched as his jaw was shattered with shrapnel. Undaunted, he carried on. He was then torn from shoulder to thigh. Staggering onward, he was hit a third time, shattering a front paw. Virtually crawling, he reached the headquarters and then fell over dead, having done his duty and saved the battalion.

There are slightly different versions of this allegedly true story. In one telling, Jack was hit twice, in the jaw and one of his forelegs. In that version, as well, he had to travel "a half mile under intense enemy fire," not four miles. Regardless, the dog performed a hero's work. The biggest misperception, however, is that Jack was awarded a posthumous Victoria Cross for "gallantry in the field." This is simply untrue, for the V.C. has never been given to an animal. As well, it is claimed that at the Imperial War Museum, there is a small wooden monument to "Airedale Jack, a hero of the Great War."

One can only begin to wonder where to begin with this legend. An examination of Appendix A in this work indicates that there is only one Airedale (actually, a crossbred Airedale) named "Jack" (dog # 54) to serve with the Sherwood Foresters. As noted in Appendix B, this unfortunate dog could hardly have been the same dog as in the story, for he was destroyed because he was of "no use." And what about Lieutenant Hunter, his alleged handler? Our Jack, above, was handled by Private Allcock. In fact, almost all of the handlers/keepers were privates or corporals, with no officers working the dogs.

It is possible that Jack was, in fact, one of the dogs for which we have no information. As noted in the appendices, there are gaps in the written record and, it is conceded, he very well might have been one of those dogs for which no record exists. However, even more telling is that Richardson does not relate this story in any of his books. One would think that a dog of such heroic measure would surely be recorded by the founder of the school, but no such recounting is to be found in any of Richardson's five books.

The inconsistencies in the distance Jack travelled, and in the extent of his injuries, suggest a certain amount of fabrication of the story. Of even greater concern is the oft-told (but false) claim that Jack won the Victoria Cross. This seems to be yet another embellishment to a fabricated story. Some apologists have claimed that Jack did not receive the Victoria Cross but that he did, in fact, receive the Dickin Medal, often referred to as "the animals' Victoria Cross." Unfortunately, the Dickin Medal was introduced in 1943 to recognize animals that served heroically with the armed forces and civil defense units during World War II. The elusive Jack, it will be noticed, is alleged to have served during World War I. Finally, when at The Imperial War Museum, the author inquired several times about the messenger dog service and the alleged tribute to Jack, but was unable to find anybody who was aware of the "small wooden monument."

None of this is to suggest that the story of Jack is untrue. Rather, it is to make clear that the story has been repeated without benefit of substantiation and the lack of evidence demands further corroboration before we can accept it as historical truth. Perhaps the story was meant to embody all that was noble about the messenger dogs and, in particular, the Airedales. As it stands at present, it is little more than romantic fiction rooted in historical truth.

There are, however, truly verifiable heroes. It is to a handful of these that we now turn.

Wolf and Prince

Two of Richardson's Airedales, Wolf and Prince, are of special interest to Canadians because of the crucial part they played in the battle of Vimy Ridge. Of equal or greater interest to military historians and Airedale fanciers is that these two were the first messenger dogs trained and sent out by Richardson. Their efforts helped to convince the recalcitrant authorities of the value of dogs in the military.

Wolf and Prince were trained at Harrow by Richardson and his wife and, as Richardson acknowledged in *Forty Years With Dogs*, the perceived need for messengers was urgent, so they worked day and night and in all kinds of environments with the dogs. The residents of Harrow grew accustomed to seeing the two speeding animals as they raced through village, town and field on their way to the designated base of operation which, in the early days, was the Richardsons' garden. Their trainer would acknowledge years later that these two were not easy to train, not because the dogs were dull, but because the trainers (Richardson and his wife) could not anticipate the conditions under which the dogs would work. Nonetheless, they were apt pupils, although Wolf did return one day with a leg of mutton that he had appropriated from a butcher shop en route. Before long, they resisted all temptations, travelling up to two miles without distraction and at top speed. They were ready to be shipped across the Channel.

They left for France at the end of 1916 and went directly to Thiepval, under escort of a gunner. There, they were "very intelligently managed," according to Richardson in *Watchdogs*. Even without the benefits of having been trained initially under war-like conditions, they settled down quickly and began working regularly. The officer in charge of the dogs, Colonel Winter, assisted Richardson with suggestions for training other dogs, which he took into consideration in subsequent work. Both dogs proved their worth before the pivotal battle of Vimy Ridge, carrying messages, under fire and over completely new territory, with speed and energy. But in 1917 they found their way forever into the history books.

The Battle of Vimy Ridge is a pivotal piece of Canadian history, in part because the country was only 50 years old but also because Canadians proved their mettle in battle under the most trying and brutal of circumstances. Vimy Ridge was a key German position that linked the Hindenburg Line with their main trench lines. British and French troops had earlier failed to take the ridge. The task fell to the Canadians under Lt. General Byng. On April 9, 1917, Canadian troops, armed with nearly 1000 artillery pieces, attacked along a six and a half kilometre front. Despite the fact that it was the first time that the Canadians had attacked together, the effort was a success, and they drove the Germans back off the ridge. Five days later, April 14, Canadian troops had gained more ground and had taken more prisoners than had any other British offensive. They paid a high price, however. There were nearly 11 000 Canadian casualties, including approximately 4000 deaths. The battle had helped to cement Canada's role in the war, albeit at a terribly high price.

And Wolf and Prince? They were the first to bring the news of the attack on Vimy Ridge. The actual military report stated that: "On the attack on Vimy Ridge the dogs were employed with an artillery post. All the telephones were broken and visual signaling was impossible. The dogs were the first to bring through news."

It was following this heroic effort that Richardson was finally invited, largely through the efforts of Colonel Winter, to formally develop a military dog program for the British.

Boxer and Flash

Boxer and Flash were two messenger dogs that worked with the 34th Division. Boxer is described as a "large, powerful Airedale," while Flash, appropriately perhaps, was a "fast, clever" brindle Lurcher bitch. Their handler, simply referred to as "Keeper W. Dixon," described his initial impressions of the two dogs soon after their arrival in France.

The two dogs I took out are doing well, I should say exceptionally well. I have not the least hesitation is saying there is not a brace of better dogs in this or any other country as Messenger Dogs. 'Boxer' the Airedale is running like an engine. The Lurcher bitch 'Flash' beats him on this week's running by 20 mins., which is not a lot considering the breeds. The General of the _____ Division said that the Airedale was the best dog he had seen.

Despite the high praise from his handler and the general, Boxer was not above temptation when it presented itself. In one instance, when he was "a bit long" on one delivery, it was discovered that he had come across a carcass of some description. Upon his arrival back in the trenches, he "tried to steal past into his bed" but was discovered. He was forgiven as his handler described the conditions as "very bad for running dogs, such a lot of rubbish and dead carcasses and abandoned cook houses, etc."

Both Flash and Boxer played a crucial role in the battle of Kemmel Hill, working under incredibly difficult conditions. Later, Dixon filed another report about Boxer.

A staunch, reliable dog, ran steadily and never let me down. Best time 3 miles in 10 minutes. On one occasion he went over the top with the Kents. Released at 5 am with important message. He jumped at me at 5:25. A tip-top performance, about 4 miles. A great dog!

Regarding Flash, he observed that "She ran every alternate week, except two, and was never once behind time."

Summarizing the dogs' work, Dixon wrote that while the times seem slow, they were really good, given the conditions. In addition to the gunfire, "they were running belly deep in mud." It would have taken a man two hours to go to the line.

Tweed

Tweed was one of the most highly respected messenger dogs trained by Richardson. An Old English Sheepdog,[29] he was a most unimpressive candidate for military work, not because of his breed (Old English Sheepdogs might look like loveable teddy bears, but people who know the breed – especially as it was a century ago – know that this is a tough, durable, working dog) but because when he was first brought in for training, he appeared completely dimwitted and untrainable. He was within days of being rejected for service. Not surprisingly, perhaps, it was Mrs. Richardson who recognized his potential and brought the shy, retiring – not stupid or slow – Tweed to maturation. As was the case with her husband, Mrs. Richardson was ahead of her time as a trainer. In an era, when harsh methods and corporal punishment were the norm in dog training, they both used persuasion and kindness to bring about results. Patiently and gently, she got him to overcome his incredible shyness and reticence and brought out his true potential. Then, he was passed over to his handler Private Reid (spelled "Read" in the Imperial War Museum's archives) who capitalized on his innate abilities even further until he became one of the best messenger dogs the Allies had.

In *Forty Years With Dogs*, Richardson speaks warmly of this most unlikely of heroes.

Tweed was a dog not easily forgotten. He was a fine, large, rough-coated English sheepdog, and a more honest looking fellow would be hard to find. His demeanour in war always seemed to me typically British, carrying as it did a quiet dignity and with no desire to quarrel, but at the same time when he did get going there was no doubt as to the certainty of his methods.

Tweed's initial shyness belied his immense courage under fire. He served for six months under some of the very worst conditions of the war, notably at Passchendaele, and never once faltered or made a mistake. As is the case of the battle at Vimy Ridge, Passchendaele looms large in the Canadian consciousness. Canadian troops performed an almost unbelievable task, but paid a tremendous price in doing so. Those who fought there could only compare it to hell. The small Belgian village of Passchendaele, near Ypres, was the site of the battle. Months of rain and millions of exploded shells, combined with the smell from the bodies of dead horses and men, made it the most impossible battlefield of the war. British Commander in Chief General Sir Douglas Haig had ordered the attack from the British front. British, Australian and New Zealand troops had battled for weeks, building up large numbers of casualties in the process. The British turned to their other Commonwealth partners, the Canadians. On October 26, 1917, Lt. General Sir Arthur Currie's Canadian Corps launched their attack. By November 7, they had achieved what the others had failed to accomplish. They had taken the village of Ypres and five square kilometres of mud. The cost was tremendous: 7000 Canadians killed and another 8000 wounded. From this one battle, only two weeks in duration, nine Victoria Crosses were awarded for gallantry.

One battalion, the 85th Canadian Infantry Battalion of Nova Scotia, sent 600 men into battle. They were really boys for the most part, many of them barely 18 years old. They were relatively new to battle, having experienced their first taste of war at Vimy Ridge. Of the 600 who went into the hell that was Passchendaele, 148 never came out and 280 were wounded. Eighty-five of the dead have no known grave. For their contribution to the battle at Passchendaele, the battalion earned the nickname the "Neverfails." It came with a high praise. A monument was erected to the 85th immediately after the war, but it eventually gave way under the elements.

Eighty-five years later, another monument was erected, a joint Canadian and Belgian effort, comprising government bodies and individual citizens, including descendants of the men who died there and the descendants of the owner of the original farm at Passchendaele where the battle was fought. A fitting tribute indeed.

General Haig would forever be criticized for his handling of the battle at Passchendaele, especially for prolonging it at such a high cost. For the Canadians who fought there, and their descendants, it is a painful memory. As is the case with Vimy Ridge, a great reputation was made, but at what price.

It was under these conditions that Tweed worked, along with his human companions and allies. Never once did he falter or make a mistake while running messages through the mud, the dead bodies and the constant bombardment. While he might have initially been shy, he ultimately proved to have nerves of steel. While most of his work at Passchendaele was of vital importance, sometimes it was of less serious nature (if any war work can be "less serious") than at other times. One night his battalion, the 13th R.H.C., had to go in and support the 3rd Canadian Division. The trenches were extremely wet and uncomfortable. The commanding officer wanted dry socks for his men, but there was no way to get a message back in daylight. Keeper Reid was asked to send his dog. Tweed did his part by carrying the message "Moving forward tonight. Send socks for men and some S.O.S. lights." It did not compare with some of his other feats, but it added immeasurably to the comfort of the troops.

In 1918, he was with a Scottish Canadian regiment at Amiens. The Allies were in a precarious situation as the enemy had broken through and cut off the British front line and were close to capturing the town. We can do no better than quote the handler's own report of what happened:

On May 2nd, 1918, I was sent to the 18th Div. There were no dogs that had been up before. On May 2nd at 10 pm the [enemy] came over on the Q.V.R. – my dog was up at their Batt. Hdqtrs. They were cut off from the London Regt.; they released Tweed with the message 'Send reinforcements and small round ammunition'. He came through a ...barrage – three kilos. in 10 minutes. The French were sent up and filled the gaps, and straightened out the line, otherwise Amiens would be in the hands of the Germans.

Not a week later, Tweed again proved his worth, as recorded by handler:

On May 8th I was with the Australians 48th Batt. They had moved forward, no runner could cross the open in the daytime – pigeons could not fly at night, they were in a bad place so they sent for Tweed. He made three runs at night, and one of the runs, he was out on patrol; they sent him back with a message 'The Germans are preparing for a raid' and spoiled the [enemy's] plans.

Tweed, who in the beginning seemed completely unsuitable for the arduous work of the messenger dog, proved his usefulness time and time again. He was a credit to the keen trainer's eye of Mrs. Richardson, as well as his handlers and himself.

Dick

In *British War Dogs* (1920), Dick's handler, Corporal Coull, states that Dick's efforts were worthy of the Victoria Cross. Dick was a black retriever (probably a Flat-coated, but the specific breed was left unmentioned). While carrying a message in the Villers-Bretonneux sector he was severely wounded in the back and shoulder. He completed his run in apparently good spirits and was sent to the kennel facilities and treated by the veterinarian. There appeared to be no foreign bodies in the wounds, so he was stitched up, left to heal and then sent back to work. He continued to perform his runs at his usual high level. He and his handler were sent to another detachment and, a few days later, it was apparent that all was not well with the dog. After a few days, the veterinarian concluded that there was some foreign body in one of his wounds and, as he was at the point of death, he was euthanized. A post-mortem revealed that a rifle bullet was resting between the shoulder and the body, while near the small of the back a piece of shrapnel was lodged close to the spine. In spite of this, he had carried out his duties cheerfully and faithfully, without complaint, until death overtook him.

CHAPTER TEN
Epilogue: World War II

World War I was, unfortunately, not the war to end all wars. Barely two decades later, the Second World War began. Colonel Richardson would live to see it. He would also witness – again – a lackadaisical government that was slow to recognize the need for a military dog program.

Germany

Between 1918 and 1939, Germany and Russia had continued to capitalize on what they had learned during the First World War. It is believed that as early as 1930, Germany had begun re-establishing its military dog program. Indeed, some historians suggest that even after the signing of the Treaty of Versailles, Germany had never stopped training war dogs. Two schools were established, one at Grunheide, near Berlin, and the other near Frankfurt. These were colossal in scale, each accommodating 2000 dogs at a time. For the most part, this was conducted more or less clandestinely, so as not to alert the Western powers as to any potential violation of the Treaty of Versailles. The dogs were presented as being in training for civil and police duty, not military. The result was that when war began in 1939, Germany had tens of thousands of dogs[30] ready for combat duty as messengers, scouts and sentries. As Britain had done during the First World War, occasional recruiting of canine soldiers was conducted through the media. The lessons learned between 1914 and 1918 had not been lost on the Germans. Dogs were omnipresent among the German troops, on every front and in every horrific concentration camp, where they instilled fear and terror among the prisoners.

German Shepherd Dogs, Doberman Pinschers, Airedales and Boxers were all in demand as war dogs. By this time, the German Shepherd Dog had become the breed of choice for the German military. Ostensibly, it was because it was the most loyal, most temperamentally consistent and the easiest to train. One believes that it might also have something to do with the fact that the German Shepherd Dog was Hitler's personal favorite breed and that the breed is indigenous to "the Fatherland." (Hitler is alleged to have given his German Shepherd bitch, Blondi, poison to kill her before committing suicide himself in his bunker). Regardless of whether or not it was the preferred breed, at least one major study suggests that the German Shepherd Dog was not the most consistently suitable breed for war work. In *The Complete Doberman Pinscher*, Gerda Umlauff reports on a study conducted by a Captain Dressler during the Second World War to determine suitability for military service. Of 16 000 dogs examined and tested (not an insignificant number), this is how the breeds fared: Airedales 33% suitable, Doberman Pinschers 32%, Boxers 32%, Giant Schnauzers 29%, Rottweilers 28%, German Shepherd Dogs 22%, all other purebreeds 18%, crossbreeds 10.5%. It would seem, perhaps, that German loyalty to the

German Shepherd Dogs might have been misplaced. It might have been somewhat disillusioning to the German military to note that the English Airedale outperformed all other purebreds (all of them German breeds) in military testing.

Of even more concern, although the German Shepherd Dog was the breed of choice for the German military, it did not perform as well on a consistent basis as did the other German breeds. One cannot help but think that there was, indeed, a misplaced loyalty to the Fuhrer's favorite.

The Soviet Union

Similarly, the Soviet Union had been busy training dogs. Fifty thousand military dogs were trained just prior to and during World War II.[31] Under the leadership of Colonel Medvedev, Director of the Central Military School of Working Dogs, otherwise known as the Red Star Kennels, the Soviets had been particularly busy, finding new ways to put them to use. Some of these were especially troubling. Whereas dogs in the modern era had been used primarily as defensive tools, e.g., as sentries, messengers and ambulance dogs, the Soviet Union had early on taken the position that dogs could be offensive weapons in war. So-called anti-tank dogs were developed as an extreme example of this stance. Perceived as being largely expendable and replaceable, the Soviets began training dogs in 1941 to carry explosives and to run under German tanks. The training was innovative, to say the least, and cringe-inducing in its cruelty. Accustomed to carrying explosives on their backs, the dogs were kept hungry and fed only under moving tanks. Thus, the unfortunate dogs learned to anticipate the weight on their backs, the rumbling of the tanks and a meal. Each dog is alleged to have carried 30 pounds (13 kg) of explosives on its back, to be detonated by wooden levers on their backpacks that hit against the underbelly of the tank as the dog ran under it, seeking food.

Hamer, in *Dogs at War* (2001), explains how the barbaric scheme backfired in "an almost slapstick twist." The idea was that once the dogs got beneath an enemy tank, the explosives would be detonated. The training proved to be too good. Because the dogs had been trained with Soviet tanks, they would not run towards German tanks as per the original plan. Rather, they worked consistently, running towards the Soviet tanks with which they had been trained. Hamer relates that this fundamental error (or, perhaps, it wasn't an error and the dogs had learned their lessons very well, indeed) was discovered on the Front. An entire tank division had had to withdraw until their very own anti-tank dogs had been shot. Despite this tragic-comic episode, the Soviets claimed that several German tanks had, in fact, been destroyed using anti-tank guns at the Battle of Kursk in 1943 and captured German documents corroborate the claim that on several occasions this most unusual and unsettling use of military dogs proved successful. Thurston, in *Lost History of the Canine Race* (1996:188), claims that the Russia still had an anti-tank dog program as late as 1993.

In addition to anti-tank dogs, the Soviets were among the first to train mine-detection dogs. It is claimed that during 1943, these dogs detected 529 000 mines and over the course of the war found over a million of them. One dog alone, a mongrel named Zucha, is reputed to have uncovered over 2000 in a week, a figure that is hard to imagine.

The Americans, British and Soviets all trained and used parachute dogs during World War II (the Americans much less frequently and not formally), but in all likelihood, the Soviets were the first to come up with the concept. Indeed, Vesey-Fitzgerald, in *The Domestic Dog*, says that they "were certainly the first to drop dogs with parachute battalions."

The Soviets trained dogs for the most inconceivable of purposes, including "spy" work. The idea was that dogs would infiltrate enemy camps and steal important documents such as maps or other items that might prove beneficial to a war effort. When reading of this "spy" training, one cannot help but think that Colonel G. Medvedev had been perhaps too much influenced by the heroics of fictional canine movie stars.

The Soviets also made solid use of sled dogs, both for offensive and defensive purposes. In five weeks in one sector of the Front, a team of dogs is credited with carrying 1239 soldiers from the battlefield in addition to hauling 327 tons of ammunition. Snow-white Samoyeds were a preferred sled dog breed, in part because they blended in so well with their environment (they are also indigenous to northeastern Siberia). They proved particularly valuable for hauling soldiers, outfitted in white, into close proximity of the enemy where they could attack and get away quickly. The Soviets are said to have also used dog drawn sleds for making night raids, when they were least expected. Similarly, two-dog teams would haul soldiers on skis, in the same fashion as modern skijoring.

Japan

Prior to the outbreak of World War II, Germany had sent a large number of war dogs to Japan. Some high estimates place the number at 25 000, while Going, in *Dogs at War* (1944), is more conservative, suggesting that the number was between 10 000 and 25 000. These apparently were mainly German Shepherds and Doberman Pinschers, although other medium and large breeds were also acquired from Germany.

The Japanese themselves organized several training facilities for war dogs in Japan. They trained the animals for the usual purposes: guard, patrol, messenger and scout duty, but also, as the Soviets and Americans did, for suicide missions. The dogs were trained to haul small carts loaded with 50-pound (22 kg) bombs that – in theory – they would rush with towards the enemy, whereupon the bomb would be detonated. The Japanese employed dogs in the Malay Peninsula campaign. Dogs were also with the troops when they went into Hong Kong.

The United States

After the attack on Pearl Harbor, the United States actively began its war dog program. The War Department designated Dogs for Defense as its official procurement agency. It wasn't until March 13, 1942, that the army formally requested trained dogs. The initial request was for 200 trained sentry dogs. Although slow to begin, once in action the number of dogs increased rapidly. Civilians donated dogs, eventually at the rate of 1500 a month. In its first two years of operation, Dogs for Defense supplied approximately 20 000 dogs for the army. Most US military dogs were trained as scouts, messenger dogs or sentries.

In the beginning, almost any dog capable of moving was considered suitable by Dogs for Defense. The list then narrowed to 32 acceptable breeds. By the end of 1944, there was a short list of five "preferred breeds": German Shepherd Dogs, Doberman Pinschers, "farm-type" Collies, Giant Schnauzers and Belgian Sheepdogs. Crossbreeds of these breeds were also deemed acceptable. For sled work, "Eskimos", i.e., the Canadian Inuit Dog, the Alaskan Malamute and Siberian Husky were preferred, while for packing, St. Bernards and Newfoundlands were the breeds of choice. It is estimated that the United States never had more than 10 000 dogs in service at any one time during World War II, but those that were saw action in North Africa, Italy, France, Sicily and the Pacific Theatre, as well as guard duty at home.

Lest we think that the Soviets were alone in their dubious and questionable use of war dogs, the Americans, once they entered the war, had their own versions of the anti-tank dog and suicide dog. In 1943, they initiated training whereby dogs with timed explosives attached to their backs would be sent to attack fortified bunkers. This operation was named "Demolition Wolf." As Hamer points out in *Dogs at War* (2001), it was doomed to failure. Oftentimes, the dogs returned to their handlers, a somewhat unnerving possibility in real combat. In addition, it was realized that under actual combat conditions, the dogs might not be convinced to actually run towards bunkers that housed the enemy, rather than Allied troops. The training was kept secret from the public and abandoned soon after it was begun. Supposedly, no explosives were ever used in training and no dogs were injured or killed during the brief duration of the training. Incredibly, according to Thurston (1996), during the 1950s, the United States seriously considered a proposal to reinstate the training, but this time by strapping small tactical nuclear weapons to the dogs.

The US had also experimented with anti-tank dogs, although it did not last. Thurston, in *Lost History of the Canine Race* (1996), points out an inherent problem with the idea: public relations. If the public had ever gotten wind of the program, it would have seriously undermined Dogs for Defense fund-raising and recruiting drives. But, as she observes, in the end, it wasn't shelved because the idea of seeing a dog blown up would have traumatized soldiers; rather, the dogs – like those of the Soviet Union – couldn't distinguish between friendly and enemy tanks.

Perhaps the most frightening consideration of military dogs during the Second World War II was a US initiative to implement a "killer dog" program in the Pacific theatre. The idea was simple and reminiscent of the Spanish and their war dogs four centuries before: packs of large, savage, attack-trained dogs would be released to kill the Japanese. It was all unbeknownst to the public, of course, and the "training," such as it was, was done in secret. The most barbaric and loathsome of "training" methods were employed, including electric shocks, beatings with bullwhips, being dragged behind galloping horses, starvation and being forced to fight for their own food. In 1943, a demonstration was presented to a group of officers. Japanese-American soldiers, outfitted from head to toe in padded protection, were wrestled to the ground and savaged by dogs. The effort was deemed a dismal failure and disbanded because, according to one military officer who witnessed the spectacle, "The performance of the animals appeared artificial and forced" (Thurston, 1996). Four hundred and fifty years after the Spanish turned their dogs on Native Americans, the world hadn't changed.

Colonel Richardson's Airedales?

There is a palpable sadness in the eighth chapter of Richardson's *Fifty Years With Dogs*. The title is "Dogs in the Second World War" and it is brief – a mere four pages. The author puts on a brave face and briefly recounts his experiences, primarily with the Toronto Scottish Regiment. He also acknowledges that it was necessary for a much younger and energetic person to take over the role that he had so competently assumed during the First World War. It helps to remember that he was 76 years old when World War II began. Nonetheless, one must wonder if, perhaps, he said this to disguise his own feelings of sadness that – once again – he had been neglected when war broke out.

After Armistice, Richardson once again retired to the life of a country gentleman, albeit this time with an Order of the British Empire (OBE), but no knighthood. Gray, in his *Dogs of War*, caustically points out that he should have retired with a knighthood, "richly as he deserved it considering all he had done for the country." He also notes that "he was grudgingly promoted to half colonel, the least that could be offered." In retirement, Richardson continued to breed, train and sell dogs for private citizens and business. Of course, they were Airedales. If one is lucky enough, one can still find copies of his advertisements in old magazines, promoting his dogs as estate guardians and personal protection dogs. They were sold across the globe, finding work in plantations, factories, prisons and wherever their services were required.

The two decades between the Armistice and the new outbreak of hostilities had seen a world of rapid change. War, as it inevitably does, had accelerated communications and transportation technology. The world was moving much more rapidly. And Richardson, who had been a middle-aged man at the outbreak of the first "war to end all wars," was now a senior citizen as the latest global war erupted.

There was another change that must have perplexed him and somewhat unsettled him. Richardson had devoted hundreds of words, and in one case a whole chapter, to championing the superiority of British breeds over "foreign breeds," especially the German Shepherd Dog. It is not uncharitable to say that he bordered on the xenophobic in that regard.[32] Between approximately 1910 and 1930, the Airedale – his personal favorite – had been one of the most popular breeds in the world. To a certain extent, Richardson had contributed to this popularity. His working Airedales had gained worldwide notice. Similarly, in the United States, another former military man, Walter Lingo, had created the world renowned Oorang Kennels and shipped dogs around the world. Between the two of them, Lingo and Richardson had helped convince the world that "an

Airedale can do anything any other dog can do," as the old adage says. Looking at the tasks for which their dogs were trained, there is little doubt that they were probably correct.

However, there are fashions within the dog fancy as much as there is in any other aspect of life. Following World War I, the German Shepherd Dog seized hold of the public fancy and has still not completely let go. Returning servicemen brought European breeds back to Britain, the United States and Canada, among them the German Shepherd Dog. But it all really began with a puppy found in a trench.

A gray puppy, found in a trench amidst gun fire during World War I, would soon become the first canine film star in history. Breed fanciers claim that Rin Tin Tin was never much to look at, but he possessed an exceptional intelligence and trainability and in the hands of Lee Duncan, he became a true celebrity. He was soon joined by another German Shepherd Dog. Legend has it that Strongheart was born in Germany during World War I, but his poverty stricken owner couldn't afford to keep him, so he was sent to a breeder in White Plains, New York. He, too, soon became a film star. The two doggy daredevils seemed capable of doing virtually everything, as long as it was heroic.

It was not long before almost every child on the planet wanted a dog like Rin Tin Tin or Strongheart. They were not alone. Max von Stephanitz, the father of the breed, had convinced the authorities in Germany that his breed was the best for police and military work. The United States and Canada have, for years, imported many, if not most, of their police dogs for the simple reason that Europe, and in particular, Germany, excel at breeding and training working dogs. Soon, police officers everywhere wanted German Shepherd Dogs. Airedales had been tried and used in the United States as well as in Europe, including Britain, but it was not long before they began to disappear from the forces. Many officers liked the psychological impact that a big German Shepherd Dog had on ne'er-do-wells and expressed their preference for that breed on that basis alone. Experience had shown that Airedales were every bit as effective as the German breeds (witness the statistics gathered in Germany during World War II, above) but one cannot deny that the lupine-looking Shepherd has a more intimidating presence than the shaggy Airedale.[33]

In Britain, the German Shepherd Dog took hold as it had done virtually everywhere else in the world. The British were a little circumspect, however, calling the dog the "Alsatian"[34] so that no stigma might be attached to the name. There was still some lingering distrust of all things Teutonic following the war. Despite the fact that the rest of the world called it the German Shepherd Dog, the British would clutch onto "Alsatian" for three-quarters of a century. Meanwhile, as had been the case in Germany decades earlier, the British Alsatian Society did as much as possible to popularize its chosen breed.

Richardson, in his final book, *Fifty Years With Dogs*, was obliged to soften his rhetoric somewhat from his previous writings. He had little choice, as the German Shepherd Dog was now the working dog *du jour*. He acknowledged that one of his colleagues, who would soon be active in mobilizing dogs for war, had "a natural bias towards this breed." He then added that "We had never considered them very suitable for peace-time work in this country, but for guard work where alertness and a certain amount of ferocity is required they are valuable." It is a back-handed compliment of the most blatant kind.

Britain had disbanded its war dog school as soon as the First World War had ended. There had been no effort made to keep it open with even the most minimum of staff. What they had in 1939 were approximately 600 dogs serving in an unofficial capacity with a few units of the British Expeditionary Force in Poland, Belgium and North Africa. Consequently, as was the case 25 years earlier, Britain was left with no military dog program in place when Germany invaded Poland. While Germany and had been experimenting and developing new ways to incorporate dogs as combat allies, it would again be two years before there were any developments in Britain.

The usual arguments were made to explain why canines were not needed. Any war that arose would not be fought in the manner of the First World War, the critics contended. It would be far more mechanized and technological, and dogs would not be as effective as they had proven to be earlier in the century. Furthermore, it was argued, warfare would be far more mobile than at any time in the past, and there was no place for dogs in that type of combat. Inevitably, as had occurred in 1914, the naysayers would be proven wrong.

Richardson had a couple of allies when he suggested that Britain reconsider its views about using war dogs. One was an "Alsatian" fancier, Major (later Colonel) James Baldwin. Another was Brigadier Murray, Director of the Veterinary and Remount Services. Furthermore, the demands placed upon the Britons would dramatically help the effort to mobilize a war dog effort.

Baldwin was, in fact, one of the first to import the German Shepherd Dog to Britain. He was passionately devoted to the breed and never failed to promote it, either in print or verbally. In *Fifty Years With Dogs*, Richardson suggests that Baldwin had worked under him at the War Dog School during the First World War and, despite his partiality towards the German Shepherd Dog, Richardson valued his experience. Baldwin also happened to be in charge of an important air field and, as such, was aware of both the sensitivity of such installations and the need for considerable manpower to keep them secure. Air fields, factories, munitions depots, naval bases: all of these and others needed to be kept safe from saboteurs and infiltrators. The use of highly trained dogs could drastically cut down the number of people needed for this task and also do it better. Together, Baldwin and Richardson were convinced that a good dog could replace six men on sentry duty.

Richardson had never stopped the breeding and training of his Airedales for military and police purposes. Early in 1939, he and Baldwin, convinced of the need for military dogs for the imminent war, began training sentries and guard dogs without help from the military brass. Early in the war, they put on a demonstration for the authorities that, for all intents and purposes, was well received and made their point. Regardless, there were no immediate steps taken towards reviving the long-dormant war dog school. Meanwhile, people who had experience with

Photos this chapter: Richardson's Airedales in training with the Toronto Scottish Regiment during World War II. All photos courtesy of the Imperial War Museum, London.
Above: Neg. #D440
Right: Neg. #D442
Below: Neg. #D443

Epilogue: World War II 163

Above: Neg. #D444
Right: Neg. #D445
Below: Neg. #D446

Neg. #D448.

military dogs continued to write to the authorities, trying to convince them of their value and offering their services.

Baldwin, in particular, was tenacious in presenting his case. Patmore, in *Your Obedient Servant* (1984), states that he wrote numerous articles asking why the British government declined to use "Alsatians" for the war effort, pointing out how useful they were to other nations engaged in battle. He even took his case to the War Office, where (according to Patmore) he pounded his fists on the table in rage. According to Warrant Officer George Clapperton of the RAF School, "He was pitching at a high level" (Patmore, 1984). Meanwhile, he had also initiated the Volunteer Trained Dog Reserve. He arranged a meeting of The Kennel Club (Britain's national dog organization) and representatives of the Royal Navy, Army and Air Force as well as the Association of Chief Police Officers in England and Wales. The objective was to form a registry of owners of trained dogs who would be prepared to offer their dogs to the services at short notice in the event of a national emergency. This was successfully achieved.

A number of other factors helped to bring the authorities to conclude that canine soldiers were a good idea. Reports of Germany's alleged 200 000 war dogs was one such consideration.

There were more concrete military concerns, as well. As Lloyd notes in "The Dog in War" (Vesey-Fitzgerald, 1948), "It was as much as anything by constant reports of 'recce patrols' not functioning according to plan, by outposts being surprised, etc. and by first hand information from responsible field officers and the persistent offers made by certain people in this country that at last the War Office decided in 1940 to start a small experimental school..." It was Colonel Baldwin who was asked by the Ministry of Aircraft Production to start up a school. A very small school was established at Aldershot, comprising a mere four dogs. Lloyd, incidentally, who had considerable stature in the purebred dog world, was invited to act as technical advisor to the school. For Richardson, it must have been déjà vu.

Despite these baby steps, it was not until 1942 that things really got underway. That year, the first trained team under Colonel Baldwin was presented. In March, Brigadier Murray presided over a meeting called at the War Office. It comprised representatives of various British army units, the Ministry of Aircraft Production and the Royal Society for the Prevention of Cruelty to Animals (RSPCA). A pivotal decision was reached: there was an immediate need for 2500 dogs to guard factories, aerodromes and other vital installations that were vulnerable to attack and sabotage. Furthermore, given the urgency of the need, there was no time to breed in order to acquire the needed dogs, a process that would also raise issues of health and hygiene during war time. The solution, exactly the same as it was during World War I, was to issue an appeal to the public.

This time, there was a difference. On the one hand, the RSPCA came under attack. Its mandate, the critics claimed, was to protect dogs and other animals, not send them off to war where they could be maimed or killed. But there was a compromising factor on the Society's side. Britain had been subject to food rationing and, it is claimed, over 200 000 dogs had been euthanized within the first two months of the restrictions in order to accommodate the demands of the new reality. There then became an option, albeit not a pretty one: dogs of a suitable size and temperament that otherwise would have been euthanized could now be volunteered to serve their country. The RSPCA also had another response to their critics: if the dogs weren't put into service, would they fare any better under the Nazis? However, the euthanization of so many dogs also meant that there was a shortage of suitable animals for recruitment. The RSPCA was aided in its efforts by the National Canine Defense League and the Animal Protection Society of Scotland and Northern Ireland. Inspectors from these organizations interviewed prospective donors and examined the dogs to determine suitability.

Lloyd tells us that in the first two weeks, 7000 dogs were surrendered by their owners. Eventually, the number rose to 10 000. Of these, fewer than 3500 were accepted. Most were rejected because they proved gun shy when tested. The appeal to the public included a list of preferred breeds including Airedales, Collies, Lurchers and various crossbreeds. There was, however, an addition since World War I: the Alsatian. Richardson must have been not a little distressed to see this, but the breed's popularity in general, its growing acceptance as a service dog and Baldwin's championing of his preferred breed could no longer be ignored. As well, the relative popularity of the Airedale – Richardson's breed – had declined since the mid-1920s. In addition to these four breeds, the army also accepted Kerry Blue Terriers, Boxers, Bull Terriers, Labrador and Curly-Coated Retrievers and various sheep dog breeds.

As a result of the appeal to dog owners, the experimental school increased the number of dogs in training tenfold almost immediately and evolved into the Army Dog Training School. As the number of dogs increased, it was moved to a number of private kennels, including those of Mr. Lloyd. Finally, when the number of dogs exceeded 250 and space became a major issue, the training centre was established in late 1942 at the Greyhound Racing Kennels at Potter's Bar, near London, after having been commandeered by the military. It remained there until 1945. The Ministry of Aircraft Production operated a school in Gloucestershire, and later during the war, others were established in Burma and Egypt.

The new facilities at Potters Bar were well equipped with up-to-date veterinary facilities and extraordinary care taken to prevent outbreak of disease. Forty members of the Women's Auxiliary Territorial Services, many of them former kennel workers (or "kennel maids," as they were called), cared for the dogs and exercised them. Training was conducted by men.

There is some confusion surrounding the initial types of training undertaken. As noted above, when the initial call went out for trained military dogs, it was for animals to guard vital areas. One would think that the first trained dogs were thus animals trained for this purpose. Indeed, Patmore states that Baldwin started training dogs in 1941 and that the first group was sent out in January, 1942, to guard prisoner of war camps, from which no one escaped after the dogs were put on duty.

Lloyd, however, provides a different sequencing of events. "It was decided, in these early days, to concentrate on two types of work which it was considered the dogs could perform efficiently…patrol work …[and] to carry messages" (1948). Later, he observes, "The Patrol and Messenger dog having proved their value, further uses were sought for the dog and it was quickly realized that ammunition and stores, dumps, factories, radio-location stations and other vulnerable points could be more effectively guarded by dogs, at a great saving of man power" (1948). It is conceivable that the first dogs used for guarding sensitive installations were, in fact, unofficial war dogs trained by Richardson and Baldwin. Or, alternately, Lloyd is using a different interpretation of "guard dog." In either of these scenarios, then, Lloyd's sequencing of training would be correct. It is hard to dismiss his version of history, for he was a technical adviser to the school.

The patrol dogs were essentially the scout dogs of later wars. In Lloyd's words, the patrol dog was "trained to accompany Recce patrols into no-man's-land – or, to state it more correctly – to 'lead' a patrol, having been trained to recognize human scent…in precisely the same manner that a gun dog recognizes game scent; on recognizing the prey the dog 'froze' on point like a Pointer or Setter" (1948). They were used with both mobile patrols and statically, i.e., at a "listening post," the latter having been established by virtue of the mobile patrol. While working on a static patrol, a dog was capable of picking up scent from 60-200 yards away, depending on the weather conditions.

Lloyd notes some of the same concerns that Richardson had encountered in the previous world war. Some commanding officers welcomed the use of patrol dogs and were pleased with the results they brought, including increased morale among the troops. Others, disinterested and apathetic, viewed them as yet another headache and were reluctant to use them and, if they did, infrequently employed them and failed to support the dog and handler.

Messenger dogs were also used (Lloyd calls them "message carriers"). Dogs were trained and handled by two soldiers, to whom the dog was equally devoted. The dog, having learned to recognize two masters, was trained to run between the two. In other words, it was the liaison dog messenger dog system. When on duty, a patrol would leave with one handler and the dog, the latter being very aware that his other master was left behind. Even though it might conceivably be hours before the dog might be put into use, and the distance a couple of kilometres between the patrol and the other handler, the dog was trained to run back quickly and without any distractions. The exercise was repeated in order to respond to the initial message. Should the patrol have moved, the dog was trained to follow the scent of a "drag" used by the handler, thereby leaving a clear scent for the dog to follow and to regain the patrol.

Building upon the experiences gained and knowledge gathered from training patrol and messenger dogs, Britain started developing other uses for their war dogs. The military police started working with dogs for perimeter defense work. The handler, a military policeman, accompanied by the dog on a short lead, patrolled the perimeter after dark, always attempting to negotiate the grounds so as to give the dog full advantage of the wind conditions. The dogs then indicated the presence of any person whose scent they picked up. As Lloyd recounts, in the early stages, the dogs sometimes apprehended innocent people, including military personnel, who either were unaware of the new security procedures or chose to ignore them. In any event, the dogs quickly proved they were more than up to the task they were assigned.

The British were also among the first to develop mine-detecting dogs and parachute dogs. There is some debate whether the Soviets or British were the first to embark on this type of training, but the latter were certainly engaged in it during the Second World War.

Mine-detecting dogs began to be trained for service in 1943. It had been found that the mechanical detector was ineffective against non-metallic and anti-personnel mines, which consequently resulted in heavy casualties. It was then recalled that, prior to the war, a Labrador Retriever had proven effective in detecting leaks in an underground BBC cable. Building on this experience, the military went to work training dogs to detect mines. The dogs, by necessity, had to be blessed with exceptional powers of scent and a keen intelligence. As well, it was quickly discovered that they had to be trained to the highest level of distraction. The work demanded intense concentration, so the dogs were, in Lloyd's words, "battle inoculated" by exposing them to Bren guns; heavy explosions at close range; low flying aircraft; tethered sheep, rabbits and game; lumps of meat, and even female dogs in estrus, while they worked.

Having met these exceptionally demanding standards, the dogs were worked in platoons, three sections of four dogs and handlers, with a fourth in reserve. It was soon discovered that, due to the intensity of the work, 20 to 30 minutes was the maximum that a dog and man could sustain the effort at any one time. When the dog detected a mine, it would sit down a few inches away to indicate the presence of the weapon. The handler then ascertained the location of the mine by gentle prodding, marked the precise location and then rewarded the dog with a piece of meat reserved especially for such work. The work was typically carried out at night, adding another difficulty for dogs and handlers. Between July, 1944, and November, 1945, four mine detecting dog platoons were employed as units of the Royal Engineers in the Northwester European theatre. The platoons were spread out among the various corps of the British army and one was attached to the Canadian army.

When reading Richardson's final book, *Fifty Years With Dogs*, one detects a sense of dismissal or contempt for some of the training that was pursued. This might be attributable to his being a senior citizen during the Second World War and therefore largely left out of the proverbial loop. Or, it might simply be that he genuinely didn't care for what was being done with the military dogs. Regardless, he ends his brief chapter about military dogs in World War II with this paragraph:

There were several experimental lines which were tested during the Second World War which might come under the heading of "Fancy." Dogs were sometimes parachuted from planes and dropped behind enemy lines, or elsewhere, for certain purposes.

Thus ends the chapter. No explanation and no context. One wonders about his use of "fancy." Does he mean it in the sense of whimsical or capricious or in the sense implying some superior skill, or difficulty? Regardless, the "para-pups" (as the parachute dogs were called by the British) were put to effective use in two capacities. Lloyd states that the elite Special Air Services (SAS – arguably the finest military unit in the world) employed them to great use behind enemy lines. Once on the ground, the dogs worked as scouts, indicating the presence of the enemy long before the soldiers themselves could have done so. Through the use of parachute dogs, many hazardous undertakings were successfully completed deep behind enemy lines.

Parachute dogs were also trained to accompany the stretcher-bearers of airborne divisions. The dogs jumped from planes, along with their handlers, but each dog with its own parachute. The dogs were immediately released from their parachute upon touching down, and having their special harnesses adjusted for work, were then given the command to quarter their ground, which they worked in much the same way that a Spaniel hunts through dense cover. The dogs were trained to notice men only in a prone position and ignored all others. According to Lloyd, the dogs quickly learned that they were to acknowledge only the wounded. The dogs worked very quickly, picking up human scent and, having done so, quickly investigated the source.

If a dog found a casualty, it would return to its handler and sit at his feet. The handler would then attach the lead to the harness and the dog would guide the handler to the casualty whereupon the dog received its reward. Dogs of a companionable, gentle nature were most adept at this type of work. They had to be thoroughly trained to ignore game and other distractions and had to be thoroughly accustomed to the noises and chaos of battle conditions. The work was usually conducted at night. In addition to the very real service the dogs provided in finding casualties, they also had a significant impact on troop morale, who realized that if they were hit and lucky enough to be merely wounded, there was a real possibility that they would be found and treated.

Almost as much care was taken with the selection of dog handlers as was taken with the selection of dogs for training. There was a certain romantic idealism at play in this regard, as volunteers with "country connections" such as farm workers, game keepers and people of similar background were the preferred choice. Others who lacked these country associations but who genuinely liked dogs and were interested in learning the necessary skills to handle them were also deemed acceptable. The implicit assumption was that, somehow, country folk had an innate gift or talent for working with dogs that their urban cousins somehow lacked. In this respect, the Second World War dog training school was no different from that run by Richardson during World War I.

In the archives at The Imperial War Museum are three volumes pertaining to the World War II War Dog School that were compiled by Monty Hunt. They contain photographs, memoirs, recollections and intimate details of the school. At the outbreak of the war, Mr. Hunt was serving with the 5th Battalion Wiltshire regiment as a corporal. In 1941, he was trained as a handler. Early in 1942, he was put on loan to the War Dogs School as a trainer and later as a driver for the commandant of the school. He has compiled what is probably the largest private collection of military dog photos and other memorabilia in the world. His materials have been on display at the War Dog Museum in New Jersey and he has had articles published in Canada and Australia and he has been interviewed by the BBC. For anybody wishing to learn more about the history of British war dogs during the Second World War, his collection is invaluable. Now in his 80s, he resides in Kent, England. Mr. Hunt was most generous in sharing some of his material with me, shipping it overseas, so that I could peruse it. I am most grateful.

A final and personal note about Airedale war dogs. The dam (mother) of my present Airedale, Katy, was sent to live with an elderly couple near Hamilton, Ontario. They had owned Collies (the wife's preferred breed) all their married life. I had a personal interest in seeing Katy's dam, whose name was Priscilla, and so I arranged to see her. Curious as to why they wanted an Airedale, as opposed to a Collie, the gentleman told me that he had served with the army in World War II and had been a dog handler with an Airedale in Africa. As a result of those experiences, he had always wanted another and now, in his senior years, the opportunity had arisen. Priscilla, the bitch, was completely bonded to her new owner and literally followed him room to room as he moved about the house.

My visit was brief, but my host related one wartime experience to me. He and his dog had happened upon, and apprehended, a trespasser. For some reason or another, the man had to leave the interloper while he went to get assistance. He had the man lie flat down on his face and stomach and gave the dog the "guard" command and left. He was unavoidably delayed for a couple of hours, but when he came back both the trespasser and the Airedale were where he had left them, the man too terrified to move and the dog ready to stop him had he tried. Colonel Richardson would have expected nothing less.

APPENDIX A
Description of Dogs Shipped From England to France and the Men Who Brought Them

The following is from The Imperial War Museum's (London, UK) archives file # 69/75/1 "GHQ Central Kennels Register of Dogs and Men." It is assumed that this represents the dogs shipped overseas between July 1917 and April 1919. The first column is the number assigned to the dog, the second is the dog's breed (or a description of the dog), the third the dog's sex (Dog or Bitch), followed by the dog's name, the owner's (keeper or handler's) name and regiment. The terms and abbreviations are as they appear in the original. The missing information is also as it appears in the original. The "X" that sometimes occurs in the dog's descriptions refers to a crossbred animal, e.g., "Old English Sheepdog X Airedale" or simply "X Collie."

#	Breed/Description	Sex	Name	Handler's Name	Regiment
1	Airedale	D	Peter	Gnr. B. Grimes	37. Res. Bty. RFA
2					
3					
4	Airedale	D	Prince	Pte. J. Coleman	2/ Yorks
5					
6	Black & White Collie	D	Smoke	Gnr. T. Slight	32/ Res. Bty. RFA
7					
8	Old English Sheep[dog]	B	Betsy	Pte. Shaylor. W.H.	3/ Suffolks
9					
10	Black Retriever	D	Sammy	Pte. W. Ramsey	4/th Royal Scots.
11	Sable & White Collie	B	Fox	Gnr. H. J. Wright	R.F.A.
12	Sable & White Collie	D	Bruce	" " "	" " "
12a	Old Eng. Sheep. X Airedale		Nell	" " "	" " "
13	Small Retriever	D	Darkie	Pte. McGregor. A.	3rd Black Watch
14					
15	X Collie	D	Jack	Pte. Brown J. H. A.	9th Royal Scots.
16	X Labrador	D	Joe	" " " "	" " "
17	Brown & White Lurcher	B	Creamy	Pte. J. Swankie	3 Black Watch
18	Brown Setter	D	Ginger	" " "	" " "
19					

20	X Irish Terrier B'dlton [Bedlington Terrier]	D	Paddy	Pte. Monoghan. M.	4. Inniskilling's
21	Bobtail Sheepdog[35]	D	Bluebell	Gnr. Firth. C.	R.F.A.
22					
23	Black & Tan Collie	D	Swift	Gnr. E. Evans	R.F.A.
24					
25					
26	Airedale	B	Vixen	Dvr. Birtles. F.	Signals R.E.
27					
28	X Bred Airedale	D		Dvr. Watts. P.	37. Res. Bty. R.F.A.
29	Irish X Deerhound	B	Deer Dane	Gnr. Young. R.	R.G.A.
30	Black Dog			" " "	" " "
31					
32					
33	X Airedale	D	Bill	Pte. C. G. Booth	52 Canadians
34	X Setter	B	Nellie	Pte. C. G. Booth	52 Canadian
35					
36					
37					
38	Black Labrador	B	Nell	L/ Cpl. J. Skinner	11th Essex
39	X Collie Retriever	B	Nellie	Pte. Town. W.	2/7th Duke of Wellington
40	Smooth Black Retriever	D	Jack	" " "	" " "
41	X Bred Airedale	B	Nellie	Pte. A. R. White	A. Coy. 2/4th Royal Berks.
42	Black X Collie	D	Jim	" " "	" " "
43	Airedale	D	Joe	Pte. W. Davies	12/ S. Wales Borderers
44	Red Collie	B	Nellie	" " "	" " "
45	Airedale	D	Togo	Pte. J. Stewart	14/A & S'Land H'l'rs
46	Irish Terrier	D	Paddy	" " "	"
47	Irish Terrier	D	Dick	Pte. H. Boxford	2/6 Sherwoods
48	X Airedale Irish	B	Bess	" " "	" "
49	Airedale	B	Lassie	Pte. J. Varney	1/ Roy. Warwick
50	Butchers Dog (red X Terrier)	D	Butcher	" " "	" " "
51	Irish Airedale X	D	Sam	Pte. E. Noble Vice. Lea.	1/5 Loyal. North Lanc.'s

Appendix A

No.	Breed	Sex	Name	Owner	Unit
52	Collie		Prince	" " " "	" " "
53	Black X Retriever Spaniel	D	Prince	Pte. G. W. Allcock	15 /Sherwoods
54	X Airedale	D	Jack	" " "	" "
55					
56	X Collie Retriever	D	Bill	Pte. Oldroyd. P.M.	49th Canadians Battllion
57	X Esquimaux Collie	D	Custard	Pte. Ferris. C.	2/4 Duke of Wellingtons
58	X Collie	D	Jack	" " "	" "
59	X Spaniel Retriever	B	Jet	Pte. G. Goldborne	6th Wilts.
60	X Collie	D	Wolf	" " "	" "
61	X Irish Airedale	D		Pte. H. Cook	1/6 Sherwoods
62	Airedale	B		" " "	" "
63	X Lurcher	D	Dane	Pte. H. Radford	8th/ S. Staffs.
64	Red Lurcher	D	Red 'Un	" " "	" " "
65	Black Bitch White Front		Tip	Pte. J. Hedley	17/ Royal Scots.
66	Collie	D	Sable	" " "	" " "
67	Irish Terrier	D	Paddy	Pte. F. Hammond	1/5/Yorks.
68					
69	Old English Sheep [dog] & Irish Terrier	D	Creamy	Pte. W. Reade	12th York & Lanc's
70					
71	Irish Terrier	D	Rags	Pte. J. Delaney	137th King's Liverpools
72					
73	Airedale	B	Myrtle	Pte. H. Hunt	20th London
74	X Bedlington	D	Winner	" " "	" "
75	Smooth Labrador Retriever	D	Feroh	Pte. D. Healy	10th Royal Fusiliers
76					
77	Airedale	D	Jock	Pte. N. Read	13. Bat. Roy. Can'n. H'rs.
78	X Irish Terrier Collie	D	Towzer	" " "	" "
79	Old English Sheep[dog]	D	Tweed	" " "	" "
80					
81					
82					
83					
84	X Collie	D	Scott	L/Cpl. R. Goodway	24/ Royal Fusiliers

85	X Retriever & Sheep [dog]	D	Gip	Pte. McGregor J.	1st Auckland Batt.
86	X Airedale Irish	B	Curly	" " "	" " "
87	Collie	B	Lassie	Cpl. Bonney. W.	2/5 King's Own
88	Retriever	B	Lill	" " "	" " "
89	Collie	D	Tricky	Pte. J. Coull	48/ A.I.F.
90	Brown Lurcher	D	Sam	" " "	" "
91	Lurcher	B	Lady	Pte. T. W. Woof	5th / Duke of Wellington
92	X Airedale Collie	D	Toby	" " "	" " "
93	Deerhound Lurcher	D	Major	Pte. S. Taylor	13th Essex
94	X Bedlington Airedale	D [?]	Maggie	" " "	" "
95					
96					
97	Airedale	B	Fatty	Pte. J. Cousall	A. Coy. 1st Irish Fusiliers
98	Brindle Terrier	D	Bob	" " "	" " " "
99	Airedale	B	Duchess	Pte. Hayes. S. R.	1st Essex Yeomanry 11/ 11/ Bat. Essex
100	Black Retriever	D	Duke	Pte. J. Waters	11th Essex
101					
102	Airedale	B	Jessie	L/Cpl. Vidler	1/ Royal West Kents.
103	X Collie	D	Rave	Pte. J. R. Jackson	1st Can'bury Inf'y Batt'n.
104	Black X Sheep Spaniel	B	Sulky	" " "	" " " "
105	Old English Sheep[dog]	D	Taffy	Pte. Cotton H.	4/ Coy/ 1st Herts.
106	Bedlington Terrier	D	Dick	" " "	" " " "
107	X Irish	B	Nan	Cpl. M. McLeod	16/ Royal Scots
108	Big X Airedale Sheep	D	Jock	" " "	" " "
109	Irish Terrier	D	Tip	Pte. J. Nicholson	D/ Coy. 10th Yorks.
110	Spaniel	B	Biddy	" " "	" " "
110a	Smooth Collie	D	Jim	" " "	" " "
111	X Bedlington & Greyhound	B	Grace	Pte. J. Ferriby	10/ East Yorks.
112	X Airedale & Irish	D	Rough	" " "	" " "
113					
114					

115 X Bred Collie	D	Digger	L. Sgt. H. Brown		21/ Machine Gun Corps.
116					
117					
118 Old English Sheep[dog]	D	Tray	Pte. Rea. W.		44th Canadian Batt.
119					
120					
121					
122					
123					
124					
125					
126					
127					
128					
129					
130					
131 X Spaniel	D	Johnson	Pte. A. Robbie		C. Coy. 1st/ 6/Blk. Watch
132 X Collie	D	Scott	"	" "	" " " " " "
133 X Collie	B	Flight	Pte. R. Errington		C. Coy. 18th D.L.I.
134 Irish Terrier	D	Mike	"	" "	" " " " "
135 X Collie Retriever	D	Curly	Pte. R. Fraser		C. Coy. 1st/ Camerons.
136 X Collie	D	Robin	"	" "	" " " "
137 X Sheep[dog]	D	Champion	Pte. C. Welham		C. Coy. 9th/ Norfolks.
138 X Welsh & Airedale	D	Lloyd	"	" "	" " " "
139 Black X Collie	D	Rook	Pte. Buckenham. H.		B. Coy.1/5 N. Staffs.
140 Irish Terrier	B	Fanny	"	" "	" " " " "
141 Golden Collie	D	Sunlight	Pte. W. J. Brooks		A. Coy.2/7. Worcesters.
142 X King Charles[36]	D	Charlie	"	" ":"	" " "
143 X Irish Airedale	D	Whitefoot	Pte. G. L. Griffiths		15/ London. Welsh
144 X Black Whippet	D	Ray	"	" "	" " "
145 X Bred Collie	D	Sulky	L/ Cpl. W. Kitchen		D. Coy. 2/5 Lincolns.
146 Lurcher	B	Sweep	"	" "	" " " "

147	Black & White X Collie	D	Domino	Pte. G. Lovegrove	C. Coy.1/16/ London
148	Welsh Terrier Airedale	D	Dick	" " "	" " "
149	X Collie	D	Pussie	Pte. T. R. Peach	8th/Batt. R. W. Kents. D. Coy.
150	Irish Terrier	D	Jimmy	" " "	" " "
151	X Bedlington	D	Blue Boy	Pte. J. Ferguson	D. Coy. 1st Gordons
152	X Airedale	D	Robb	" " "	" " "
153	X Old Sheep[dog] Irish	D	Swift	Pte. T. E. Gregory	C. Coy. 2 Roy'l Sussex
154	X Spaniel	D	Drummer	" " "	" " "
155	Lurcher	D	Bugler	Cpl. W. Taylor	1/6 Batt. Manchester
156	X Collie		Willard	" " "	" " "
157	X Collie	D	Bonnie	Pte. S. Boreham	B. Coy. 9th Suffolks
158	X Airedale	B	Raider	" " "	" " "
159	X Sheep[dog]	D	Tom	Pte. R. R. Windle	C. Coy. 8/ Border Regt.
160	X Airedale	B	Rab	" " "	" " "
161	X Irish	D	Paddy	Pte. M. Dempsey	B. Coy. 2nd. Roy. Mun'. Fus.
162	X Old En. Sheep & Irish	D	Glen	" " " "	" " "
163	Airedale	D	Fortune	Pte. H. E. Stephens	C. Coy. 1st/ 7 Middlesex
164	X Collie	D	Cosy	" " " "	" " " "
165	Airedale	D	Jack	Pte. G. Murray	2nd/ West Yorks.
166	Sheep[dog]	D	Shag	Pte. G. Murray	2nd/ West Yorks
167	X Collie	D	Fox	Pte. Fletcher A. R.	B. Coy.4/ Can . Rifles
168	X Collie Setter	D	Dandy	" " " "	" " "
169	Airedale	D	Boxer	Cpl. W. Dixon	A. Coy. 4th/ No'h'd. Fus.
170	Brindle Lurcher	B	Flash	" " "	" " "
171	Collie	D	Trusty	Pte. N. Brown	11. A & Suth'd H'la'drs
172	X Airedale	D	Peter	" " "	" " "
173	Brindle Bull	B	Bully	Pte. D. Bruce	11. Royal Scots.
174	X Airedale	D	Prince	" " "	" " "
175	Collie	D	Bruce	Pte. Bevinston	B. Coy.2/5 S. Staffs.

176	X Bred Collie	D	Surefoot	" "	" "
177	Collie	B	Mop	Pte. A. Mathieson	7/ Seaforth H'ldrs.
178	X Irish & Collie	B	Nell	" " "	" " "
179	Mastiff & Sheep[dog]	D	Bruno	Pte. J. Dunn	A. Coy. 14/Welsh
180	X Collie	D	Wolf	" " "	" " "
181	Brown Greyhound	D	Sandy	L/Cpl. A. Dowdeswell	5/ Royal Berks.
182	Black Lurcher	D	King	" " "	" " "
183	Brindle & White Lurcher	D	Seagull	" " "	" " "
184	X Airedale & Old En. Sheep.	D	Blinker	Pte. H. Robbins	D. Coy. 18th. Batt. A.I.F.
185	X Retriever & Old En. Sheep.	D	Knight	" " "	" " "
186	X Black Lurcher	D	Solomon	" " "	" " "
187	X Collie	D	Runner	Pte. J. Stretton	A. Coy. 1/8 Lanc's. Fus'lrs.
188	Irish X Airedale	D	Nipper	" " "	" " "
189	X Collie	D	Volunteer	" " "	" " "
190	X Airedale	D	Badger	Pte. H. Johns	5th/ Canadians
191	X Collie	D	Scott	" " "	" "
192	X Old English Sheep	D	Merry	" " "	" "

THE REMAINDER OF THE DOGS LISTED WERE SHIPPED TO THE CONTINENT WITHOUT "OWNERS". THEREFORE, SOME INFORMATION IS INCOMPLETE.

Dogs # 193-204 are listed as "Came out without owners. Arrived here June 3, 1918."

#	Description	Sex	Name
193	X Grey & White Old En. Shp.	D	Smoke
194	X Poodle	D	Coffee
195	Sable & White Collie	D	Victor
196	Collie. R't'r. Spaniel.	D	Tom
197	X Smooth Collie Lurcher	D	Yellow
198	Airedale (short face)	D	Rocket
199	Airedale (long face)	D	Jam
200	Collie. W. Blaze & Paws	D	Thunder
201	Small Smooth Collie Terrier	D	Bob
202	X Deerhound Lurcher	D	Ronald
203	X Collie Retriever	D	Moses
204	Large German (Collie Esquimaux) [sic]	D	Fritz

Dogs # 205-216 are listed as "Came out without owners. Arrive her arrived here [sic] June 16. 1918."

#	Description	Sex	Name
205	X Blk, Collie Retriever	D	Rex
206	Tri Colour Collie (Blk. & Tan)	D	Jo
207	Brown Collie	D	Snipe
208	Lurcher Collie	D	Famous
209	Black Lurcher	D	Blk. Tiger
210	Pale Colored Airedale	D	Jake
211	Dark Sable & White Collie	D	Bobbie
212	Small Brindle & White Lurcher	D	Johnny
213	Black & White X Spaniel	D	Feathers
214	X Spaniel	D	Snowball
215	Black & Tan Collie	D	Lammie
216	Black Retriever	D	Curly Boy

Dogs # 217-228 are listed as "Came out without owners. Arrived here June 25.6.18 [sic]."

#	Description	Sex	Name
217	Sable Collie	D	Yellow Tiger
218	Dalmation [sic]	D	Fitz
219	Curly Retriever	D	Black Peter
220	Working Collie	D	Pierrett

221 Airedale   D   Forward
222 Airedale   D   Mr. Blunt
223 Airedale Cur   D   Cocoa
224 Irish Terrier   D   Paddy
225 Sable Collie   D   Ben
226 Lurcher   D   Lizard
227 Blk. Sheep Dog   D   Billy Goat
228 Irish Terrier   D   Michael

Dogs # 229-240 are listed as "Came out without owners. Arrived here 29.6.18"
229 Black & White X Collie   D   Spotty
230 Irish & Airedale   D   Hefty
231 X Collie Retriever   D   Rusty
232 B & W Lurcher Cur   D   Little George

Beginning with Dog # 233 and ending with Dog # 240 there is a new heading called "Qualification."

#	Description	Sex	Name	Qualification
233	Fawn X Lurcher	D	Vulcan	V. Good.
234	L. Fawn Lurcher	D	Rapid	V. Good
235	Bk. Retriever Lurcher	D	Hanky	V. Good. Excellent
236	Fawn Lurcher Cur	D	Skim	V. Good
237	Fawn Lurcher Cur	D	Lynx	V. Good
238	Retriever	D	Ink	Good Dog
239	Smooth Retriever	D	Blake	Good Dog
240	Brindle Lurcher	D	Hurry	Good Dog

Dogs # 241-252 are listed as "Came without owners. Brought by Cp. Taylor 18.7.18"
241 Black Lurcher   D   Fatty
242 Airedale   D   Curley Coat
243 Airedale   D   Tip
244 Rough Black Lurcher   D   Sailor
245 Airedale   D   Crack
246 Airedale   D   Long Tail
247 Black Lurcher   D   Valiant
248 Airedale   D   Moses
249 Lurcher Cross   D   Tortishell [sic]
250 Yellow Lurcher   D   Slick
251 Airedale   D   Dale

252 Tricolor Collie   D   Roman

Dogs # 253-264 are listed as "Brought out without owners 10. 8.18"

253 Yellow Lurcher   D   Fleet
254 "   "   D   Wolf
255 Rough Yellow Lurcher   D   Barrie
256 X Bred Airedale   D   Cutter
257 Spaniel   D   Coffee
258 Small Blk. Lurcher   D   Slipper
259 Black & Tan Lurcher   D   Bruce
260 Irish Terrier   D   Michael
261 Airedale   D   Prince
262 Yellow Collie   D   Honey
263 Yellow & W. Collie   D   Arrow
264 Blk. & Tan Collie   D   Bob

Dogs # 265-276 are listed as "Brought over from England 16.8.18."

265 Blk. & White Collie   D   Swallow
266 Sheep Dog   D   Nightshade
267 Black & Tan Collie   D   Tweed
268 Airedale   D   Max
269 Retriever   D   Jerry
270 Collie   D   Flight
271 Dalmation [sic] X   D   Spotty
272 Lurcher   D   Laddie
273 Airedale   D   Joseph
274 Airedale   D   Grissle
275 Retriever   D   Longtail
276 Lurcher   D   Yellow Streck [sic]

Dogs # 277-292 are listed as "Came over from England 31.8.18"

277 Deerhound   D   Hero
278 German Sheep Dog[37]   D   Hun
280 Brindle & White Lurcher D   Stump
281 Airedale   D   Jo
282 X Bred Bulldog   D   Bobs
283 Deerhound   D   Ronald
284 Sable & W. Collie   D   Snipe

285 Small Yellow Lurcher	D	Frolic	
286 Bk. & Tan Collie	D	Go Bang	
287 Small Bk. Lurcher	D	Fatty	
288 Yellow & Br'dle Lurcher	D	Jip	
289 Small X Bred	D	Cocktail	
290 Black Lurcher	D	Invader	
291 Bk. Collie Retriever	D	Ebony	
292 Curly Retriever	D	Curley	

Dogs # 293-304 are listed as "Came over from England 14.9.18."

293 Bk. & W. Collie	D	Rover	
294 Airedale	D	Duke	
295 Fawn Lurcher	D	Smiler	
296 Black Lurcher	D	Coal	
297 Airedale	D	Mustard	
298 Deerhound	D	Athol	
299 Old. Eng. Sheep[dog]	D	Smokeball	
300 Old Eng. Sheep[dog]	D	Don	
301 Sable Collie	D	Buttercup	
302 Airedale	D	Corker	
303 Old. English Sheep[dog]	D	Lion	
304 Brindle Lurcher	D	Dick	

Dogs # 305-316 are listed as "From England 28.9.18."

305 Sable Collie	D	Diamond	
306 Grey Sheep Dog	D	Starlight	
307 Pointer Cross	D	White Fang	
308 Airedale	D	Johnny	
309 Cream Bull Terrier	D	Byng	
310 Retriever Cross	D	Bluewater	
311 Dark Grey Sheep Dog	D	Foch	
312 Black & Tan Collie	D	Flyer	
313 Retriever	D	Black feather	
314 Airedale	D	Tags	
315 Retriever Cross	D	Running Water	
316 Brown Collie Retriever	D	Cinders	
317			
318			

319
320
321
322

Dogs #323 -324 are listed as "From England 12.10.18. Conveyed by Lloyd & Cook."

323	Large Collie Cross	D	Hero
324	Spaniel	D	The Black Prince
325	Red Sable Collie	D	Quaker
326	Airedale	D	Jim
327	Small Bk. & White Collie Cross	D	White Toes
328	Airedale	D	Glasgow Jack
329	Cross Bred Bull Terrier	D	Bully Beef
330	Sable Collie	D	Dandy Lion
331	Collie	D	Dart
332	Airedale	D	Sure
333	Black Curly Retriever	D	Sambo
334	Cross Bred Airedale	D	Nailer

Dogs # 335-346 are listed as "From England 26.10.18 Conveyed by Lloyd, Shaylor [?] & Hoad [?]."

335	Sheep Dog	D	Sprinting
336	Cross Bred Foxhound	D	John Peel
337	Lurcher	D	Trumps
338	Cross Bred Lurcher	D	Racer
339	Airedale	D	Joker
340	Irish Terrier	D	Yellow Tail
341	Black Lurcher Cross	D	Blackamoor
342	Welsh Terrier	D	George
343	Sheep Dog	D	Greybeard
344	Irish Terrier	D	Trot
345	Black Lurcher	D	Pershing
346	Cross Bred Foxhound	D	Jethro

APPENDIX B
Casualties to Dogs

The following is from archival material (file # 69/75/1) housed at The Imperial War Museum, London. It is a list of all the above dogs, noting the casualties. The comments are verbatim. When reading this, it is useful to bear in mind the following observations from Richardson's *Forty Years With Dogs* as one notes the designation of certain dogs as "Useless," thereby justifying their being killed or given away. Remember that this is the first time in British history that an official, organized dog program had been used. Richardson is writing in reference to his visit to the troops in France.

> *The keepers were glad to see me....and my visit encouraged them in their difficult task. Many of them had, when the first drafts went out, great obstructions to contend within the management of their charges. Commanding officers of those battalions to whom they were first sent very often made light of the dogs, or else ignored them, or worse still rather cynically set them to tasks under impossible conditions.*

Dog #	Comments.
1	Gassed 1.5.18. Returned GHQ, got fit & again goes to Section 2 as 60.
2	
3	
4	Gassed 1.5.18. Returned to GHQ, got fit & again goes to Section 2 as 62.
5	
6	
7	
8	Returns from No. 2 Section 19.9.18.
9	
10	
11	
12	Missing in line.
12a	Returned in season 9.6.18. Given to Capt. Harris 20.2.19.
13	
14	
15	Lost in line July 1918.
16	Returned 5/7/18. Shot by O.C.'s orders 24.7.18.

17	Shot in line Sept.
18	Missing Early Oct. (Killed) with Runners.
19	
20	
21	Missing, found and Returned to GHQ Kennels 15.5.18. Goes up again to [illegible] as 127.
22	
23	
24	
25	
26	Returns 16.10.18
27	
28	Missing in line July 1918
29	Returns from Sect. 1 9.6.18 as useless. Sent to GHQ or [illegible] for Col. Ailes.
30	Returned from Section 1 20.6.18.
31	
32	
33	Destroyed by O.C.'s orders 18.4.19
34	
35	
36	
37	
38	
39	Given to Col. Nissen. No use to the service.
40	Killed by bomb during training.
41	Returned as of no use 9.6.18. Given to Mr. Wood Assistant Camp Commandant GHQ
42	Died at Section 1 [illegible].
43	Missing in line Nov. 1918
44	Missing in line Nov. 1918
45	
46	
47	Returns [illegible]
48	Shot 22.8.18 by OC's orders
39	
50	Returns from 2 Sctn. Destroyed 23.9.18.

51	
52	
53	
54	Returned to GHQ Kennels & Destroyed by OC's orders. No use up line 28.6.18
55	
56	Shot in line
57	Lost in line Sept.
58	
59	Shot by OC's orders. No use.
60	
61	Given to Lt. Col. [illegible – Rherjutt?]
62	Missing in line. Nov. 1918.
63	Missing in line. Nov. 1918.
64	Missing in line. Nov. 1918.
65	Returned to GHQ Kennels 20.6.18 after being missing in line from July 18. In Whelp.
66	Lost in line. May 1918.
67	
68	
69	Missing.
79	
71	
72	
73	Missing 3.6.18.
74	Lost April 1918.
75	Missing.
76	
77	Given to Col. Dodd.
78	Given to Col. Drake.
79	
80	
81	
82	
83	
84	

85	Returned 1.11.18.
86	
87	Lost in line May 1918.
88	Missing in line beginning of July. Found again.
89	
90	Missing in line. May 1918.
91	Killed in line. Nov. (early).
92	Killed in line. June 1918.
93	
94	Shot by O.C.'s orders. 24.7.18.
95	
96	
97	Given to Col. Whitehead of GHQ being no use to service.
98	
99	Wounded 12.5.18 & returns to GHQ Kennels. 24/6/18 in whelp. Sent to No. 13 Vetry. Hosp'l. 3.8. 18 Returns [illegible] 10.10.18 Destroyed 18.2./19. O.C. orders.
100	Lost in line. May 1918.
101	
102	Destroyed by O.C.'s orders 2.11.18.
103	Returns from [illegible] 19.9.18 Goes to Lovats Scouts. Reported missing end of Oct.
104	
105	
105	
107	Lost in line some time April-May.
108	
109	
110	Lost in line Aug.
110 a	Lost in line.
111	Missing in line April. Killed.
12	Returned to GHQ Kennels as useless 9.6.18. Shot by O.C.'s orders 4.7.18.
113	
114	
115	Returned 26.7.18 Wounded. Evacuated to hos C. H. Depot 28.7.18. [There is an entry that says "Killed 20.7.18". That has been scratched out and replaced with "Died 8.8.18".]
116	

117
118 Returned to kennel 24.6.18 Destroyed 8.2.19 by order of O.C.
119
120
121
122
123
124
125
126 Missing in line July 1918.
127
128
129
130
131 Lost in line.
132
133 Missing.
134
135 Lost in line Aug. 1918.
136 Returned 5/7/18 useless afraid of shell fire. Given to Major Williams.
137 Return from No. 2 Sctn. 19.19.18
138
139 Return from Sctn. 2 19.9.18.
140
141 [illegible – either "lost" or "killed" end of June in line.]
144 Shot by O.C.'s order no use.
143 Missing in line. Aug 1918.
144 Went through gas before going to Section, Afterwards Killed in line July 1918.
145 Becomes 52 21.10.18.
146 Returned, in Season 20.6.18. Destroyed by order of O.C. 23.8.18.
147 Returned to GHQ useless 12.9.18. Given away.
148 Given to Cpt. Barker as no use to service. Again given to Capt. Barker by Lt. Col. Ailes.
149 Lost in line.
150

151	
152	Wounded May '18. Evacuated by ADVS.
153	
154	Missing in line about beginning July. Found again.
155	
156	Lost in line early July 1918.
157	Given to major [illegible] 10.10.18.
158	Returned 5.7.18 as useless. Shot by order of O.C. 27.7.18 useless.
159	Returned gassed 1.5.18. To GHQ got fit & goes to Sctn. 2 as 61. Returns & again goes to [illegible]. Later reported missing.
160	Killed in line.
161	Missing in line Nov. 1918.
162	Missing about June 1918.
163	
164	Shot by order of O.C. No use to service.
165	Lost in Line Oct.
166	Returns from 2 Sctn. 19.9.18 Given to Major Williams 10.10.18.
167	Taken away by Cpt. [illegible] 28.8.18 [illegible]
168	
169	
170	
171	Killed in line.
172	Killed in line.
173	Lost in line.
174	Lost in line.
175	
176	Destroyed by O.C.'s order being useless.
177	
178	Shot being useless 25.6.18 by O.C.'s orders.
179	
180	
181	
182	Destroyed by O.C.'s orders June 14.18 [sic]. Useless, has fits.
183	Destroyed June 3. 18 as of no further use.
184	

Appendix B 189

185	Missing in line Nov. 1918.
186	
187	
188	Wounded. Returns 10.8.18. Goes to to [sic] 13 Vet'y Hosp'l 12.9.18. Return from Hosp'l 10.10.18 goes as 20 16.10.18
189	Lost in line Sept.
190	
191	
192	Returned to GHQ Kennels useless.
193	Returns from No. 2 Sctn. 19.9.18.
194	
195	
196	
197	
198	Missing in line beginning July 1918. Found again.
199	Missing in line beginning of July 1918. Found again.
200	
201	
202	Died in line.
203	Missing in line Nov. 1918.
204	
205	
206	
207	
208	
209	From No. 2 Section 19.9.18. Killed on Railway 3.10.18.
210	
211	Lost in line Sept.
212	
213	Lost in line July.
214	Came back from Section 3 4.10.18 Destroyed by order of O.C. 10.10.18.
215	Lost in line.
216	Destroyed 12.9.18 by O.C. orders.
217	Destroyed 12.9.18 by O.C. orders.
218	Lost in line.

219	
220	
221	
222	
223	Missing in line End of Oct.
224	
225	Returned from 2 Sctn. 19.9.18 Goes to 3 Sctn. 5.10.18 as 129.
226	
227	Given to Col. [illegible] 4.10.18
228	
229	
230	Destroyed by Sgt. McLeod Aug. 13 1918.
231	Destroyed by order of O.C. useless.
232	
233	
234	
235	
236	
237	
238	Destroyed by order of O.C.
239	Destroyed By O.C. orders.
240	Died in line Aug. 1918.
241	Returns from Sctn. 2 19.9.18.
242	Comes from Sect. 3 4.10.18 to be kept for No. 2 Sctn. as 98 21.10.18 Returns 23.11.18.
243	
244	
245	Lost in line Sept.
246	
247	
248	
249	Returns from No. 1 Sctn. 19.9.18 Goes to No. 2 Sctn. again 20.9.18. Returns 23.11.18.
250	
231	Returns 1.11.18
252	

253 Reported missing.
254
255 Lost in Line. Found and returned to GHQ Central kennels 5.10.18 later given to Major Williams 10.10.18.
256
257 Destroyed by order of O.C. 8.2.19.
258
259 Destroyed 23.9.18. after being tried at no. 2 Section.
260 Becomes 82. returns with d'temper [distemper] 2/10/18.
261
262 Killed on railway line night of 29.8.18-30.8.18,
263 Killed "   "   "   "   "
264 Returns from Sctn 2 19.9.18.
265 Becomes No. 1 13.9.18
266 Becomes 62 26.8.18.
267 Shot by order of O.C. 22.8.18
268 Becomes 24 13.9.18
269
270 Becomes 134 23.8.18. Destroyed by orders of O.C. 1.12.18.
271 Becomes 16 13.9.18
272 Killed (suffering from Dist[emper]) 6.9.18
273 Died 17.9.18
274 Pneumonia on first coming out. Sent to No. 3 Vet'y Hos'l. Dies in Hos'l.
275 Killed on railway night 29-30.8.18.
276 Sunstroke on first coming over. Sent to No. 3 Vet'y Hos'l. Destroyed 8.9.18.
277 Given to Field Marshall Sir Douglas Haig. Nov. 29.
278 Became 74 13.9.18. Believed killed in line about Oct. 18.
279 Becomes 97 20.9.18. Returns 23.11.18.
280 To No. 1 Section as 15 20.9.18.
281 Becomes 96 20.9.18. Returns 23.11.18.
282 Given to Major General Sir Arthur A. M. Stuart 25.10.18.
283 Becomes 76 5.10.18 Died 7/1/18 [sic – presumably it was the 7/1/19].
284 Becomes 52. Later becomes 74. 21.10.18.
285 Becomes 131 5.10.18.
286 Becomes 63 13.9.18.

287	Destroyed 19.9.18.
288	Missing. Believed killed 29.9.18.
289	
290	Becomes 39 13.9.18.
291	Becomes 67 20.9.18.
292	Becomes 77 21.10.18 Destroyed 24.10.18 by order of O.C. No use.
293	
294	
295	Sent to Sctn. 2 as 80. Returns 23.11.18.
296	Died Sep 29 1918.
297	
298	Given to Col. Thompson 16.11.18.
299	Given to Capt. Dunsterville 21.2.19.
300	
301	
302	
303	Left as 60 20.9. 18.
304	
305	Left as 81 5.10.18
306	Given to Col. Thornton 27.10.18
307	Goes as No. 3 11.10.18
308	
309	Sent to Sctn. 1 as 42. Nov 1918 died at Section.
310	
311	Left as 75 5.10.18.
312	Goes to Section. 3 as 42. 5.10.18
313	
314	Goes to Section 3 as 107 5.10.18.
315	Destroyed by order of O.C. 8.2.19
316	
317	
318	
319	
320	

321	
322	
323	
324	
325	Goes up as (4) 16.10.18
326	
327	Goes up as 5 16.10.18
328	
329	
330	Goes up as 6 16.10.18
331	Destroyed 24.10.18 No use.
332	
333	
334	
335	
336	
337	Destroyed by O.C.'s orders 23.11.18
338	
339	Given to Capt. Hogg 21.1.19.
340	
341	
342	
343	Destroyed by O.C.'s orders 23.11.18.
344	
345	
346	Destroyed 8.2.19 by O.C.'s orders.

APPENDIX C
Unregistered Dogs and
the Men Who Brought Them

In the Imperial War Museum's archives (file # 69/75/1 – Messenger Dog Service (France) July 1917-April 1919) there is a list of "Unregistered Dogs and Who Brought Them." We assume that these were dogs taken to the front unofficially and with no military role. Some, it seems, were found by the troops and kept as companions. Below is the list with information as it appears in the files.

Number or Reference Mark	Description of Dog	Sex	Name of Dog	Owner's Name	Reg't or Unit
U. R. A	Belgian Fawn	D	Foxy	Spr. G. Lister	47/ Signal Coy. R. E.
" " B	Big Upstanding Grey Prick Ears	D	Pick	Sp'r. G Lister	47/ Signal Coy. R.E.
" " C	X Airedale	D	Tom	Pte. H. Radford	8/ S. Staffs.
" " D	Chow	D	Chow	Sgt. J. W. Clarke	22/ London
" " E	Airedale	D	Jack	Pte. J. Hedley	17/ Royal Scots.
" " F	Airedale	D	Buller	Cpl. W. Bonney	2/5 King's Own
" " G	X Whippet	D	Swallow	Pte. Rea. W.	44th Canadian . Batt.
" " H	X Old. En. & Italian G'hound[38]	D	Sharp	Pte. J. Ferriby	10/ East Yorks.
" " I	Collie		Clever	Pte. J. Delaney	
" " J	X Airedale Irish	D	Pat	Pte. S. Taylor	13th/ Essex
" " K	Airedale	D	Jack	Pte. W. H. Shaylor	3rd Suffolks.
" " L	Black X Bred Terrier	D	Nigger	Gnr. T. Slight	32/ Res. B'T'Y. R. F. A.
" " M	Borzoi Lurcher	D	Sailor	Gnr. C. Firth	28/ Res. Bat'y
" " N	Irish Terrier	D		Pte. A. R. Fletcher	B. Coy. 4/ Can'dn. Mt'd. Rifles
" " O	X Bloodhound	D	Duke	Pte. P. M. Oldroyd	44? Canadian Batt.
" " P	Liver Colored X Span'l Setter	D	Gas Dog	Pte. F. Waters	11th Essex
" " Q	Black & Tan German Scheoefer [sic]	D	Brought from down the line by Major Waley. Given name of Tilley.		

"	"	R	Black & Fawn	D		Brought here by Lieut. A. Morgan. Supposed German dog. Given name of Roach.
"	"	S	German Bk. & Tan Bitch	B		Brought down the line by Sgt. Wright.
"	"	T	German Dog	D	Kaiser	Brought down the line from No. 3 Section.
"	"	U	Black Lurcher	D		Brought here from H. Depot. Etaples.
"	"	V	French Sheep Bitch[39]	B	Marie	" " by Major Waley.
"	"	W	German Blue Roan	D	Rudolph	" " by Sgt. Nunns.
"	"	X	Black Dog. Old Eng. Shp.	B	Nell	From Le Touquet.

APPENDIX D
Casualties to Unregistered Dogs

In The Imperial War Museum's archives (file # 69/75/1) there is a list of "Casualties to U. R. Dog" (the "U. R." presumably referring to "unregistered – see above). It suggests the fate of many dogs that found themselves in the midst of the war. The entries are as they are recorded in the original.

U. R. A Died. Congestion of bowels.
"   "   B Returned 16.10.18
"   "   C
"   "   D Killed in line Aug. 1918.
"   "   E
"   "   F
"   "   G Killed
"   "   H
"   "   I Returned as useless. Shot by O.C.'s orders.
"   "   J Returned as of no use.
"   "   K Returns. Wounded. When well again goes up to Section 1 as 44. Again returns 5/7/18.
"   "   L Reported missing end of [illegible]
"   "   M Missing in line.
"   "   N Destroyed by O.C.'s orders.
"   "   O Missing in line [illegible]
"   "   P Lost from compound. (Gassed dog).
"   "   Q Killed in line.
"   "   R Shot by O.C.'s orders 27.7.18. Useless.
"   "   S
"   "   T
"   "   U Shot by order of O. C. No use.
"   "   V Shot by order of O. C. No use.

Endnotes

1. We mustn't take this too literally. "Greyhounds" and "Mastiffs," as used in the 15th century, might not mean the same breeds that we know today by those names.
2. This raises an interesting possibility. There is a breed called the Cane Corso ("running dog"), the only coursing Mastiff in the world. Its ancestry has been dated to AD 600 in the breed's native Italy. It weighs 40 kilos (88 pounds) and up, with some large males weighing in excess of 50 kilos (110 pounds). Nobody has ever considered that these were what the Spanish brought with them, but it is worth pondering.
3. As is the case with so much of this history, there are discrepancies. Vesey-Fitzgerald, in *The Domestic Dog – An Introduction to its History* (1957:138) claims that the number of dogs was 100, not 800.
4. The Barbet is a French water dog, probably ancestral to the Poodle. In some accounts of this story the breed is actually called a "Poodle." Gray, in *Dogs of War*, states that Poodles have been great favorites of French officers right up to the modern day and that, historically, "Many French officers went into battle accompanied by their Poodles" (1989). More often than not, they were probably Barbets. Despite the popular misnomer "French " Poodle, the Poodle is actually of German origin, while the Barbet – as previously noted – is French.
5. The Cuban Bloodhound no longer exists as a breed. It is believed that the dog was a cross between the Bloodhound and the Dogue de Bordeaux and was used to track runaway slaves. The Bloodhound would have provided the desired nose, the Dogue de Bordeaux the aggression.
6. Also sometimes called the Molosser or Molossian Hound in the cynological literature.
7. This includes a large number of European and Asian breeds that are characteristically pure white or predominantly white, stand between 66 and 82 centimetres at the shoulder and weigh 36 to 63 kilograms. This group includes the Great Pyrenees (Pyrenean Mountain Dog), Kuvasz, Maremma, Akbash, Polish Tatra, Komondor, and the Slovak Tchouvatch, among others. Their job was to protect flocks of sheep and goats against predators such as wolves and bears.
8. This is a dubious assertion, as many fanciers recognize that the Mastiff was near extinction at the end of the 19th and beginning of the 20th centuries and that the breed has been largely reconstructed since that time using other large breeds such as the Great Dane and Saint Bernard.
9. Dogs, of course, were not the only animals pressed into service during the First World War. Horses and pigeons were also common, although donkeys, mules, camels and oxen saw action, in addition to countless mascots of various persuasions.
10. One wonders if Fitzgerald's claim for 1848 is a typographical error, i.e. the "1848" was meant to be "1884." It seems likely, given his usual thoroughness and accuracy in his writing.
11. Today, Germany recognizes nine breeds as being suited for police and military service: the Airedale, Rottweiler, Doberman Pinscher, Giant Schnauzer (or Munchener), Boxer, Hovawart, German Shepherd Dog, Belgian Malinois and Bouvier des Flandres.

12. The story of how the manual was found was related in *The American Kennel Gazette,* September, 1941. It was found during the 1920s in the farm cottage of a young woman in New Jersey. She lived alone, bred German Shepherd Dogs, was apparently on too friendly terms with a French veteran, drove her Model T with reckless abandon, wore pants and smoked. In brief, she was far too European and cosmopolitan for small town New Jersey in the '20s. She was eventually driven out of her home while rumors circulated that she had been a German spy. One of the youngsters who found the manual, as well as some other papers relating to the training and use of German war dogs, wrote a two-part article for the magazine. He believes that she had been given the manual by her French veteran friend who had either found them in a trench, or taken from a prisoner or cadaver, regardless of the fact that they were not to be taken to the front lines. He did not believe that she had been a spy.

13. In *British War Dogs* (1920), Richardson quotes from a translation of a German document pertaining to the training of messenger dogs. It was taken from a German headquarters. In virtually every respect, it is similar to the one described by Lewis, except the desired breeds listed are "German sheep dogs [i.e., the German Shepherd Dog], Dobermannpinschers [sic], Airedale terriers, and Rottweilers." This discrepancy is hard to explain except, perhaps, that over the course of time the standards changed. In Richardson's account, two German breeds, the Doberman and Rottweiler, replaced the Scottish Sheepdog (or Collie). The Airedale and German Shepherd Dog remained preferred breeds.

14. The reference to "Mastiff" is questionable. The Great Dane, a German breed – not Danish – was sometimes called the Ulmer Mastiff and was very popular at this time. It is hard to imagine the Mastiff keeping pace with Setters over a two kilometre distance, which leads one to wonder if the "Mastiffs" were Great Danes or some other breed.

15. Max von Stephanitz, the "father" of the German Shepherd Dog, gives the number as 28 000. Of these, 7000 died in action.

16. This undoubtedly is a type indigenous to Continental Europe known as the Matin, or Matin Belge. Common in Belgium and The Netherlands, it is a type of large (45-55 kilograms) Mastiff type, bred for strength and freighting ability, rather than the show ring.

17. This is a somewhat confusing term, as there is a breed called the Dutch Shepherd, very similar to the Belgian Shepherd. In almost all certainty, one of these two breeds is meant, not the ubiquitous German Shepherd Dog.

18. This story appears in both *Forty Years With Dogs* and in *Fifty Years With Dogs*. Remarkably, in the former the dog's name is Masher, in the latter, Johnny. One can only wonder.

19. What breed this is is uncertain; it might be the Belgian Sheepdog – Groenendael, Malinois, Tervuren or Laekenois – or the Bouvier des Flandres.

20. The use of muzzles is interesting for another reason. Trainers of protection or attack trained animals will often train their dogs in man work with a muzzle. The belief is that it keeps the dogs from becoming "sleeve happy," i.e., dependent upon attacking and working the padded arm. In this way, the dog has to learn to rely on other means of combating the decoy or agitator.

21. Waley doesn't state this, but it seems apparent, from archival photos and written accounts by the handlers, that when it was not possible to have three dogs of the same breed per handler, there

was a concerted effort to have dogs of approximately the same size.

22. One of the most respected trainers in North America once expressed the same sentiment to me. As he quaintly put it, "There would be something seriously wrong with either the dog or me if he [the dog] chose to listen to me instead of pursuing a bitch in heat."

23. Gray reports that despite all these safeguards, rabies did find its way to the British mainland, but it was through dogs smuggled in illegally in 1918 on returning troopships and in at least one airplane.

24. We can make an interesting observation here. The Germans, during World War I, used coercive methods of training. There is a photograph that shows two German soldiers removing food from a container carried by an Airedale. The dog's tail is completely clamped between its legs, indicating stress and/or fear. It is evident that it has been trained by coercive means, something that does not usually work with the breed. Compare that picture with those of Richardson's dogs, which invariably appear happy, confident and relaxed.

25. This is not to suggest that all dogs displaying these characteristics are trained using punitive methods. Some individuals of some breeds, such as the hounds, do not take to repetitive obedience training as do others, such as the Belgian Malinois, one of the finest working dogs in the world. Then again, the Malinois could not be expected to perform as well as a Bloodhound in the latter's domain of expertise.

26. Many trainers today still use food as a training aid, but many others are vehemently opposed to the use of food, claiming that the dog works only for food and, once it is removed, will not work. It seemed to work for Richardson, although he also used an abundance of praise. At the time of his training, food as a motivator was probably rarely used, as most trainers still used compulsion and "correction," often a euphemism for corporal punishment.

27. This is another instance in which Richardson's recounting of events differs from source to source. This quotation is from *Watchdogs: Their Training and Management*. In *Forty Years With Dogs,* he quotes the general as saying "if only one dog out of four gets through, I am satisfied." A minor quibble, perhaps, but a bit disconcerting.

28. This number is suspect. Richardson claims, in *Fifty Years With Dogs*, that he shipped 30 dogs at the end of the first month, but according to Major A. S. Waley (IWM 69/75/1), who was in charge of the dogs in France, 74 dogs and 30 men arrived in July, 1917, the first such group. This is more likely the correct number, as each keeper or handler had two or three dogs. Richardson might have confused the numbers.

29. In most references to Tweed, he is referred to as an Old English Sheepdog or "Bobtail," another name for the breed. The official records of the Messenger Dog Service, housed at the IWM, record him as being an Old English Sheepdog. In at least one place, however, he is called a "Highland Sheepdog," which implies a Bearded Collie, a different but somewhat similar appearing breed. A picture of Tweed that appears in *British War Dogs* suggests an Old English Sheepdog.

30. One estimate claims that 50 000 dogs were ready to enter battle in 1939, another claims as many as 200 000 were ready.

31. Thurston, in *Lost History of the Canine Race* (1996:188) states that "While Hitler's army numbered at least thirty thousand German Shepherds, Russia had the most respected canine force on the Continent, totaling well over a million animals." It is unclear where she got this figure, and

what it actually implies. Similarly, while German Shepherd Dogs predominated among the Germans during World War II, other breeds were used.

32. Richardson wasn't, and isn't , alone in this attitude. Col. David Hancock, a contemporary British writer of several scholarly – albeit controversial – dog books, holds similar views. In *The Heritage of the Dog* (1990), he laments the influx of "foreign breeds" on to British soil and the usurpation of the former roles of indigenous breeds. Regarding the Airedale, he writes "The Airedale has given valuable service to man – but is no longer utilized – the German Shepherd reigns supreme." Elsewhere, he writes that "It saddens me to look at the registration tables for 1985 and see that against over 21,000 German Shepherd Dogs, over 9900 Dobermanns [sic – this is the proper spelling of the breed's founder's name and the spelling that is used in Europe], and 6800 Rottweilers, we can muster only 1300 Airedales and 752 Bullmastiffs, our two famous native guarding breeds, both the choice of gamekeepers all over the British Isles." One wonders if this type of concern is inherent in retired British military officers.

33. The German Shepherd Dog would continue to reign as the service dog of choice into the 1980s, when other breeds, including the Belgian Malinois and Labrador Retriever, would start usurping that role. The Malinois, a high energy worker, is becoming the favored breed for protection work and crowd control, while the Lab works in other capacities, e.g., narcotics and bomb detection. In Guide Dog work for the blind, the Golden Retriever and Labrador Retriever now far outnumber the German Shepherd Dog, although some people still prefer the GSD because if its deterrent effect on wrongdoers, much as police officers do. Every dog must have its day, but the German Shepherd's seems to be waning.

34. In some cases, the breed was called "the Alsatian Wolfdog." In fact, that was actually the name of a breed monograph published in 1923. The most absurd arguments were made to convince people that the breed had "wolf blood." In one laughable example, a man remarked how his Borzoi, aka "Russian Wolfhound" until the 1930s, attacked a German Shepherd Dog. This was proof: his dog, bred to hunt wolves, attacked the dog, therefore it must be "part wolf."

35. "Bobtail Sheepdog" is another name for the Old English Sheepdog.

36. This is a remarkable entry. The Cavalier King Charles Spaniel is a toy breed, bred solely for companionship and with the gentlest of dispositions, that weighs a maximum of 8 kilograms. One wonders what the other part of him was.

37. This is a most interesting entry because it is likely referring to a German Shepherd Dog. Richardson, in one of his books, insists that only indigenous British breeds were employed by the War Dog School and that no foreign breeds were used, a statement clearly meant to include the German Shepherd. It is clear from this entry that at least one found its way to France.

38. This is an improbable cross. Italian Greyhounds weigh, on average, 2.7 kilos (six pounds) to 4.5 kilos (10 pounds) compared to the 29.5 to 36 kilos (65-80 pounds) for the Old English Sheepdog. In all likelihood, the alleged Italian Greyhound cross was, in reality, a Whippet. The Italian Greyhound resembles a Whippet put through a compactor. Whippets weigh approximately nine to ten kilograms.

39. This, in all likelihood, was a Briard, a French herding breed that won considerable praise as a war dog during WW I.

References

Archival Material

The Imperial War Museum, London (UK) Department of Documents
File # 69/75/1 (Major A. S. Waley)
1) Messenger Dog Service (France) July 1917-April 1919
2) GHQ Central Kennels Register of Dogs & Men
3) GHQ Central Kennel Index of Personnel

The Imperial War Museum Film and Video Archives
IWM 235

National Archives and Records Administration, Washington, D.C.
Collection #4248 (History of Military Use of Dogs)

Books, Articles and Personal Communications

Baynes, Ernest Harold. *Animal Heroes of the Great War*. The MacMillan Company. 1926.

Bennett, E. E. "Employment of Dogs for Military Services." *Journal of Royal United Service Institution*. Vol. XXXIII. 1889-90.

Collon, Dominique. Personal communication. March, 2003.

Downey, Fairfax. *Dogs for Defense – American Dogs in the Second World War, 1941-1945*. New York, NY: Trustees of Dogs for Defense. 1955.

Flamholtz, Cathy. *A Celebration of Rare Breeds*. Ft. Payne, Alabama. 1986.

Fleig, Dr. Dieter (translated by William Charlton). *Fighting Dog Breeds*. Neptune, New Jersey: TFH Publications. 1996

Gersbach, Robert and Theo. F. Jager. *The Police Dog*. Canandaigua, New York: The Deming Press. 1910.

Going, Clayton, G. *Dogs at War*. New York: The MacMillan Company. 1944.

Gray, Ernest A. *Dogs of War*. London: Robert Hale. 1989.

Green, Miranda. *Animals in Celtic Life and Myth*. London: Routledge. 1992.

Hamer, Blythe. *Dogs at War*. London: Carlton Books. 2001.

Hancock, Colonel David. *The Heritage of the Dog*. Alton, Hantshire. Nimrod Press Limited. 1990

Horning, Dr. J. G. "Training the Real Dogs of War." *American Kennel Gazette*. February 1, 1928..

Hutchinson, Walter (ed.). *Hutchinson's Dog Encyclopaedia* (three volumes). London: Hutchinson. 1934/35.

Jager, Theo. F. *Scout, Red Cross and Army Dogs*. Rochester, N.Y: Arrow Printing. 1917.

Lewis, Alexander G. "'For Amy Use Only'. Germany's Methodical Planning Is Shown in its Secret Orders for Courier Dog Units in the First World War." *American Kennel Gazette*. September, 1941.

Lloyd, H. S. "The Dog in War" in *The Book of the Dog*. Brian Vesey-Fitzgerald (9ed.). London: Nicholson & Watson. 1948.

n. a. "Dogs in War." *Journal of the Military Institution*. September, 1896.

Patmore, Angela. *Your Obedient Servant*. London: Hutchinson. 1984.

Richardson, Edwin Hautenville. "The Employment of War Dogs, With Special reference to Tripoli and Other Recent Campaigns." *The Journal of the Royal United Service Institution*. Vol. LVI. December, 1912.

War, Police and Watch Dogs. London: William Blackwood. 1910.

British War Dogs: Their Training and Psychology. London: Skeffington. 1920.

Watch-Dogs: Their Training and Management. London: Hutchinson. 1923.

Forty Years With Dogs. London: Hutchinson. 1929.

Richardson, Edwin Hautenville and Mrs. Blanche Richardson. *Fifty Years With Dogs*. London: Hutchinson. 1950.

Thurston, Mary Elizabeth. *The Lost History of the Canine Race*. Kansas City: Andrews and McMeel. 1993.

Trew, Cecil G. "With War Dogs Through the Ages." *American Kennel Gazette*. February 1941.

Varner, John Grier and Jeannette Johnson Varner. *Dogs of the Conquest*. Norman, Oklahoma: University of Oklahoma Press. 1983.

Vesey-Fitzgerald, Brian. *The Domestic Dog – An Introduction to its History*. London: Routledge and Kegan Paul. 1957.

Vesey-Fitzgerald, Brian. (editor). *The Book of the Dog*. London: Nicholson & Watson. 1948.

Watson, Walter. "Hull Police Dogs – a description of the methods of training." *The Kennel*. 1910.

Index

Battles/Wars

American Civil War, 24, 25, 34
Balkan War, 81, 86
Battle of Aboukir, 21
Battle of Agincourt, 30
Battle of Antwerp, 50
Battle of Castiglione, 21
Battle of Kemmel Hill, 150
Battle of Kursk, 156
Battle of Ligeand, 50
Battle of Louvain, 50
Battle of Marengo, 21
Battle of Namur, 50
Boxer Rebellion, 43, 93
Crimean War, 50
Herrero Campaign, 36
Malay Peninsula Campaign, 157
Passchendaele, 118, 151, 152
Pearl Harbor, 55, 157
Rotenturm Pass, Romania, 38
Russo-Japanese War, 50, 51, 77, 92
Russo-Turkish War, 91
Seminole War of 1835-1842, 23
Siege of Liege, 50
Spanish-American War, 54
Spanish Conquest, 11, 17, 18, 19, 20
Turko-Italian War, 52, 53, 82, 83
Vimy Ridge, 99, 149, 151, 152
Wars of the Roses, 21

Books by Col. Richardson

British War Dogs, 17, 18, 21, 36, 45, 50, 62, 68, 84, 87, 90, 97, 99, 103, 105, 116, 118, 130, 132, 134, 135, 137, 153, 200, 201
Fifty Years with Dogs, 59, 64, 65, 66, 67, 70, 82, 85, 98, 100, 101, 122, 132, 137, 141, 159, 160, 161, 168, 200, 201
Forty Years with Dogs, 59, 60, 61, 64, 66, 68, 74, 78, 82, 83, 86, 87, 89, 95, 97, 102, 130, 131, 149, 151, 200, 201
War, Police and Watch Dogs, 34, 70, 126, 132
Watch Dogs: Their Training and Management, 125, 126, 128, 131, 132, 149, 201

Breed Names

Airedale Terrier, 35, 36, 38, 40, 42, 43, 46, 50, 51, 52, 53, 55, 63, 70, 73, 82, 84, 85, 86, 87, 88, 89, 93, 94, 95, 98, 99, 100, 102, 107, 108, 109, 110, 112, 113, 114, 117, 125, 126, 130, 131, 132, 134, 135, 138, 140, 142, 143, 145, 147, 148, 149, 150, 155, 156, 159, 160, 161, 162, 163, 164, 165, 169, 199, 200, 201, 202
Akbash, 27, 199
Alaskan Malamute, 158
Alaunt, 18, 19
Barbet, 21, 199
Basset Hound, 61
Beagle, 128
Bearded Collie, 140, 20
Beauceron, 45
Bedlington terrier, 125, 134, 135
Belgian Shepherd, 45, 128, 158
Bloodhound, 21, 24, 25, 61, 66, 73, 74, 77, 79, 85, 86, 121, 130, 199, 201
Border Collie, 73, 126, 132, 140
Borzoi, 202
Bouvier des Flandres, 129, 199, 200
Boxer, 128, 155, 166, 100
Briard, 45, 202
Bulldog, 125, 126, 143

Bullmastiff, 31, 62, 130, 143, 202
Bull terrier, 125, 126, 130, 143, 166
Canadian Inuit Dog, 158
Cane Corso, 199
Cavalier King Charles Spaniel, 202
Chow, 128
Collie, 74, 75, 76, 77, 78, 79, 86, 113, 125, 126, 130, 131, 132, 140, 143, 145, 158, 165, 169, 200
Crossbreed, 18, 24, 25, 27, 52, 82, 86, 126, 128, 132, 140, 143, 148, 155, 158, 165
Cuban Bloodhounds, 23, 24, 25, 199,
Curly-coated Retriever, 130, 133, 166
Dalmatian, 125, 128
Dandie Dinmont Terrier, 64
Doberman Pinscher, 25, 51, 84, 126, 128, 129, 155, 157, 158, 199, 200, 202
Dogue de Bordeaux (French Mastiff), 16, 26, 27, 31, 32, 64, 199
Dutch Shepherd, 50, 200
Eskimo, 125, 158
Flat-coated Retriever, 126, 130, 133, 153
German Shepherd Dog (also, Alsation Wolfdog), 25, 40, 42, 43, 45, 51, 84, 109, 126, 128, 129, 155, 156, 157, 158, 159, 160, 161, 164, 165, 199, 200, 201, 202
Giant Schauzer, 128, 155, 158, 199
Golden Retriever, 129, 133, 202
Great Dane, 65, 130, 133, 143, 199, 200
Great Pyrenees, 46, 47, 199
Greyhound, 17, 18, 125, 128, 132, 199
Groenendael, 128, 200
Hovawart, 199
Irish Setter, 130
Irish Terrier, 94, 118, 123, 124, 125, 134, 135
Irish Wolfhound, 16, 18, 65, 113, 130, 133
Italian Greyhound, 202
Kangal, 27
Kerry Blue Terrier, 166
Komondor, 199
Kuvasz, 199
Labrador Retriever, 25, 129, 130, 133, 166, 167, 202
Laekenois, 128, 200

Lurcher, 73, 113, 125, 130, 131, 132, 143, 145, 165
Malamutes, 130
Malinois, 25, 129, 199, 200, 201, 202
Matin Belge, 200
Maremma, 52, 53, 83, 199
Mastiff, 11, 15, 16, 17, 18, 20, 21, 26, 27, 28, 29, 30, 41, 53, 130, 134, 143, 199, 200
Molossus, 26, 27, 199
Neapolitan Mastiff, 26, 27, 30, 31, 32
Newfoundland, 66, 130, 158
Old English Sheepdogs, 40, 55, 62, 86, 125, 126, 130, 132, 140, 150, 151, 166, 201, 202
Pit Bull, 31
Pointer, 41, 125, 166
Poodle, 22, 42, 199
Retriever, 73, 74, 86, 125, 126, 133, 143, 145, 153
Rottweiler, 25, 128, 155, 199, 200, 202
Rough Collie, 73, 126
Samoyed, 157
Scotch Collie, 33, 43, 66
Scotch Terriers [sic], 40
Scottie, 70
Scottish Deerhound, 64, 65, 120, 125, 130, 132, 133
Sealyham, 70
Setter, 41, 125, 133, 166, 200
Siberian Husky, 158
Smooth Collie, 126
Spinone, 52
Springer Spaniel, 61, 125, 126, 129, 168
St. Bernard, 51, 130, 158, 199
Staffordshire Bull Terrier, 126
Tatra, 199
Tchouvatch, 199
Tervuren, 128, 200
Tibetan Mastiff, 27, 30
Weimaraner, 129
Welsh Terrier, 125, 130, 134, 135, 140
Whippet, 125, 128, 202
Wire-haired Fox Terriers, 70

Other Uses for Dogs

Badger baiting, 11
Bear baiting, 11, 29, 30, 31, 64
Bull baiting, 11, 18, 29, 31
Hunting, 18, 27, 29, 34, 52, 107, 128, 130, 132, 168
Jaguar baiting, 31, 64
Lion baiting, 29, 30, 64
Mascots, 24
Pit dog fighting, 11, 34
Search dogs, 77
Shepherding, 29, 34, 52
Tracking, 19, 24, 61, 80, 84, 91

Names of Dogs

Beaufort, 29
Benny, 65
Bercerillo, 18, 19, 20
Blondi, 155
Blue Boy, 135
Boadicea (Perra de la Reine), 80, 81
Bob, 89
Boxer, 150
Carlo, 77
Dick, 153
Don, 54
Flash, 150
Frigate, 61
His Lordship, 29
Jack (Airedale), 135
Jack (Airedale hero), 147-148
Jack Thyr, 29
Jim, 88, 89
Jo, 83
Johnny, 64, 65, 200
Katy, 169
Laddie, 79
Lady Ashton, 64
Lassie, 126
Leoncico, 19
Lloyd, 135
Lorna, 64
Maida, 64
Major, 132
Malcolm, 64, 65
Masher, 200
Moustache, 22
Paddy, 118
Prince (Airedale), 99, 149
Prince (Irish Terrier), 123, 124
Priscilla, 169
Prusco, 48
Rin Tin Tin, 160
Robbie, 77
Saida, 64, 65
Sanita, 36, 74, 75
Spot, 24
Strongheart, 160
Tweed, 62, 126, 150, 151, 152, 201
Warrior, 79
Whitefoot, 135
Wodan, 29
Wolf, 99, 149
Zucha, 157

Names of People

Aldrovandrus, Ulysses, 19
Alexander the Great, 26, 30
Alleyn, Edward, 29
Aristotle, 26
Assurbanipal, 15, 26
Baldwin, Maj. James, 161, 164, 165, 166
Bennett, E.E., 41, 73
Charles I, 29
Charles V, 20
Columbus, Christopher, 17, 18
Columbus, Diego, 19
Czar Nicholas of Russia, 69, 78
Dowager Empress Marie, 78, 84
Duncan, Lee, 160
Dupin, Lt., 77
Edward I, 29
Edward VII, 78
Elizabeth I, 21, 29, 30
Empress Eugenie, 80
Evans, Rev. Vivian, 66
Franklin, Benjamin, 22, 23
Haig, Gen. Douglas, 151, 152

Haking, Brig. Gen. R.C.B., 90, 94, 95
Hamid, Sultan Abdul, 79, 80
Hammurabi, 16
Henry VII, 29
Henry VIII, 11, 20, 29
Hitler, Adolf, 155, 156, 201
Horning, Dr. J.G., 68, 69
Hunt, Monty, 169
Hunter, Lt., 147, 148
James I, 29, 30
Julius Caesar, 11, 28, 91
Jupin, Lt., 33, 43
Keller, Count, 77, 78
King Alfonso of Spain, 81
Legh, Sir Peers, 30
Lingo, Walter, 159
Lloyd, H.S., 165, 167, 168
McClay, William, 23
Medvedev, Col. G., 156, 157
Megnin, Paul, 45, 98
Murray, Brig., 161, 165
Napoleon, 21
Nicholson, Charlotte, 60, 61
Ponce de Leon, Juan, 19
Queen Alexandra of Russia, 84
Quintus Aurelius, 65
Reid, Pte., 151, 152
Richardson, Angus, 62
Richardson, Blanche, 62, 63, 64, 70, 99, 100, 151, 152
Richardson, James Nicholson, 60
Richardson, Joshua, 60, 61
Richardson, Rev. John, 60
Robin Hood, 21
Varro, Marius Terentius, 26
Von Bungartz, Herr, 35, 36
Von Donat, Karl, 33, 34
Von Stephanitz, Max, 43, 51, 160, 200
Waley, Alec, 101, 106, 107, 108, 109, 110, 113, 114, 115, 116, 118, 120, 121, 123, 200, 201
Winter, Col., 99, 150

Organizations (Dog)

American Kennel Club, 128
Animal Protection Society of Scotland and Northern Ireland, 165
Berlin Sporting Club, 41
British Alsatian Society, 160
Canadian Kennel Club, 128
Der Verein fur Deutsche Schaferhunde, 36
Dogs for Defense, 157, 158
German Shepherd Dog Club of America, 55
Home for Lost Dogs (Battersea), 125, 147
Kennel Club (British), 65, 70, 128, 164
Mastiff Club of America, 28
National Canine Defense League, 165
RSPCA, 122, 123, 124, 165
Village Clubs (Germany), 35, 42
Volunteer Trained Dog Reserve, 164

Training Schools & Kennels (for War Dogs)

Aldershot, England, 165
Army Dog Training School, England, 11, 166, 169
Bulford, Salisbury Plain, England, 103
Central Military School of Working Dogs (Red Star Kennels), Russia, 156
Chantilly, France, 98
Etaples, France, 111, 120, 121, 129
Frankfurt, Germany, 155
Grunheide, Germany, 155
Lechernich, Germany, 35, 74
Matley Ridge, New Forest, England, 103, 133
Nieppe Wood, France, 119, 122, 124, 127, 131, 135
Royal Air Force Police Dog School, England, 11
Satory, France, 45, 47
Shoeburyness, England, 95, 99, 100, 101, 103, 120
Tsarskoe Selo, Russia, 83

War Work Performed by Dogs

Ambulance/Red Cross/Mercy, 33, 35, 42, 43, 44, 46, 48, 50, 51, 53, 54, 73, 74, 75, 76, 80, 84, 85, 91, 92, 93, 94, 97, 98, 100, 107, 108, 147, 156, 169
Anti-tank, 156, 158

Attack/Protection, 17
Draught, 46, 47, 48, 49, 50
Guard/Watchdog, 17, 24, 25, 26, 29, 31, 44, 46, 47, 51, 53, 84, 85, 86, 91, 94, 97, 101, 103, 113, 121, 128, 130, 132, 138, 142, 143, 144, 147, 157, 158, 169
"Killer" dogs, 158
Liaison, 110, 111, 121, 167
Messenger/Courier, 24, 33, 35, 37, 39, 40, 41, 43, 45, 46, 48, 50, 54, 61, 62, 73, 74, 80, 84, 91, 92, 93, 94, 99, 100-101, 104, 106, 107, 109, 110, 113, 115, 116, 117, 118, 119, 120, 121, 122, 123, 124, 126, 127, 129, 131, 132, 133, 134, 137, 138, 139, 140, 142, 144, 147, 148, 149, 150, 151, 152, 156, 157, 158, 166, 167, 201
Mine Detection, 25, 156, 167, 168
Pack/Carrier dog, 36, 40, 43, 45, 47, 50, 51, 53, 73, 84, 91, 92, 158
Parachute dog, 157, 167, 168
Perimeter Defense, 167
Policing, 38, 43, 48, 86, 87, 88, 89, 128, 131
Scout/Patrol, 20, 22, 35, 42, 43, 46, 48, 54, 73, 82, 83, 88, 91, 93, 95, 98, 147, 157, 158, 166, 167
Sentry, 17, 24, 25, 34, 35, 42, 43, 44, 45, 46, 48, 50, 51, 52, 53, 54, 73, 74, 80, 82, 83, 86, 91, 93, 94, 95, 97, 98, 100, 102, 103, 115, 121, 130, 132, 134, 138, 142, 143, 144, 147, 156, 158, 161
Sled pulling, 49, 130, 157, 158
"Spy" dogs, 157
Taster, 17

Various

Armor (suits for dogs), 17
Dickin Medal, 148
Escaupil, 19, 20
Firepots mounted on dogs, 17
Gunfire, acclimatizing dogs to, 39, 41, 49, 84, 99, 108, 113, 114, 132, 139, 140, 141, 145
Injuries/Casualties to dogs, 40, 41, 50, 107, 115, 116, 117, 118, 119, 121, 124, 135, 140, 147, 148, 153

Manuals, German (care & training), 38, 39
Media attention to dogs, 38, 45, 48, 77, 80, 82, 84, 103, 120
Nikias (statue), 26
Rabies, 122, 123, 201
Soul of the dog, 66, 67, 68
Wolf, 26, 27, 29, 31, 64, 128, 199, 202